NEHRU AND PLANNING IN INDIA

About the Authors

N.B. Das Gupta (*b.* 1924) M.A., Ph.D. Former Reader and Head of the Department of English, M.M.H. College, Ghaziabad, author of seven books; a regular contributor to different journals on literary, social and economic topics.

J.L. Raina (*b.* 1937) obtained his Ph.D. in Sociology from the Institute of Social Sciences, Agra University, Currently, Dr. Raina is Head, Department of Sociology, M.M.H. (P.G.) College, Ghaziabad.

H.M. Jauhari (*b*, 1940) M.A., M.A.S., LL.B. Labour and Taxation Law consultant.

B.M. Jauhari (*b.* 1942) M.A., Ph.D. Head of Economics Department, M.M.H. College, contributed about 30 articles in various journals and books, completed two U.G.C. research projects. He is also a visiting faculty to Institute of Management Studies, Ghaziabad.

NEHRU AND PLANNING IN INDIA

Proceedings of the National Seminar on Pandit Jawaharlal Nehru,
Planning Commission and Planned Development in India
Ghaziabad, 1989

N.B. Das Gupta
J.L. Raina
H.M. Jauhari
B.M. Jauhari

CONCEPT PUBLISHING COMPANY, NEW DELHI 110059

ISBN 81-7022-451-9

First Published 1993

Published and Printed by
Ashok Kumar Mittal
Concept Publishing Company
A/15-16, Commercial Block, Mohan Garden
NEW DELHI-110059

Lasertypeset by
Microtech Advance Printing Systems (Pvt.) Ltd.
H-13, Bali Nagar
NEW DELHI-110015

DEDICATED TO THE MEMORY OF A
GREAT SON OF INDIA
PANDIT JAWAHARLAL NEHRU

FOREWORD

This collection of essays and speeches by distinguished academicians was prepared on the occasion of a two-day National Seminar on 'Pandit Nehru, Planning Commission and the Planned Economic Development in India'. The Seminar was organised by the Indian Centre for Socialist Studies, Ghaziabad in collaboration with the Planning Commission of India and was held at Ghaziabad on March 29 and 30, 1989. The publication assembles the excellent working-papers prepared and text of speeches delivered. The Nehru Centenary Year offers us the opportunity to look into the basic approach of Nehru, our achievements – 'the tasks done and the tasks which remain still to be accomplished'. This is an occasion for self-introspection; a year when we can call upon ourselves to look at the forty-one years of our Independence in the changing perspectives. This publication reflects not only the insights of a superb group of eminent academicians as diverse as Shri Tarlok Singh – the grand old man of Indian Planning – and Prof. Y.K. Alagh – my colleague in the present Planning Commission, but also projects outstanding professionalism of men working at the Centre for Socialist Studies.

This collection not only highlights the views on planning held by men of different pursuits, but also attempts to come to grips with the fundamental questions that must be addressed to adjust planning to a new technological era which maintained the basics of planning in tact. This volume, I'm sure, will be of great use to all those persons who are assessing the major challenges facing the process of planning.

The Centre and people connected with the publication of this Document deserve the thanks of all of us for this timely and important effort.

I am most grateful to the Indian Centre for Socialist Studies, Ghaziabad – a Centre sincerely and earnestly devoted to the spread of Socialist Ideology – for having asked me to write a foreword to this collection. I wish the Centre all success.

New Delhi
November 29, 1989

ABID HUSSAIN

PREFACE

Our aim in collecting the essays and speeches by different Indian academicians in this volume is a double one: to look into the history of the Planning Commission in diverse perspectives with the study of Pandit Nehru at the Centre – the study of his multi-centered personality, his ideals, his attitudes and approaches to various problems of the teething India – and to offer an exploration of our various failures, our inability to attain the goals set out by Pandit Nehru – in fact – an exposition of our sincere self-introspection. To that end, we have drawn together some of the leading contemporary Indian academicians – who might give the reader – whether he be a specialised student or a general reader – some sense of the lively issues in the current ferment of Indian affairs. Naturally we have essays by Sri Tarlok Singh – who very beautifully and in clear words – spells out not only the beginning of the Planning Commission (he has been associated with it since its inception), but also the various pitfalls of our experiments. We have the then member of the Planning Commission – Prof. Y.K. Alagh who recaptures, Nehru's vision of a technologically progressive India – free from bureaucratic controls. He warns against the intermediaries and quotes Nehru to caution us against the so-called practical and hard headed politicians – who often are devoid of any humane sense. The collection also contains a speech by Dr. N.B. Das Gupta where he tries to present a new historical perspective – (new in the sense that it is a departure from the official one) of our freedom movement.

The Indian Centre for Socialist Studies, Ghaziabad, in collaboration with the Planning Commission, organised a two-day National Seminar on Pandit Nehru, Planning Commission and the Planned Economic Development in India, at Ghaziabad on March 29 and 30, 1989, and all the articles were read out in that Seminar. The book seeks to pay homage to Nehru not with aphorism and uncritical bias, but with an effort to present the personality of the great leader in its true perspective. The purpose of this book is to provide an up-to-date exploration of the current dialogue on Planned Economy of India.

We express our deep sense of gratefulness to Shri Abid Hussain (Former Member, Planning Commission), former Ambassador to the U.S.A. who has very kindly gone through the compilation and has written an encouraging foreword to it.

We express our thankfulness to Concept Publishing Company, New Delhi which has made the publication of this volume possible. We also take this opportunity to thank Prof. B.S. Mathur, former Vice-Chancellor, Meerut University who has always been a source of inspiration to the Centre. We also express our sincere thanks to Dr. M.M. Mathur (Former Director ICSSR), Mr. Devendra Rai (Liaison Officer Indian Centre for Socialist Studies) and Mr. C.R. Pillai. Lastly we offer our sincere thanks and gratefulness to all the contributors whose valuable papers are included herein.

EDITORIAL BOARD

CONTENTS

SECTION III
Agriculture

SECTION IV
Nehru: Panchsheel and Secularism

SECTION V
Freedom Movement and the Personality of Nehru

LIST OF CONTRIBUTORS

Shri Tarlok Singh
Former Member Planning Commission

Prof. Y.K. Alagh
Professor of Economics,
Sardar Patel Institute of Economic & Social Research, Ahmedabad

Prof. S.S. Mohapatra
Former Member of Parliament

Dr. Yashvir Tyagi
Reader,
Department of Economics,
Lucknow University

Dr. B.M. Jauhari
Head of Economics Department,
M.M.H. College,
Ghaziabad

Prof. Ruddar Datt
Principal,
School of Correspondence Courses & Continuing Education,
University of Delhi

Dr. A.D.N. Bajpai
Reader, Department of Economics,
R.D. University,
Jabalpur

Prof. A.K. Singh
Professor of Economics,
Giri Institute of Development Studies,
Lucknow

Prof. Jagdish Prakash
Professor of Commerce and Business Administration,
University of Allahabad

Prof. Lallan Prasad
Professor of Economics,
South Campus,
University of Delhi

Dr. S.C. Mathur
Former Head of Political Science Department,
M.M.H. College,
Ghaziabad

Prof. G.S. Bhalla
Former Member, Planning Commission.
(Currently Professor & Head, Centre for Regional Development, J.N.U., New Delhi)

Dr. B.B. Singh
Principal, M.M.H. College, Ghaziabad

Dr. R.C. Gupta
Head of Geography Department,
S.D. College, Ghaziabad

Ms. Indira Priyadarshini
Student of M.A. Economics,
Sambalpur University

Ms. B. Ghousia
Student of B.A.
Karnataka University

Ms. Supriya Deshpande
Student of B.Com
Gulbarga University

Dr. V.K. Parkhomenko
Former Cultural Secretary,
Soviet House of Culture, New Delhi

Shri I.K. Gujral
Former Minister of External Affairs,
Government of India

Dr. G.N. Srivastava
General Secretary,
Indian Institute of Non-Aligned Studies,
New Delhi

Shri H.M. Jauhari
Labour & Taxation Consultant

Dr. N.K. Gupta
Head of Political Science Department,
S.D. College, Ghaziabad

Dr. N.B. Das Gupta
Former Head of English Department,
M.M.M. College, Ghaziabad

Dr. J.L. Raina
Head of Sociology Department,
M.M.H. College, Ghaziabad

Shri A.K. Khare
Department of Zoology,
Meerut College, Meerut

Shri Jagdish Kodesia
Chief Editor,
Indian Farmer Times,
New Delhi

Dr. L.B. Ram
Former Head of Hindi Department,
M.M.H. College, Ghaziabad

Dr. Harish Sharma
Former Head of Hindi Department,
M.M.H. College, Ghaziabad

INTRODUCTION

The Nehru Centenary Year offers us an opportunity to look back to our past and to look forward to the future. We achieved our Independence in 1947 with a hoary and blood stained past, when for very many years our country was steeped into the darkness of hell and abysmal chaos and confusion. We inherited a legacy of a corrupt foreign government which immensely enjoyed the exploitation of our golden land bringing in a sea of horrors and griefs to all of us.

Before Independence, the Indian National Congress under the presidentship of Subhash Chandra Bose, in the late 30s appointed a National Planning Committee with Pandit Jawaharlal Nehru as its Chairman. Bose and Nehru were confident that sooner or later the Britishers would be forced to quit India and that Indians themselves were to look after the building and the development of a New India. Hence after the achievement of Independence, Pandit Jawaharlal Nehru took it upon himself to see to the formation of Planning Commission. Here in this volume we have a rare collection of essays and speeches by different academicians, who have a double purpose to look into the history of Planning Commission in diverse perspectives with of course, Pandit Jawaharlal Nehru at the Centre and the study of his ideals and exploration of his multi-centred personality and also to find out the various pitfalls of our planning with an eye to the proper development of building of the future India. In a way the compilation is an exposition of our self introspection – a study not only of the lively issues tackled during the last fortytwo years – many of which are very much alive even today; but also of the multifarious problems being felt by the new generation after we achieved Independence.

The compilation may well be sub-divided into various sections:

1. Nehru and Planned Development
2. Industry
3. Agriculture
4. Panchsheel and Secularism

5. Freedom Movement and the personality of Nehru.

Mr. Tarlok Singh, the grand old man of Planning in India, who is still very much active despite his age, while inaugurating our National Seminar, spells out the beginning of Planning in India and draws our attention to the late 30s when the first National Planning Committee was formed. He readily points out the uniqueness of Nehru's vision for a New India where a deep concern with the well-being of the rural population (Mahatma Gandhi's teachings) harmonised with the humane quality of the Soviet Five-Year Plans. Nehru, Mr. Tarlok Singh points out, was deeply familiar with the discussions in U.K. and Europe on the problems of Planning in market economies operating under diverse conditions of democracy. In fact Nehru looked forward for a comprehensive planning for the scientific development of New India, for employment and for social services. Nehru had to face tremendous problems because of the partition of India and because of the harrowing distresses of the people who came to be known as refugees. The immediate problems were – rehabilitation of displaced persons, integration of princely territories, but more than these, the creation of a new faith for the reconstruction of a New India on democratic lines with Socialism as her ultimate goal. Mr. Tarlok Singh points out to the objectives of different five-year plans in India. He rightly states that Nehru's deepest concern was for the achievement of a true and real national synthesis. It is a fact that the different plans helped to integrate diverse activities. Nehru laid stress on the development of Science and Technology but not at the cost of literature and arts. In this sense he was to a large extent a follower of Rabindra Nath Tagore. Here is a man, Mr. Tarlok Singh points out, who has the deepest knowledge of Marxism and pre-war Western Socialism and he, therefore, repeatedly stresses that the means of production should be socially owned and controlled for the benefit of the society as a whole. He recognises the fact that the basic and machine building industries are the "root and base of industrial growth" and that these must be built first and they should be placed within the public sector. In other areas of industry, for practical reasons, he finds a great deal of room for private industry. He prefers mixed economy and is against the complete nationalisation of industries to start with. The mixed economy for him is but a stepping stone to the ultimate socially controlled economy where every man is assured of a job, of proper living, of real education and of true freedom of expression. In the field of agriculture, he maintains the necessity of ceilings on agricultural holding and proposes a package of measures for the protection of tenant cultivators. The basis for agricultural economy should be cooperative farming.

Mr. Tarlok Singh, thereafter, draws our attention to the need of reappraisals and revolutions i.e. self introspection. In a letter to the State Chief Ministers in 1963, Pandit Nehru points out to the vast gap of professed ideals and their implementation.

Prof. Y.K. Alagh – a leading economist – draws our attention to the deep concern of Nehru about the application of reason and science to the core problems of the Indian Economy and Society. Prof. Alagh removes a misgiving common amongst Indians that Nehru's fixation, to be entirely fair to the man, was the birth of a new man in a new society. Industrialisation or technological development was only the method to reach the ideal of creation of a new humanity. In this century, Prof. Alagh very correctly points out, we cannot do away with science and technology. Today the need is for a complete integration of various disciplines of life, where science, technology, humanities, music, and arts are properly harmonised. Nehru wanted the harnessing of modern technology to the economic development of this country. It is quite fruitless to argue about the small scale industries and the heavy industries. Both are important. Science cannot be ignored. We are not to find faults with science. Science, in its true perspective, is a body of systematised knowledge. Nehru repeatedly points out that we can use science either to make a heaven or to destroy the humanity. Therefore, he regards the use of technology essential for the construction of a New India. In his various speeches, he points out how India has suffered long because of the lack of proper knowledge of science and technology. Not only technology should be the base of wealth creation, but it should also be the basis of socio-political change. Nehru does not support the protection of out-moded industries, "I am all for tractors and big machinery, and I am convinced that the rapid industrialisation of India is essential to relieve the pressure on land, to combat poverty and raise standards of living, for defence and a variety of other purposes. But I am equally convinced that the most careful planning and adjustment are necessary if we are to reap the full benefit of industrialisation and avoid many of its dangers". Another important thing about Nehru, points out Prof. Alagh, is the vital importance of planning to the anti-colonial struggle. "The objective for the country as a whole, was the attainment, as far as possible of national self-sufficiency. International trade was certainly not excluded, but we were anxious to avoid being drawn into whirlpool of economic imperialism". Prof. Alagh also points out that with Nehru, planning was not an end in itself. It was a method to overcome constraints to our rapid development with the goal to bring about the real fruits of socialism to every individual. Hence his vision of a technologically progressive new India was not that of bureaucratic controls, but of a socially directed process of integrated scientific and technological knowledge with the central concerns for every Indian.

Prof. S.S. Mahapatra in his paper on 'Indian Planning at a Glance', presents a comprehensive study of Indian Planning – analysing various plans and exploring the various gains, pitfalls and limitations. He rightly cautions that results depend more on deeds than on words and platitudes.

Dr. Yashvir Tyagi talks about Nehru's vision of planned development of India. He seeks to identify the impact of Nehru-Mahalanobis strategy on the post-Nehru planning and its influence on the course of Indian economy. Dr. Tyagi refers to the Fabian-Marxian influences on Nehru. At the same time he refers to the Gandhian impact on him. The emphasis on heavy industries and a scientific temper is the basis of Nehru-Mahalanobis strategy. Nehru understood well the dynamics of international power equations. Hence he talked about the firm foundations of heavy industries under the state control. But the welfare of the common man was never lost sight of in the economy of Nehru and P.C. Mahalanobis.

Dr. B.M. Jauhari speaks about 'Planning and poverty eradication – retrospect and prospect'. He puts his finger at the right spot claiming that the main objective of planning, should be the eradication of poverty. Unfortunately even after so many years of India's Independence, poverty is the basic sore of our country. Dr. Jauhari points out that we always complain of India being over populated. This is correct, but at the same time this malady exists in all the developing countries. What we need, he points out, is not merely the proper planning, but the need of the moment is the proper utilisation of our enormous resources. If the utilisation is properly done, if corruption is eradicated, if the leakages are set right, much of the scar of poverty can be healed up.

Prof. Rudra Datt argues in his paper on Gandhi and Nehru – Planning for poverty removal – that the Nehru Model of development had many serious distortions and deviations during the process of implementation. He emphatically points out Nehru's failure to provide a national minimum and to attain full employment. According to Prof. Rudra Datt these failures are due to the neglect of agriculture and small scale industry. Nehru, according to the Professor, himself recognised the reasons of his failures a few years before his death. Prof. Datt also points out that the Janata Party coming to power for a short period equally failed to make any break-through in implementing the Gandhian model of development (the Janata Party Leaders called themselves staunch Gandhites). The learned author here pleads for a reconciliation of the two models. According to him Nehru spoke for the heavy industry while Gandhi sought to provide for a better deal to the poor man. Therefore, if the two models are harmonised together and synthesised into a new whole, perhaps India can have a very bright future.

Dr. A.D.N. Bajpai brings out a challenging paper where he places on record the planning as conceived and done by Pandit Nehru and the disparities which are very much visible at present in spite of the best efforts of the planning stalwarts. He again and again refers to the dire necessity of the soul and body put together. In India, Planning is well conceived, allocations made, but the common man, who is to be associated with the planning manoeuvre, is often forgotten and left out – the result being the non-implementation of the planning – but with the misspending of the total allocation.

The section – 'Industry' – begins with a paper by Dr. A.K. Singh. Prof. Singh is his paper studies Nehru's ideas on Socialism and the place of mixed economy in the achievement of the socialist ideals. He refers to the origin of Nehru's socialism and points out the influence exerted on him by Fabian Socialism and Marxism. As far back as in 1930 in the Karachi Session of the Indian National Congress, Nehru moved the resolution on the Fundamental Rights of the people and stressed on the nationalisation of the key industries and the services. He wanted the abolition of private property except in a restricted sense and the replacement of the then existing profit system by higher ideals of cooperative services. He also stressed on the ideals of Panchayati Raj institutions. But for the attainment of socialistic ideals, he advocated the introduction of a mixed economy. During his lifetime, refers Prof. Singh, he nationalised a number of key industries and he laid foundations for the start of Unit Trust of India, which is playing a vital role in our present day economy. Dr. Singh points out that Nehru was a pragmatist, he was never an orthodox in any of his approaches. Perhaps Nehru was orthodox only in one approach – approach for the attainment of the Socialistic ideals in a new India.

Prof. Jagdish Prakash, in his paper seeks to present the vision of Nehru and his efforts to build up a New India. He points out that Nehru from the very outset expressed himself in favour of the state taking up more and more industries for the construction of a New India and against private capitalism – India being the first country to emerge from the colonial status into an independent sovereign State after the Second World War and the Britishers had left a garbage of spoils, disaster, sufferings, illiteracy and backwardness coupled with abject poverty. Nehru felt that only by rapid industrialisation, India could emerge as a free nation with noble ideas. He did not like to handover the Indian economy to the private capitalists who, according to him, would ruin the country completely. Nehru declared in May 1956, "I want this House to realise how vast and unexploited a field lies there for the public sector to occupy". But at the same time he stated, "May I say here, that while I am for the public sector growing, I do not understand or appreciate the condemnation of the private sector". Prof. Jagdish Prakash points out, "It was this strong conviction and vision of Panditji of a just, self reliant, technically advanced with scientific fervour and modern economy that placed public sector at the centre of India's development." Nehru, however, made it clear – "while the public sector must obviously grow and even now it has grown absolutely and relatively – the private sector is not something unimportant. It will play an important role though gradually and ultimately it will fade away. But the public sector will control and should control the strategic points in our economy".

Prof. Lallan Prasad talks about the policy perspectives of our industrial growth. His paper is rather a historical sketch where he refers to how the traditional industries like textiles, jute and rubber were retrograded in background, while engineering, petroleum and electronic industries were given powerful incentives. He also talks about the somewhat injudicious policy of Licence Liberalisation, which has also pushed back our industrial growth.

Dr. S.C. Mathur brings out before us the place of mixed economy, industrialisation and the use of technology in the process of rebuilding India. He justly refers to Nehru's ideas of socialism and the inspiration that Nehru secured from the Soviet Union, "The Five Year

Plans have completely changed the face of Russia", Nehru writes, "From a feudal country, it has suddenly become an advanced industrial country. There has been an amazing cultural advance and the social services, the system of public health and accident insurances are the most advanced in the World". Dr. Mathur believes that Nehru wanted to achieve these ideals through the five year plans in India. He also points out that the Soviet Union has, since Nehru's time, offered India assistance in building 70 large industrial enterprises and other projects in the public sector.

The section on 'Agriculture' is broadly covered by Prof. G.S. Bhalla, Dr. B.B. Singh, Dr. Rajpati Ram and Dr. R.C. Gupta.

Prof. G.S. Bhalla in his paper stresses on the fact that with Nehru the greatest ideological commitment was the achievement of economic and social freedom as represented by socialism. In his paper he points out both to the achievements and failures of our economic planning and seeks to make a detailed attempt to critically analyse Nehru's ideas on role and importance of agriculture in the national economy and his contribution to the agricultural planning in India. Prof. Bhalla introduces the paper with a detailed account of the conditions of Indian peasantry in the free India. Next he discusses the implementation of the agrarian policies after independence. Thereafter, he evaluates the agricultural planning and policies during Nehru's period. Lastly he sums up his ideas with a pointer to the future and the lapses which are occurring daily in our implementation of Land Reforms.

Dr. B.B. Singh and Dr. Rajpati Ram come out with sound conclusions in their paper on Rural Infrastructure and Agricultural Development in a Backward Economy. Creation of rural infrastructure is indeed basically important for any strategy of agricultural development. The paper deals with conceptual framework, methodology and inter-relations and makes an indepth study of agriculture and allied issues. It is a bold attempt to tackle the problems of agriculture, to lift it from a backward to a highly developed stage.

Dr. R.C. Gupta, seeks to analyse the suitability of Nehru's economic policies to the development of modern India. He refers to the different facts of Indian Economic situation, agrarian, industrial private sector, public sector and cottage industries. He says that the basic flaw in Nehru's economic policy is the minimisation of the need of growth of agriculture. He is one with Gandhiji that agriculture and cottage industries should be given top priority.

The fourth Section contains the first three prize winning essays in order of merit on Nehru and Panchsheel. It also contains stimulating papers by Dr. V.K. Parkhomenko, Shri I.K. Gujral, Dr. G.N. Srivastava, Shri H.M. Jauhari and Dr. N.K. Gupta.

Dr. Parkhomenko details out in his paper the friendly and brotherly relations of the Soviet Union and India and the contributions of Pandit Nehru to the attainment of these relations. Nehru visited the Soviet Union three times and was always deeply impressed by the great achievements of the Soviet Union both in artistic and in scientific fields, and was also deeply moved by the feelings of profound interest and sympathy of the Soviet people towards India. In hours of trials and tribulations, the Soviet Union has always extended its warmth and its strong hand of cooperation to India for the alleviation of her difficulties.

Mr. I.K. Gujral takes up the study of secularism and Nehru. He is not at all obsessed with the economic policies of Nehru. He pleads for a secular India where the rights of the minorities are to be properly protected and where religious sentiments are not to pollute the political climate. Nehru, he points out, objected to, "flirtations with all religions". Nehru was against the astrologers or the miracle makers. But at the same time he never villified any religion. He was for value based politics. Mr. Gujral concludes, "The British had legitimised communal politics with a purpose. Its continuity now is highly damaging and must end".

Dr. G.N. Srivastava in his paper details the contribution of Pandit Nehru in building NAM as an effective international forum for peace and mutual cooperation. Nehru indeed was an internationalist in out look and desired that the globe should be free from tension, distrust and hegemony of any form. NAM, to be precise, is the symbol of Nehru's faith and belief.

Mr. H.M. Jauhari deals with the secular ideals of Nehru. He unfolds some facts unknown to many of us. Secularism is the basis of our national life and Pandit Nehru had been a staunch believer in this creed – a national necessity.

Dr. N.K. Gupta tries to present a study of Nehru's socialism, its origin and the development that it took during his life time. He expresses his belief that Nehru's Socialism can only be termed as Nehruist.

The final section starts with a speech by Dr. N.B. Das Gupta. Dr.

Das Gupta, in his paper on 40th Anniversary of Indian Independence seeks to present a new perspective to the study of Indian freedom movement – a perspective that is opposed to the official history available in our country. He constantly refers to the struggle of the common man for the freedom of the country which is often forgotten by our traditional and official historians. He says, "It is seldom the record of the people, it is seldom the record of the suffering humanity". He also points out to the rather unfortunate fact that many of the historians refer to the revolutionaries as terrorists. We often forget, he says, the freedom upsurges of the peasants and the tribals. We often forget the Moplahs, the Indigo-Resistance movements: We forget the names of Birsa Munda, Phadke, Khudiram and various others. We do not even pay proper homage to Bhagat Singh, Sukhdev, Rajguru, Surya Sen and a host of other revolutionaries who were not terrorists but who sacrificed themselves for the cause of their motherland.

We also tend to forget the movements of the working class and the peasantry. In fact, Dr. Das Gupta points out, that our worthy books of history are mostly class histories and not the real account of our freedom movement. Thus we do not accord proper place to the role of the 1942 upsurge, the mass movements for the release of I.N.A. heroes and the great liberation upsurge, which has just been glossed over as RIN mutiny.

Dr. J.L. Raina, in his article "Nehru on Education" very vividly recaptures the basic ideas of Nehru on education. He points out at the very outset that Nehru did never jot down his ideas and ideals on education, they are to be collected from his various addresses on different occasions. Nehru wanted to build a new India, out of a heap of ashes and broken images; hence he wanted the creation of a new man – a personality with social awareness, a personality with devotion, discipline and dedication – with a keen eye on the integration and the synthesisation of the diverse forces of Indian Culture.

Shri A.K. Khare has something interesting to present in his paper on Nehru and Science. He seeks to point out how Nehru was drawn towards science, and at the same time how he was deeply conscious and aware of the possibilities of the colossal misuse of science.

Mr. Jagdish Kodesia, talks about the multi-coloured personality of Pandit Nehru and the deep popularity he enjoyed with the Indian masses. He gives certain instances drawn from his personal experiences and observations how Nehru could create a spell of magic over his audience, which more than once used to be in lakhs.

Dr. L.B. Ram 'Anant' seeks to find out Nehru's real ideas about nation, nationality and integration. Dr. Ram presents the ideas of Dr. B.R. Ambedkar regarding nation and integration. The paper evokes some radical questions which might disturb our common ideas about integration.

Dr. Harish Sharma presents a lyrical study of the literary genius of Nehru. Nehru was a great statesman, a staunch humanist, but he was also a great literary artist. Dr. Sharma, very ably, draws our attention to this rather little-known or forgotten side of Nehru.

Lastly 'The Man Alive – The Man Immortal' wherein Dr. Das Gupta presents a collection of quotations from Nehru's different writings and speeches, with suitable punctuations that bring out the real Nehru with his incredible great heights, his doubts, his imbalances, self-introspection. It is a fitting tribute to the Man Alive – the Man Immortal.

SECTION I

NEHRU AND PLANNED DEVELOPMENT

1

JAWAHARLAL NEHRU AND THE PLANNED DEVELOPMENT OF INDIA

TARLOK SINGH

I feel deeply honoured in being asked to give the opening address at the Nehru Centenary seminar convened by the Indian Centre for Socialist Studies. An occasion such as this provides an opportunity to relate the present to the past and, to an extent, also to look at the future.

Twenty-five years after the passing of Jawaharlal Nehru, through all the changes that have since occurred, we are struck by the deep impact he made on his times, the main paths of progress that he marked out for the country, and the sense of continuity which marks the growth and evolution of the economy and polity of India. These attributes are testimony to Nehru's sound assessment of the needs of India and his carefully considered response.

The economic perspective of the freedom movement was formulated decisively during the thirties, between the Karachi Congress in 1931, Faizpur Congress in 1936, and the setting up of the National Planning Committee in 1939. Against the background of Gandhiji's deep concern with the well-being of the rural population, Nehru's had been the dominant influence in defining and articulating economic and the social policies for the future. Thus, when freedom came, Nehru's mind was fully prepared on many of the basic issues.

Jawaharlal Nehru was ahead of his contemporaries in perceiving the necessity of planning for the economic and social reconstruction of India. He had witnessed the powerful impact of the earlier Soviet Five-Year Plans. He was familiar with the discussions in U.K. and Europe on the problems of planning in market economies operating under conditions of democracy. The National Planning Committee made it possible for him to bring a large number of scholars, scientists, experts and social workers to think together about future economic and social development. Thus, from an early stage, the need for national planning became a point of common agreement among thinking people. Post-war reconstruction plans in Britain and elsewhere had also proceeded in terms of comprehensive planning for employment and social services. The belief in planning was reinforced by the series of independent documents which followed the Bombay Plan. With the setting up of the Planning and Development Department in the Government of India in 1944, planning became a part of the system of government and administration which India inherited at independence.

One of the first initiatives taken by Nehru after the formation of the Interim Government was the setting up of an Advisory Planning Board to review the work done by way of post-war reconstruction. This review pointed to the need for a new agency for planning to be called the Planning Commission. However, this step had to wait until the immediate problems of rehabilitation of displaced persons, integration of princely territories, and the making of the Constitution had been dealt with. The formal setting up of the Planning Commission came as a sequel to the promulgation of the new Constitution. In the Resolution of the Government in March 1950 setting up the Planning Commission, Nehru took care to relate its objectives not only to the immediate tasks of planning and harnessing of natural and human resources, but also to the longer term goals embodied in the Fundamental Rights and the Directive Principles of the Constitution. This perspective and the ethos has been an important contributory factor in the continuity of planning in India.

In a federal system, co-operation in national development between the Centre and the States is an imperative condition for the success of national planning. To an extent such co-operation is secured through the greater capacity of the Centre in providing financial support. The roots of Centre-State co-operation, however, have to be deeper. They have to be sought in shared objectives and a sense of common values. It was this aspect that Nehru stressed on every occasion. The Resolution setting up the Planning Commission had proceeded on this assumption. The Government of India could take the initiative to set up the Planning Commission only by virtue of the provision in the Constitution which made Economic and Social Planning an item in the Concurrent List. The setting up of the National Development Council in 1952 was a logical corollary of this fact. In the very first meeting of the National Development Council, Nehru spoke of it as a forum for intimate co-operation between State Governments and the Central Government for all the tasks of national development. The Council was set up with three objects: to strengthen and mobilise the effort and resources of the nation in support of the Plan; to promote common economic policies in all vital spheres; and to ensure the balanced and rapid development of all parts of the country. From these objectives flowed the functions of the Council, namely, to review the working of the National Plan from time to time; to consider important questions of social and economic policy affecting national development; and to recommend measures for achieving the aims and targets of the National Plan.

Between November 1952 and November 1963, during Nehru's life-time, the National Development Council met 20 times. Its meetings marked significant stages in the evolution of national planning. The Council proved to be an effective means of cooperation and coordination in areas of development which involved both the Centre and the States. In areas of economic and financial policy which fell more directly within the sphere of the Centre, specially in the Ministry of Finance, the role of the Council has been somewhat secondary.

The Planning Commission and the National Development Council were the two main pieces of planning machinery evolved during Nehru's time and at his instance. Through them, Nehru stressed the role of planning as a means for achieving a larger national synthesis. This aspect was of crucial significance in the early years of planning and nation-building, and appeared then to be its decisive role. Nehru's personal identification with Planning and its main instruments gave tremendous strength to them and helped the Centre and the States and public opinion generally to think and work towards a national consensus.

We may ask how Nehru viewed the process of planning. On many occasions he emphasised the need for precision, avoiding mere wishfulness. Planning involved the interlocking of production, consumption, employment and other facets of development like transport, social services, education and health. Statistics were essential for achieving such interlocking. Hence the consistent support he extended to the work of the Indian Statistical Institute and the National Sample Survey. Secondly, planning implied taking a long-term, view, having before the mind a picture of what was to be achieved over a period. The picture would change as we move forward. Therefore, planning had to be in nature both continuous and responsive to new needs and new challenges. Fourthly, planning meant moving continuously from the political to the economic and social plane. Finally, though planning helped to integrate diverse activities, it was only a part of the total national endeavour. In his role as nation-builder, Nehru identified himself simultaneously with variety of movements of change-social, economic, scientific and technological, literary, artistic and others. Together they added up to the scheme of creative national endeavour.

In speaking of the need for a perspective, Nehru emphasised that there should be a clear view of the structure of the society we wished to achieve. His own picture, he insisted, was 'definitely and absolutely a socialistic picture of society'. He did not use the expression in a rigid and dogmatic sense. He accepted the view common to Marxism and pre-war western socialism that the means of production should be socially owned and controlled for the benefit of society as a whole. He had in mind, particularly modern industry. His commitment was by no means unqualified. He distinguished heavy and machine-building industries from light and consumer goods industries. Basic industries and machine-building industries were for Nehru the 'root and the base of industrial growth' and these must be built first. For basic and machine building industries, future expansion should in the main be in the public sector. In other areas of industry, for practical reasons, he saw a great deal of room for private industry. He was opposed in principle to nationalisation of existing industries because they would be technologically behind. The public sector should advance faster, both absolutely and relatively to the private sector, but in the areas allotted to it, the private sector should be allowed to function freely. The essential aim in Nehru's mind was that economic power should not be concentrated in private hands, economic power should be dispersed, and no monopolies should be allowed to develop.

In his picture of the future, Nehru gave the first place to industry, science and technology. He expected that these together would have decisive influence in changing social structure and social attitudes and behaviour. Perhaps he under-estimated the extent to which scientific and technological progress itself depended upon social and structural changes. He looked to the processes of democracy to create pressures for social change. He was confident that through planning under democracy it would become possible to counter the pulls in favour of an acquisitive society.

Nehru was clear in his mind that while the future depended on industry and technology under Indian conditions, agriculture remained the foundation for industrial, and economic development. In particular, until the rural population was brought into the mainstream, the barrier of underdevelopment could not be crossed and the entire economy would be held back. In the long run, agriculture itself would depend on progress in industry. Nehru gave his full support to agricultural extension, grow more food programmes, and community development. Development in rural areas could not go far without local participation, local leadership, and responsible local institutions. Strengthening of cooperatives and panchayats at the base of rural society and the development of Panchayati Raj institutions therefore became an integral part of Nehru's picture of the future and, at every step, he extended the utmost support to these institutional developments.

Nehru had long held that the agrarian structure in India was largely built on feudal traditions and was inequitable. There fore, he gave his full support to proposals for land reform urged by the Congress Agrarian Reforms Committee and to the recommendations, in particular in the Second Plan. Despite differences at the highest levels, he maintained the necessity of ceilings on agricultural holdings and the package of measures proposed for protecting the tenant cultivator. The prolonged food deficit led him to a firm belief in the need for cooperation in all forms, including operations of farming. Cooperative farming undertaken on a voluntary basis, and supported by incentives and demonstration, became accepted policy. However, towards the close of the fifties, as forces opposed to it became stronger, within and outside the Indian National Congress, there was a measure of retreat. Perhaps Nehru himself felt that the ground had yet to be adequately prepared. Nevertheless, he continued to educate the country on the necessity of cooperation in varied forms for building up the rural economy.

The design of development which Nehru presented through his speeches was reflected in the Plans. It was weak in some respects. It did not give sufficient attention to employment and the utilisation of human resources. The problem of eradication of illiteracy was left to the distant future. Lags between development of economic infrastructures and social services were accentuated. Poverty, like unemployment and under-employment, tended to be seen as long-term problems, dependent for their final solution on the growth of the economy as a whole. Practical difficulties in finding foreign exchange for import of fertilizers were for long a source of weakness for rapid agricultural development.

Even during Nehru's lifetime, certain contradictions and imbalances had emerged in the pattern of development that was taking shape. The food problems remained acute and food aid was an essential element in securing relative price stability. Much of the industrialisation was being accomplished through inflows of external resources. While technological self-reliance gradually advanced, economic self-reliance was still a long way off. Then structural changes contemplated in the scheme of agrarian reform were proceeding only slowly and implementation of the legislation which had been enacted in the states left much to be desired. Nehru had himself become increasingly conscious that the benefits of development were not flowing sufficiently to the weaker groups in the community. Imbalances latent within the economy came to a head with the prolonged stagnation in agriculture and the new burdens of defence which the country was called upon to bear in the early sixties. Thus, even in Nehru's own life-time, the stage had come for a thorough reappraisal of the goals of planning and of planning methods and priorities.

Reappraisals and revaluations are a necessary part of the process of planning. They are a means for correcting imbalances and setting fresh courses that may be called for in the course of development. There would be general agreement that by and large the directions which Nehru gave to planning and the economy have proved their worth. We owe to them the impressive growth of infrastructures, of science and technology, and the resources of manpower. Some reason for doubt exists in respect of the place given to agriculture. Perhaps, if a more integrated view of agriculture and industry had been taken, agriculture would have received greater support, more favourable price policies would have been adopted,and agrarian changes would have been speeded. Thereby greater progress might have been achieved in agriculture. The view which Nehru expressed about agriculture and small industries providing some kind of balance to the growth of large scale industries and specially of heavy industries did not sufficiently acknowledge their critical role in the economy. Large and small industries have to be seen together as part of a unified industrial structure, with shifts stimulated and aided within the structure as technology and organisation advance. Likewise, agriculture and industry have to be constantly seen together in the scheme of technical change.

Some of the consequences of choices made in Nehru's time became clear only in later years. Thus, the gap between the organised sector, specially the public and the corporate sector, and the vast array of unorganised activities, in terms of income and productivity levels, has profound implications for poverty and employment. The need to put much larger resources into the unorganised sector and to deal directly with the problems of poverty and employment is now perceived more clearly than before. Faced with problems presented by landless labour and marginal and small farmers, the need for co-operative and group action is not less urgent than before, although the forms have to be adapted to present needs and realities. The growth of inequalities is a visible consequence of the patterns of development in a mixed economy to which no direct answer seems to be presently available. With greater concentration of resources on accelerated development in the more backward regions and on the weaker groups in society, some of the harsher consequences of greater inequality within the economic system might be countered. Higher priority to social and human resources development would make for greater equity and strength for the economy as a whole.

The passage of years has left the main framework of ideas represented by Nehru and the Plan with which he was associated largely in tact. They represent the structure on which new policies and directions have to be built in to provide for changing conditions, new technological possibilities, and pressing social demands. The coming years will certainly demand more rapid social, economic and technological changes and more sensitive approaches to social, human and regional issues in development.

2

NEHRU : Planning Commission and Planned Economic Development

Y.K. ALAGH

Nehru was centrally concerned about applying reason and science to the core problems of the Indian economy and society. Technological progress was a fixation, but the real target was a new man. Industrialisation was the method. But the driving concern was to get the country out of its stagnant rut into a dynamic process of thought and action. One sees in his thinking concerns which are refreshingly contemporary. Technical progress through scientific education and thinking, industrialisation as a dynamic process, social action through consensus and socialism with a human face, all so pressingly contemporary in the Perestroika and Twenty-first Century paradigms. Frank Moraes in his biography of Nehru, had correctly argued that his contribution would only be evaluated when the generation of young persons he had influenced would cross their forties and start playing a leadership role in Indian society. A core of inter-related economic ideas underlies Nehru's economic thinking through a long period. This comes out very strikingly if one compares sections of *The Discovery of India* (Ch. VIII and X) and one of his last overall analysis of his own policies and views contained in the article on *Changing India,* published after the Chinese invasion in *Foreign Affairs* (April 1965). Nehru seems to be a case of the proposition of J.M. Keynes, that "in the field of economic and political philosophy there are not many who are influenced by new theories after they are twenty-five or thirty years of age."[1] The cut-off point was latter for Nehru, but during the past thirty years of his life, his economic ideas show a remarkable consistency.

2. To Nehru, the harnessing of modern technology to economic development was very important. There were two implications of

this. The first was an acceptance of the emphasis on heavy industries in the process of industrialisation of India. While there has been considerable controversy in India on large scale *vs.* small scale industrialisation, Nehru himself had clinched the issue in his own mind even in his early economic thinking. This was perhaps one of the few economic *choices* he really made. Discussing the issue of the big machine *vs.* cottage industries, he stated emphatically that "it is not a mere question of adjustment of the two forms of production and economy. One must be dominating and paramount with the other as complimentary to it, fitting in where it can. The economy based on the latest technical achievements of the day must necessarily be the dominating one."[2] The second, wider implication of this approach was his emphasis on scientific education and research. He seems to have a particular fascination for the idea that under "proper" social conditions, experimentation with the machine would inculcate the "scientific temper" and widen the experience and outlook of men.[3] Formal economics is now accepting this idea in the shape of the productivity implication of a "learning theory approach".

3. Technology was the basis of wealth creation:

> "The search for the sources of India's strength and for her deterioration and decay is long and intricate. Yet the recent causes of that decay are obvious enough. She falls behind the march of technique, and Europe, which had long been backward in many matters, took the lead in technical progress. Behind this technical progress was the spirit of science and a bubbling life and spirit which displayed itself in many activities and in adventurous voyages of discovery. New techniques gave military strength to the countries of Western Europe, and it was easy for them to spread out and dominate the East. That is the story not only of India, but of the whole of Asia."[4]

It was however also the basis of socio-political changes:

> "In these days of very rapid technological advance, no man knows what the world will be like even a short time hence. We are technologically backward. Therefore, sometimes, when we discuss big problems, we discuss them in a rather static way forgetting that the very ground underneath our feet is changing and slipping

away. Unless we move with it, we may tumble down or be left behind. We are not emotionally aware of what is happening from day-to-day in the field of technology. It may well be that in the course of the next ten or twenty years, this technological advance may change the whole aspect of things in the world, and that will affect the life of human beings tremendously. It will affect their social structure. Ultimately, it must affect their political structure also. Anything may happen. We cannot bind the future, but for the present, we have to deal with facts as they are."[5]

4. Technical change was however a dynamic process. The emphasis on modernization that we are talking of again now and that this involved *change* was a bugbear for Nehru. And so:

"The real question is not one of quantitative adjustment and balancing of various incongruous elements and methods of production, but qualitative consequences flow. The economic and political aspects of this qualitative change are important, but equally important are the social and psychological aspects. In India especially, where we have been wedded for too long to past forms and modes of thought and action, new experiences, new processes, leading to new ideas and new horizons, are necessary. Thus we will change the static character of our living and make it dynamic and vital, and our minds will become active and adventurous. New situations lead to new experiences, as the mind is compelled to deal with them and adapt itself to a changing environment."[6]

And again:

"The history of science shows that it does not simply better the old. It sometimes upsets the old. It does not merely add new truths to the old ones but sometimes the new truths and thereby upsets the way of men's thinking and the way of their lives. Science, therefore, does not merely repeat the old in better ways or add to the old but creates something that is new to the world and to human consciousness.

If we pursue this line of thought what exactly does the spirit of science mean? It means many things. It means not only accepting the fresh truth that science may bring, not only accepting improving the old but being prepared to upset the old if it goes against that spirit. It also means not being tied down to something that is old because it is old, because we have carried on with it but being able to accept its disintegration; it means not being tied down to a social fabric or an industrial fabric or an economic fabric if it goes against the new discovery."[7]

Those who would quote Nehruite planning to argue that he was supporting protection to outmoded industries would do well to read what he had to say in 1946:

"I say this because I am to some extent, if I may venture to say so, of a scientific bent of mind and I try to thinking more in dynamic terms than in static terms. The existing industry today that most people think of — capitalists, socialists, or communists — is something of which they think in static terms, as if the thing must go on and on, while as a matter of fact the thing is completely out of date and most of it should be scrapped.

It you think in a somewhat dynamic way, you can see that we are at one of the major ages of transition when completely new sources of power are being tapped, something of the nature of the Industrial Revolution or Electrical Revolution, but something even more far-reaching. If somebody at the time of the Industrial Revolution was thinking in terms of the pre-industrial age and talking about acquiring this or that, he would have been completely out of the picture some time later when the new age come and there were new industrial age and whether it takes ten, fifteen or twenty years — I doubt if it will take more than — many of our methods of production will become completely out of date, and what you are thinking of acquiring today may have no value at all. That is a warning. I hope it does not frighten people and make them think that they should not invest money in any industry. But one has to be very wide awake today about these changes and one must think in terms of the future rather than the past, because the past is dead and gone and we cannot go back to it, and even the present is a rapidly changing present. If you approach it in terms of the future, then many of the present conflicts seem out of place; or, at any rate, they assume a new aspect and you get out of the rut of your old mode of thinking."[8]

5. The urge to go to the 21st century has roots in the yearnings of the early years of independence. To Nehru, however, machine building infrastructure development and self-reliance were important as methods of technological self-reliance in a large economy, aiming at autonomous development. Planning was the method to achieve these objectives.

> "I am all for tractors and big machinery, and I am convinced that the rapid industrialisation of India is essential to relive the pressure on land to combat poverty and raise standards of living, for defence and a variety of other purposes. But I am equally convinced that the most careful planning and adjustment are necessary if we are to reap the full benefit of industrialisation and avoid many of its dangers."[9]

and again:

> "The three fundamental requirements of India, if she is to develop industrially and otherwise, are a heavy engineering and machine-making industry, scientific research institutes, electric power. These must be the foundations of all planning, and the national planning committee laid the greatest emphasis on them. We lacked all three, and bottlenecks in industrial expansion were always occurring."[10]

Nehru was clear in his economic choices in favour of self-reliance and critical of those who took a short cut to industrialisation:

> "Not, if we think in terms of building our industry, we must give up the idea of continually getting machines from abroad. We must build them here. Sometimes, our Government Departments, who have a peculiar way of calculating things, try to show that it is cheaper to get things from abroad than to order them here. That I call a perverted approach. Anything that comes from abroad is more expensive than the one produced by Indian labour, even though it may cost ten times as much. I do not say we should always do it. I stress it because this business of getting things from abroad needs to be looked into from the point of view of the human problem in India, the problem of employment, production and building up our economy. We must aim at

producing the machines and all the basic things here. We might get them from abroad to begin with, but we should not go on getting them in this manner. For ultimately, our basic industries are as essential as the development of power."[11]

The origin, of course, went back to the anti-colonial struggle:

"The objective for the country as a whole was the attainment, as far as possible, of national self-sufficiency. International trade was certainly not excluded, but we were anxious to avoid being drawn into whirlpool of economic imperialism."[12]

6. The emphasis on planning and on socialism as an objective was clear. However, on *methods* the great man could be electic. Thus

"I wish to lay stress here on our approach to planning I mean the democratic approach. This approach has also to be statistical approach, that is, an approach based on statistical information, not on vague ideas and ideals. Statistical data have to be collected, and sample surveys and calculations made at every stage, to calculate our actual resources, the employment potential of the plan, the production rate, and the commodity balances. For, it must be remembered, planning does not merely mean putting up a factory here or a factory there. Planning implies the interlocking of the production, consumption, employment and a large number of other things, such as transport, social services, education and health. The whole thing has somehow to be brought together. Of course, human relationships in a vast country of three hundred seventy million people cannot be dealt with in a mathematical way. There are numerous uncertain factors, the coming of the monsoon, for instance. Yet the element of uncertainty and error can be greatly reduced by planning."[13]

But planning was not an end in itself. It was a method to overcome constraints to development sequentially:

"Gradually, though the painful processes of thought we have proceeded along the path of planning. And I have no doubt that we ought to continue this and learn more and more, often make mistakes, nevertheless growing progressively a little more expert at this business of planning. We want to arrive at a stage when we can assess, more or less accurately, what the next stage is going to be and to provide for it and to visualise our problems in advance, to take appropriate action to meet them before events force our hands. After all, that is the object of planning."[14]

Socialism was an objective, but there was electism in methods:

"Now, we have said that our objective is a socialist pattern of society. I do not propose to define in precise terms what socialism in this context means, because we wish to avoid any doctrinaire thinking, any rigid thinking, because even in my life time I have seen the world change so much, and I have seen so many other changes that I do not want to confine my mind to any rigid dogma. But broadly speaking, what do we mean when we say our objective is a "socialist pattern of life"? Surely, we mean a society in which there is a social cohesion, which is without classes, where there is equality of opportunity and the possibility for everyone to live a good life. Obviously, this cannot be attained unless we produce the wherewithal to achieve these standards to enable us to lead that good life. So, we have to lay great stress on equality. on the removal of disparities, and it has to be remembered always that socialism does not consist in the spreading out of poverty. The essential thing is that their must be wealth and production."[15]

7. The only issue on which there was to be no compromise was advancement through technological progress. Planning and the necessary degree of social control were to be handmaidens to this objective. Thus:

"For instance, if I may put one aspect of the case before the House, I think that the progress of technology and of science is so enormous and so rapid that within a fairly short space of time, let us say, 15 years, the whole conception of modern industry will have changed completely. New sources of power will be discovered and those sources of power will upset the methods of production that exist today, much more so than the Industrial Revolution did 150 years ago in England and in the rest of Europe.

All these enormous changes are going to take place and I find that many of us, whether we call ourselves socialists, communists, capitalists or by any other name, are singularly unaware of the big changes that are taking place. They are so unaware of this that they think merely in terms, not of the greater wealth coming into existence by fresh methods, but rather only of changing the ownership of industry, which, of course, may be important from the point of view of advancing towards equality.

Distribution is very important, but what is far more important is the dynamic future. In the changed situation all over the world, new sources of power might completely revolutionize our agriculture as well as our industry. Therefore, what I think is most important for the State is that whatever may happen to the existing sources of production these new and novel sources of production should always remain in the hands of the State. We should not allow them to go into private hands and thus become private monopolies. And in regard to the existing sources, we should proceed step by step, and avoid any drop in production or disturbance of the economic structure, as far as possible.[16]

8. There was in Nehru a genuine concern about the need for a peaceful transition through consensus in the development phase. There is frequent emphasis on the "*social*" implications of economic ideas and programmes. Forced with a direct issue the late Prime Minister was liable to discuss it sometimes along "wider" national, international or even philosophical lines. The earlier method of "democratic collectivism" remains later in the shape of "democratic socialism" and the "mixed economy". Equality of opportunity for all remains a basic theme. This concern for a consensus comes out strikingly in his own words when he was writing about the work of the National Planning Committee set up by the Congress Party before independence under his direction.

> "So one thing led to another and it was impossible to isolate anything or to progress in one direction without corresponding progress in another. The more we thought of the planning business, the vaster it grew in its sweep and range till it seems to embrace almost every activity. That did not mean we intended regulating and regimenting everything, but we had to keep almost everything in view even in deciding about one particular sector of the plan. The fascination of this work grew upon me and, I think,

upon the other members of our committee also. But at the same time, a certain vagueness and indefiniteness crept in; instead of concentrating on some major aspects of the plan, we tended to become diffuse. This also led to delay in the work of many of our sub-committees which lacked the sense of urgency and of working for definite objective within a stated time.

Constituted as we were, it was not casy for all of us to agree to any basic social policy or principles underlying social organisation. Any attempt to discuss these principles in the abstract was bound to lead to fundamental differences of approach at the outset and possibly to a splitting up of the committee. Not to have such a guiding policy was a serious drawback, yet there was not help for it. We decided to consider the general problem of planning as well as each individual problem concretely and not in the abstract and allow principles to develop out of such considerations."

9. Nehru's vision of a technologically progressive India was not that of bureaucratic controls, but of a socially directed process of integrating technology with the central concerns of Indian development, namely the interface of modern methods of production and organization with vast areas by passed in the colonial era, where our great resources and population concentration lie. Modernization, therefore, has to be with the sense of priorities and this is all that planning is about. Control is not an end in itself but resources have to be directed to areas of concern whether they are rehabilitation of sick industries which meet the needs of the average Indian, critical infrastructure and intermediates, agro-based development of exports and global presence in selected sectors. His advice to those who would shy away from such problems is as relevant now as then. Thus:

"As I am sitting here, member of your Federation who was moving or supporting a resolution finished up by saying something about the practical approach to things, because, of course, industrialists and businessmen take pride in being practical: politicians also talk of being practical. What amazes me, however, is that these men whose God is 'being practical' are sometimes most amazingly ignorant of people and of what is happening around. Their idea of being practical is to imagine that the world never changes and follow something that they and their forefathers have done in the past: that is being practical, just, as, if I may refer to the class to whom I might be said to belong, the politicians are very hard-headed and practical men too. Being hard-headed and practical people they are forced to bring about wars in the world: and dealing with terrific problems they work hard and earnestly, fail to solve them and then have another war and create more problems and so on. So the cycle goes on and we are all trying to be practical. Now, surely, there is something wrong about this approach to things. So I have become a little weary of people who call themselves practical and hard-headed. That hard-headedness often represents a complete lack of resilience."[17]

NOTES

1. *The General Theory of Employment, Interest and Money,* pp. 383, 384.
2. *The Discovery of India,* p.415.
3. *Ibid.* pp. 416 and 525, also Government of India, Publications Division, *Jawaharlal Nehru's Speeches, 1949-53.* Speech at Silver Jubilee Celebration of the Central Board of Irrigation and Power, Nov. 17, 1952; p. 67.
4. *The Discovery of India,* p.41.
5. *Speech in Lok Sabha* on December 15, 1952.
6. *The Discovery of India,* p. 415.
7. Speech at the *Opening Ceremony of the Fuel Research Institute,* Digwadih, April 22, 1950.
8. *Jawaharlal Nehru's Speeches, Sept, 1946 — May 1949,* Vol. I, pp.99.
9. *Discovery of India,* p. 412.
10. *The Discovery of India,* p. 417.
11. Speech delivered at the *National Development Council Meeting* on November 9, 1954; p. 18.
12. *The Discovery of India,* p. 404.
13. Speech delivered at the *National Development Council Meeting,* January 20, 1056.
14. Speech delivered in the Lok Sabha initiating the Debate on the Second Five Year Plan, May 23, 1956.
15. *Speech delivered in the Lok Sabha* initiating the Debate on the Second Five Year Plan, May 23, 1956.
16. *Jawaharlal Nehru's Speeches Vol. I,* Sept. 1946 — May 1949 pp. 113, 114. *A speech delivered in the Constituent Assembly,* New Delhi, Feb. 17, 1948.
17. Jawaharlal Nehru's Speeches Vol. I, Sept. 1946 — May 1949, pp. 133, 134. Speech delivered at the Twenty-Second Annual Meeting of the Federation of India Chambers of Commerce and Industry, New Delhi, March 4, 1949.

3

INDIAN PLANNING AT A GLANCE

S.S. MOHAPATRA

The basic point that I want to emphasise in this article is that Indian Planning has lacked a clear understanding of the objective, priorities strategy and budgeting of good planning. With the passage of time the new colonist hold on the Indian elite has been strengthened through foreign aid and collaboration. Perhaps the greatest failure of India's planned development is the failure of our so called planning experts to understand the economic science that obtain in India.

The fundamental effect of a socialistic economy is control of means of production and distribution. This has not been done since the beginning of the first Five Year Plan. The Government has been always playing in the hands of the capitalists who hold the means of production. Even the public sector has been a total failure because of corruption and mal-administration. The total loss in the public sector is in the tune of thousands of crores of rupees during the last 30 years. Our steel plants have always been in loss compared to this significant sector in Japan. It is India which supplies iron-ore to Japan and the funniest part is that Japan sells steel at a cheaper rate than India.

Our power generation has been erratic and on the verge of collapse. When Khruschev and Bulganin visited India in 1955 they had told Jawaharlal Nehru that the life line of country's progress was power generation and India should attach more importance to it. Jawaharlal Nehru under-estimated Khrushchev's advice and had never thought of nuclear power generation in those days. The Damodar Valley Corporation failed to meet the demand.

When Subhash Chandra Bose was the Congress President he had nominated Jawaharlal Nehru as the President of the Planning Organisation, and gave suitable directions in this regard. Nehru was influenced by the planned economy as was adopted in USSR and had asked P.C. Mahalanobis to go to Russia and study the economy. Nehru's conception was socialism whereas Bose had thought of a regimented economy. Bose had dictatorial tendencies which was reflected in his political and economic thoughts. But Nehru was different. Jawaharlal Nehru's democratic nature was reflected in all aspects of Indian Political economy. He thought it was always good to take all the sectors together. His committee comprised of both capitalists and socialist thinkers. Whatever it is, when Jawaharlal Nehru became the Prime Minister of India, he was not able to put through his ideas because of pressures and counter-pressures from various economic groups in the country.

In India the agricultural economy has been in shambles. The only one country where agricultural economy has been boosted is China. The Chinese first plan began with a psychological ground work of the anti-corruption drives and national self defence. The First Plan lasted from 1953 to 1959. The Second Five Year Plan was executed between 1958 and 1962. Then there was a period which was called the leap forward between '58 and '60. The magnitude of the success of the great leap forward may be incurred from the increased output in agriculture and industry between 1958-78. The production output of cotton, Tobacco, production of wheat, coal and generation of electricity was manifold. As back as in 1958 the electricity production was around 20 billion kWs.

In India the First Five Year Plan was agriculture oriented but it failed due to land holding system. Nehru could neither go for collectivisation nor for good co-operative movement. It was a hotch potch.

The organisation and machinery of planning in China begins with the National People's Congress, which is the apex of planning body and the supreme planning authority, and includes the State Council which is headed by the Vice-Premier, the Provincial Planning Commissions in the different provinces which are responsible to the State Planning Commission at the Centre, and the lower organs of the Government.

China adopted both long-term and short-term planning and direct and indirect planning. The long-term plans were usually spread over a period of one year. Both the long-term and short-term plans are prepared even today by the Provincial Planning Commission at the provincial level. Their long-term plans generally cover a period of 12 to 15 years.

Most planning in China is direct planning. The basic units which produce goods and services under socialist or cooperative enterprise usually formulate their own plans. This is, in effect, direct planning.

The units working under the capitalist or semi-capitalist system are not allowed to plan for themselves. It is the administrative organs which prepare the plans for these units. This, in effect is indirect planning.

The planning procedure in China resembles the planning procedure adopted by the USSR. In China, it is the State Planning Commission, under the direct control and supervision of the Vice-Premier which prepares programmes for economic development. However, these economic development programmes are governed by the major decisions of the National People's Congress, which is the supreme planning authority in the country.

In China, physical and financial planning is undertaken simultaneously. The Chinese planners try to maintain a balance among raw materials, manpower and investment: and they lay emphasis on the supervision of plan implementation. The inspection teams undertake on-the-spot investigation and actually demand and get reports on the results of plan implementation.

The Soviet Union has accumulated vast experience of planning. It was while the Soviet planning system was being established and developed that the main feature of Socialist planning, which are of international significance, took shape. Moreover, the experience of Soviet planning is inseparable from the historical course that the Soviet economy has followed since the Great October Socialist Revolution in 1917. At each stage in the development of the Soviet economy there have been specific tasks to fulfil and correspondingly the modern planning system gradually emerged.

The main results of the sixty years of planned socio-economic, scientific and technological development in the USSR are:

- creation of a socio-economic system based on public ownership of the means of production and on planned methods of economic management.
- elimination of the exploiting classes and the building of a socialist state of the whole people founded on the common interests of all social strata and all nationalities in the country.

The success of the economic planning in a country is the well being of the people and eradication of unemployment, checking of inflation food, clothing, houses for everybody. Here is a Table 3.1 showing the unemployment figures of India which will speak for itself.

TABLE 3.1: Unemployment Figures in India

Educational levels	No. on Live Register as on 30-6-1988. (in thousands)
Matriculates	9676.2
Persons who passed Higher Secondary (including Intermediates/under-graduates)	4192.2
Graduates (including Post-Graduates) Total	2812.4
(i) Arts	1303.3
(ii) Science	557.2
(iii) Commerce	497.2
(iv) Engineering	57.9
(v) Medicine	27.6
(vi) Veterinary	1.1
(vii) Agriculture	27.0
(viii) Law	12.6
(ix) Education	290.3
(x) Others	38.1

With the growing unemployment every year simultaneously with the growing population it is no wonder that Indian economy will collapse in a few years. Our international debt is hundreds of billions of dollars. It is the kindness of God that India has not reached the stage of Latin American countries, but the fact is our economy is in shambles.

To conclude I am not going to be optimistic about the future economy of the country unless the very attitude is drastically changed. Communist Governments in East European countries are falling like cards every day. In USSR long lines for buying food stuff is seen in market; not that people have no money; they have, but the goods are not available. Seventy years of practice of socialist economy in USSR has failed and that the text of communist manifesto which envisaged a dictatorship of the proleteriat, is fast dying out.

What India wants today is complete overhaul of economic system and a good-bye to the Public Sector. Margret Thatcher has done well by denationalising British Airways. Today the BA has improved 200 per cent according to a national survey conducted in UK. Socialism under the high breed bureaucracy cannot be successful. It requires a mental training of attitude and perspective for the leadership. The socialistic economy of egalitarian type will suit India, which again depends on a committed leadership to transform the social progress.

The spectre of high inflation is once again haunting the economy thereby posing a big challenge to the Government. The price stability was enforced in 1988-89 despite being a post drought year.

The general index of wholesale prices – with the new base 1981-82 = 100 – has risen by 6.6 per cent between the end of March and September 9, 1989 as against the increase of only 3.9 per cent during the corresponding period of last year. Increase in prices has been particularly strong during the past three months.

The liquidity growth during the current fiscal year till Sept. 8, 1989 has been of the order of Rs. 14,445 crores recording a growth rate of 7.6 per cent against Rs. 12,246 crores with 7.5 per cent growth rate during the corresponding period of 1988. This strong liquidity growth has come on the top of fairly substantial increase in liquidity during the past several years.

Experts fear that the rate of inflation might reach the level of 7 to 8 per cent by the end of this month and after the elections there will be such a psychological pressure in the trade and market that even after the arrival of new crops by November, there may not be any tangible fall in price level. If this happens, not only there will be budget deficit for 1989-90 which will go up substantially from the targeted level by the end of the fiscal year but also there will be an impact on the Eighth Plan investment projections as the figures are based on 1989-90 prices.

The new Government led by V.P. Singh as PM is fully aware of it. As a Finance Minister he shook the vitals of the capitalists in India and the country has now reposed faith in him. His Deputy Choudhary Shri Devi Lal is a people's man with zeal of a titan to serve the rural masses. But the results will depend more on deeds than on words.

percent according to a national survey conducted in [illegible]. So [illegible] under the [illegible], a [illegible] coming [illegible] regains [illegible] national [illegible] of a [illegible] and [illegible] for the leadership [illegible] of [illegible] India, which [illegible] a [illegible] leadership [illegible] of [illegible] or some [illegible] challenge to the Government. The [illegible] being [illegible] [illegible].

The general index of wholesale [illegible] per cent between the end of [illegible] and September [illegible], 1989 as against [illegible] only 8.9 per cent during [illegible] period [illegible] has been [illegible] during the last [illegible] months.

[illegible] growth during the current [illegible] year till September [illegible] of the order of [illegible] per cent as against [illegible] corresponding period of 1988. The [illegible] on the top of fairly substantial increase in [illegible] during the past several years.

[illegible] that if the rate of inflation [illegible] each [illegible] there will [illegible] a [illegible] in the trade [illegible]. That [illegible] of [illegible] the [illegible] to [illegible] price [illegible] only [illegible] will be [illegible] a [illegible] [illegible] level [illegible] the [illegible] that [illegible] will [illegible] on the Eighth Plan [illegible] as the figures [illegible] based on 1989-90 prices.

The new [illegible] by V.P. Singh [illegible] is [illegible] Finance [illegible] the capitalists [illegible] India [illegible] [illegible] is [illegible] with [illegible] the [illegible] masses. But the results will [illegible] more [illegible]

4

NEHRU'S VISION OF PLANNED DEVELOPMENT OF INDIA

YASHVIR TYAGI

During the Centenary year of Jawaharlal Nehru, a renewed interest in his ideas about diverse subjects is only to be expected. However, it is also true that some of these elaborations, re-appraisals and re-examinations of his profound vision and his unique experiments in nation building, are more ritualistic than academic. But as a perceptive columnist in the *Economic and Political Weekly* has remarked, "The Nehru Centenary has thus a great relevance. It should provide ample food for thought on the dialectical causation of history, and on the contradictions which are its staple".[1]

With the advantage of the hindsight of the closing years of the 20th century, it is possible to have a critical look at the Nehruvian path of development with a view to finding out if it has stood the test of time. Another important issue is to identify the impact of 'Nehru-Mahalanobis' strategy on the post-Nehru planning strategies and their influence on the course of Indian economy and whether these influences have, in general, been benevolent or malevolent for the health of the country's economy. A third question of importance is that, when the Indian economy is poised for a big leap forward and the country is being described in international media as an emerging super-power; whether the Nehruvian strategy has the basic strength and the resilience to enable India to march into the 21st century as a country free from its age-old affliction of poverty and take her rightful place among the comunity of nations with a thriving self-reliant economy.

There have been scholarly treatises on the Nehru-Mahalanobis strategy of planning and its various critiques. However, if there can be an agreement on the underlying causes of structural backwardness of Indian economy which are basically manifested in the shortage of capital and the predominantly low productive agriculture, it can be said that "even a more pragmatically inclined politician than Nehru could well have opted for the same set of arrangements for promoting economic development."[2]

The multi-faceted vision of Nehru was shaped by diverse influences. Foremost among them was socialist ideology of both Fabian and Marxist variety. His upbringing and Western education nurtured a liberal outlook in him. His idealist passions were tempered by his experience of working among the poor peasants of Indian villages with Gandhiji as his Guru. Nehru viewed planning basically as a means to enable an underdeveloped agrarian economy like that of India to usher into an industrial society without either the rigours and inequities of capitalism of the regimentation and violence or collectivist-communism. This middle path of development is called a mixed economic system. The profound wisdom of Nehru in opting for this course for Indian economy has been proved right by the course of events over the years which have made possible the convergence of the two competing economic systems and the emergence of a system based on the concept of a welfare state deriving legitimacy from the freely expressed democratic will of the citizens and coordinating and balancing the activities of the public and private sectors in enhancing the material welfare of the country. This is precisely what Pandit Jawaharlal Nehru attempted through the instrument of Five Year Plans. In these respects Nehru can be said to have been ahead of his times and this ability gave him the hall mark of a visionary. In the light of these considerations we can attempt to delineate the contours of the Nehruvian strategy of development in a planned framework.

The theoretical underpinning of this strategy were provided by the famous Mahalanobis model. As has been described earlier, given the constellation of economic social and political conditions at the time of its formulation, the soundness of this approach cannot be faulted. It is to the credit of Indian planners, that starting from a simple limited sectoral model, they have attempted to build sophisticated plan models incorporating new techniques and elements.

Another major plank of Nehruvian approach was his emphasis on 'cultivating a scientific temper'. Nehru had a great faith in the ability of science and technology to transform society. He said, "In modern life, science and the progeny of science, techniques and technologies etc. are of the highest importance. They govern our lives and conditions of our living today". Nehru took keen personal interest in promoting and patronising the scientific disciplines and their activities. The spectacular achievements of the Indian scientists owe a great deal of debt to Pt. Nehru.

Although Nehru was a staunch votary of individual freedom, the result of planning on a vast scale were expanding bureaucratic controls that have to a great extent hampered the growth of Indian economy. People's active participation in the planning process both at the formulation and implementation level is crucial for the success of plans and Nehru understood them well. It is for this reason that he initiated community development programmes and laid great emphasis on co-operatives. It is another story that owing to the vested interests and their stranglehold on the levers of power, these programmes could not deliver goods to the extent desired.

Nehru understood well the dynamics of international power equations and the many faces of imperialism and capitalism. Therefore, he pursued a vigorous foreign policy to consolidate the newly independent, developing countries of Asia, Africa and Latin America. The much talked about South-South cooperation and the collective self-reliance of developing countries was first visualized by Jawaharlal Nehru.

In the present circumstances, one can say that the basic approach of Nehruvian strategy of economic development is still valid and it needs to be made free of the distortions that have crept into it. There is a need for a renewed commitment and national consensus on the basic premises of planning. Planning has to be geared up towards increasing the welfare of common people. In the name of faster growth planning should not be allowed to be used for enrichment of privilleged few. At a time when there is 'plan weariness' and the utility of planning is being questioned by academicians and politicians, it is incumbent upon Indian intelligentsia having faith in an orderly development to demonstrate that planning is still a better alternative to unplanned growth. Pandit Jawaharlal Nehru has bequeathed us a legacy which needs to be preserved and nurtured and used in the way he would have liked us to do.

NOTES

1. *Economic & Political Weekly*, December 10, 1988.
2. Chakravarti Prof. S.: *Development Planning*, Oxford 1988, p.9.

5

PLANNING AND POVERTY ERADICATION : Retrospect and Prospect

B.M. JAUHARI

The first and foremost and one of the most avowed goals of planning and economic development in India has been the eradication of poverty. But even after the completion of the seven plans, the task of poverty removal appears to be far more complex, difficult and beyond perceptible imagination. Poverty is a global phenomenon, but its peculiarity portrayal and permeability differ from society to society. "Poverty is real and illusive, it is relative and absolute, it is life giving, life denying, life harassing and paradoxically life sustaining". The intensity and volume of poverty, unfortunately, is quite alarming and staggering in India. Can we at all say that poverty in India is a product only of the present century? No, it is not. To be precise the origin of poverty must be associated with the dawn of British imperialism in India. During the decades of the alien British rule, the disease became acute and beyond any imaginable perceptions. All the developing nations of the globe, to be on the right track, are poor mainly because of the (mis) rule of the foreign rulers.[1]

I

Colonilism, indeed, had been a significant contributing factor to the economic degeneration of African, Asian and Latin American countries. But sad as it is, the modern growth economists have maintained a discrete silence on this issue. Thus poverty is being attributed to religious attitudes and social institutions. Vera Anstey has this to say "The population problem lies at the root of the whole question of India's economic future. It is difficult to avoid the conclusion that no matter how productivity is increased, economic organisation is improved, public health is promoted or industrialisation progresses, the standard of life of the masses will not and cannot be raised to a satisfactory level until changes have been introduced which will enable the size of the population to be better adjusted to economic resources". However, we cannot reject the view in the light of our own experiences during the post Independence era. Poverty, to be precise, is both the cause and consequence of population explosion in the third world countries. Under the circumstances of economic insecurity, the poorer classes tend to associate economic security not with a reduction, but with an increase in the number of children. The poor have no other economic asset than their own labour and the larger the number of earners in the family, the greater is the amount of family earnings. The lower survival rate further reinforces the preference for children. Our own experiences on this score confirm this view-point. India has passed through all such trials and tragedies and is even passing through this demographic trap.[2] A comparative picture of population statistics in 1947 and their counterparts at present tells about the demographic trends and their precise relationship with the programme of economic development and growth. Malthusian demon still hangs over our heads as a sword of democles. The same analysis can be applied to all other third world countries of Asia, Africa and Latin America. And then we have to compare our demographic and economic performance with the developed and highly industrialised economies. While our population had become a hurdle to the growth process, the developmental efforts and gains in the developed countries are not being multiplied at a desired pace mainly due to an almost stationary population growth. What a paradoxical situation! Population growth in some societies is a boon but a curse in others as it involves the issue of an optimum size.

The incidence of poverty has not diminished in spite of about four decades of planned, "pull up" programmes for the people below the poverty line. When there is a substantial concentration of the population at the poverty line, as in our country, small changes in the level of consumption can shift a large number of people above or below it. No other country perhaps is so rich as India in poverty studies. Several attempts have been made from Dada Bhai Naoroji down to Dandekar and Rath, Ahluwalia, Sen and Dharam Narain, to estimate poverty in our country. Poverty was typically measured with such crude indices as the percentage of people below the poverty line or the aggregate income gap (the sum over the poor of the amounts by which their incomes fall short of the poverty line).

The census of 1981 in India sent a wave of disappointment amongst the demographers, planners, social reformers and politicians because the family planning programme had failed to bring down either the growth rate or the size of population. It is commonly agreed that chronic poverty is the major cause for increase in population and family planning programmes could have little effect on population. The aforesaid census revealed that the net increase in the population of India during the decade 1971-1981 was 135.6 million or 24.75 per cent over the last decade. A prominent feature of this growth is that the land per man is decreasing and density of population is increasing. Two factors which significantly affect the poverty in India are – very poor land-man ratio and the illiteracy of women.[3] Population, therefore, is both the cause and effect of poverty.

The family planning programme has miserably failed in India. The enormous expenditure involved in this effort has gone into the drain. The 1991 Census figures also reveal a dismal picture on the population front – another twenty-five per cent growth in our population over the 1981 figures. It is catastrophic indeed. We cannot march onward if we fail to control the size of our population. There is a general impression that free India has conquered the battle against hunger though the war against poverty has not been won yet. The National Sample Survey (1983-84) has disclosed very unfortunate figures: 19 per cent of rural population either did not get two square meals a day or got it only for part of the year and four per cent of the urban population did not have two square meals on any day. Despite large expenditures by the Government on anti-poverty programmes, the proportion of the people living below the poverty line has not gone down between 1983-84 and 1990-91. Close to 50 per cent continue to be poor, about 20 per cent of them not having two square meals a day. The pursuit and promotion of elitist consumerism in this situation seems to be not merely inappropriate but also grossly vulgar and anti-social.

II

The phenomenal increase in population is an obstacle to economic growth and development and in fact obstructs it in more than one ways i.e. (1) generates and pushes up the demand; (2) curtails export prospects; (3) accelerates imports; (4) supply becomes tight and its management quite difficult; (5) leads to inflationary spiral – mild or wild; (6) creates unemployment of human resource; (7) leads to disequilibrium in plan process; and (8) warrants heavier social expenditure on education, health, hygiene, medicine, housing, sanitation, recreation etc.

We have, undoubtedly, attained a lot during the process of planned economic development. Some of the statistics are quite revealing and praiseworthy if we compare them either with the developed or even the developing countries for the same period. The consistent rate of growth of Indian economy is one very significant parameter, the food self sufficiency is another, our industrial achievements are yet another, the savings rate, creation of infrastructure, expansion of medical facilities and many more.[4] But the stature of the heroes of economic growth has been drastically shortened by the villain of alarmingly high rate of population growth. This dark and dismal side confirms our belief that Malthus is very much alive even today. The percentage of people below the poverty line has increased to 48.1 or even 50. Thirty second round of the National Sample Survey on household expenditure (1977-78) arrived at these figures relating to the number of people below poverty line for all states of India (Poverty line of Rs. 65.00 per capital per month at 1977-78 prices). The figure was brought down to 37 as per the official record during 1984-85. The figure would further come down to 25 by the end of the seventh five year plan (1989-90). The issue becomes more complex and complicated in the light of the steep decline in the value of money and the sharp price rise.

Delivering the Dr. C.D. Deshmukh Memorial Lecture in New Delhi on January 14, 1988, Dr. Malcohm Adiseshiah observed that although records show that there is a percentage reduction of those living in poverty, the absolute number of the poor – "those going to bed every night hungry" – is 270 million. He also made a very revealing observation that the cited statistics were based on the National Sample Survey of individual and household expenditure at current prices, conducted for the years which happened to register bumper harvests, and that it meant the intervening years must have seen a sharp rise in the percentage and number of people living in poverty.[5]

It can be inferred from the aforesaid description that there is a lot of politics and economics involved in the actual and factual assessment of poverty in India. We could not develop any absolute fool proof and commonly acceptable measurement so far. But it is again a well known fact that poverty in its worst form is in existence in India even after four decades of developmental planning and that its extent and gravity is still beyond any conceptual comprehension. Only the poor knows the meaning and content of poverty.[6] It is a very unfortunate situation and makes the mockery of our declared socio-economic goals and constitutional obligations.

III

All poverty eradication programmes, therefore, become of utmost importance – the first and foremost priority – if we have to exist as a civilized society. Poverty must be eradicated at the fastest speed. The measures cannot be one or two but a package. The eminent economist Mr. Tarlok Singh summed them up in these words, "Eradication of poverty is bound up at the same time with (i) agrarian reform (ii) agricultural development policies and (iii) comprehensive development, region by region, including agriculture, small industries, social services and economic infrastructure". Poverty eradication, therefore, calls for a new approach, a new strategy indeed a 'big push' approach once for all. It cannot be eradicated in instalments and in half-hearted manner. "There are two forms of poverty in India today – the poverty of hungry millions who seldom know where and when they may find their next morsel, and the poverty of thought of a band of poverty eradicators, who have only theoretical perception of poverty". It is the latter type of poverty which has become more chronic and should, therefore, be handled in a suitable manner.

Two very effective methods of poverty alleviation are – population control and a rapid rate of economic growth. Growth with equity should become the basis of socio-economic transformation. Grassroot planning[7] and participation of the masses should become a reality rather than a slogan or convenience. The government must ensure that the poverty alleviation measures are real, effective and reach to those people for whom they are actually meant. Economic development and social upliftment should proceed simultaneously. Such schemes should lay more emphasis on relief in kind and avoid cash relief which are usually misused. The experience of the past decades has shown that the quantum of relief which the beneficiary actually gets is much less than the amount proposed, announced and sanctioned i.e. the lion's share is pocketed by the middlemen (official or political). Poverty eradication programmes lead to the enrichment of those people who are already rich. It is a very sad commentary on our affairs and involves the 'national character'. If the Government and the people fail to undo all this, poverty eradication programmes should be entrusted to private, social, charitable, missionary and humanitarian institutions without any further delay.

The budgets of the Government of India (1988-89, 1989-90, 1990-91, 1992-93) contained important poverty alleviation measures. It has become an annual ritual. The states have also come out with a sizeable amount of their budgetary outlays for poverty schemes. A number of schemes have been announced for the benefit of marginal farmers, landless workers and low income people. The Intensive Rural Development Programme (IRDP) a major programme for relief to the poor, aims at providing income generating assets to identified families below the poverty line. It comprises of subsidies and institutional credit at cheaper rate. The Rural Landless Employment Guarantee Programme (RLEGP) is another landmark and aims at improving and expanding employment opportunities for rural landless labour. The project is fully financed by the Centre. Similarly the National Rural Employment Programme (NREP) has an objective of generating additional gainful employment to unemployed and under-employed in the rural areas. It also improves the nutritional standards of rural poor. Besides these there are also many more concessions, subsidies, tax relief and rebates which benefit the poor both in urban and rural areas.[8]

But again the same question remains – how many of these budgetary benefits shall filter down and reach the poor finally and ultimately? If implemented sincerely and honestly, a sizeable number of people must cross the poverty line. It is a big question mark and the hall-mark of our progress, national life, social and economic commitment, national polity and character.

The next five year plan (Eighth) has already begun and with it has begun a search for a new approach to poverty removal. But to-day we have a political vacuum with no single political party able to govern the country. We to-day face a grave political and constitutional crisis. It is already changing our priorities and goals. We to-day stand at cross roads with political and economic impasse. In our country unfortunately politics takes precedence over everything else. Hence poverty removal programmes will go into the background. The makers of our political destiny never visualised this situation.

Pandit Jawaharlal Nehru, the architect of New India had initiated the process of planned economic development in India with the sole object of poverty eradication. He rightly said in Bombay on May 20, 1936, "if the Congress has grown stronger, it is because I raised the issue of socialism. To-day the masses have come nearer to the Congress . . . . . I myself have derived strength for what little I do because I have seen the sufferings and poverty of the peasants and the workers".[9] Nehru's convictions were born out of his passionate concern for the poor and his dedication that the Government must improve the lot of masses. Nehru had rightly merged his own personality with that of an average Indian and could rightly understand the pains and pangs of poverty. It was this honest and sincerity of purpose which compelled him to initiate the poverty alleviation programmes as the centre and crux of the planned economic programme in free India.

NOTES

1. The Indian Economic Journals and Conference Volumes 1987-1988.
2. *Southern Economist* — Jan. 1, 1989.
3. Seventh Five Year Plan.
4. Indian Year Book 1986-1987 to 1991.
5. *Times of India.*
6. Sen, A.: *Poverty & Famine: An Essay on Entitlement & Deprivation* (1984).
7. Ahluwalia, S.M.: *Agricultural Change & Rural Poverty* (1986).
8. Union Budgets 1988-89, 1989-90, 1990-91.
9. Akbar M.J.: *Nehru — The Making of India.*

[illegible] Poverty [illegible]

[illegible] poverty [illegible] the [illegible] The [illegible] but [illegible] New [illegible] development [illegible] May [illegible] the [illegible] many [illegible] what [illegible] and the [illegible] out of [illegible] and [illegible] understand the [illegible] poverty [illegible] India.

[illegible]

[illegible] Jan. [illegible]

[illegible]

6

GANDHI AND NEHRU: Planning for Poverty Removal

RUDDAR DATT

A debate has been going on in our country about the Gandhian approach to development versus the Nehruvian approach. In fact, the advocates of both the approaches have been passionately arguing for and against, but the need of the hour is to find points of commonality so that a strategy of development can be adopted within the framework of a mixed economy and a democratic political set-up.

Points of commonality between Nehru and Gandhi.

It would be in the fitness of things to first identify the socio-political framework in which both Gandhi and Nehru intended to function.

First, Gandhi and Nehru both believed in a Mixed Economy framework. Gandhi did not believe in total nationalisation of the means of production. Gandhi propounded his theory of trusteeship which urged upon the capitalists to voluntarily share their wealth with the toiling masses. This voluntary surrender would avoid a bloody revolution, but if the capitalists refused to do so, the State, according to Gandhi, was within its rights to nationalise any undertaking or industry in social interest. To Gandhi, however, nationalization was only a necessary evil, an intermediate stage. The ultimate goal was trusteeship.

Contrast it with the Industrial Policy of 1956, carved out under the stewardship of Nehru, in which the State reserved for it the right to take over the ownership and control of any undertaking, if social compulsions persist. The nationalisation of State Bank of India, the Life Insurance Companies, the takeover of coal mines, the takeover of 20 major commercial banks, all were motivated by protecting social interest and the State has been able to exercise control for the welfare of the working class and the society.

Gandhi did not want the abolition of the Zamindari system without compensation. Nehru adopted the Gandhian model and proceeded with Zamindari Abolition in the Gandhian sense and measures were taken to abolish Zamindari with compensation.

Secondly, Gandhi did not want the State to become an instrument of oppression. So, he ultimately wanted to operate in a political system which provided broader consultation, more especially with the rural and weaker sections of the society. Nehru adopted parliamentary democracy as the political framework in which Indian society would function. The interests of the weaker sections were sought to be protected with the help of the institution of parliamentary democracy.

Thirdly, Gandhi wanted that all basic industries, defence industries and public utilities be controlled by the state. Nehru incorporated it in the Industrial Policy of 1956.

From the above, it may be inferred that Nehru inherited the economic and political framework from the Gandhian school of thought, since he was himself a close disciple of Gandhi.

Both Gandhi and Nehru were motivated towards planning for poverty removal. Gandhi asserted that all planning policies should be tested by the following touchstone:

> "Whenever you are in doubt, or when the self becomes too much with you, apply the following test. Recall the face of the poorest, and the weakest man whom you may have seen, and ask yourself, if the step you contemplated is going to be of any use to him. Will he gain anything by it? Will it restore him to a control over his own life and destiny? In other words, will it lead to Swaraj for the hungry and spiritually starving millions? Then you will find your doubts and yourself melting away".

Nehru in his presidential address before Lucknow Congress (1936) considered the establishment of a socialist society as the only means of ending poverty, unemployment and degradation of the Indian people. To quote Nehru:

> "I am convinced that the only key to the solution of the world's problems and of India's problems lies in the socialism, and when I use this word I do so not in a vague humanitarian way but in the

scientific, economic sense. Socialism is, however, something even more than an economic doctrine; it is a philosophy of life and as such also it appeals to me. I see no way of ending the poverty, the vast unemployment, the degradation and the subjection of the Indian people except through socialism. That involves vast and revolutionary changes in our political and social structure, the ending of vested interests in land and industry, as well as the feudal and the autocratic Indian states system. That means the ending of private property, except in a restricted sense, and the replacement of the present profit system by a higher ideal of cooperative service. It means ultimately a change in our instincts and habits and desires. In short, it means a new civilisation, radically different from the present capitalist order."

It would be, therefore, relevant to understand Nehru and Gandhian Models of Development and study their points of similarity and difference. It would also be relevant to examine whether a reconciliation of the two models is possible. But while analysing these models, it would be pertinent to keep a few things in mind. Firstly, besides the removal of poverty, there were other objectives which had also to be accomplished, viz., industrialisation to remove our backwardness, self-reliance, more especially in food and defence to free ourselves from dependence on imperialist nations and also to further socialist policies in a mixed economy framework attached with a democratic political structure.

Nehru Model of Development

The development of the Indian economy during the first 25 years of planning was guided by Nehru Model of Development which intended to make heavy industry the foundation of the economy and Nehru wanted the foundation to be strengthened at an early stage so that the economy is able to reduce the dependence on foreign aid.

A strong foundation is also important from the point of view of defence, without which the question of economic development becomes irrelevant. The Nehru strategy of development has made India the tenth most industrialised nation in the world. Reviewing the overall achievements of planning in the first five plans, the Janata Party's Sixth Plan draft conceded:

"It is a cause of legitimate national pride that over this period, a stagnant and dependent economy has been modernised and made more self-reliant".[1] More specific achievements of Nehru model of development are:

(a) Considerable rise in agricultural productivity per hectare on account of application of seed-fertiliser technology making the country self-sufficient in food and also to accumulate huge reserves of foodgrains;
(b) Impressive industrialisation in the capital goods sector through a leading role given to the public sector, this has resulted in the diversification and expansion of India's industrial capacity. India is now self-sufficient in consumer goods and in basic commodities like steel and cement, while the capacity of new industries like fertilisers is rapidly expanding;
(c) Development of economic infrastructure in the form of irrigation, power, transport and communications etc. which provides the base for rapid economic growth; and
(d) Growth of science and technology and the development of technological and managerial cadres to run a modern industrial structure.

Weaknesses of Nehru Model of Growth

Nehru model of growth based on heavy industries has established many weaknesses. It has failed to provide a national minimum level of living despite almost three decades of planning. More than 40 per cent of the population now lives below the poverty line. The number of unemployed and under-employed is quite high and has been increasing continuously. Inequalities of income and wealth have worsened and there is a growing concentration of economic power in the hands of a few. Land reforms have not been properly implemented, resulting in much dissatisfaction in rural area. Above all, the country has been moving from one shortage to another and has been subjected to vicious inflationary pressure.

The Gandhian Model of Growth

Gandhi was not a professional economist and had not systematically developed a model of economic growth. But he advocated a philosophy with regard to the development of Indian agriculture, industries etc. Acharya S.N. Agarwala brought out the Gandhian Plan in 1944 and reaffirmed it in 1948. These publications form the basis of Gandhian model of growth.

The basic objective of the Gandhian plan is to raise the material as well as the cultural level of the Indian masses to a basic standard of life within a period of 10 years. The Gandhian Plan aims primarily at improving the economic conditions of the 5 lakh villages of India and, therefore, it lays the greatest emphasis on the scientific development of agriculture and of the cottage industries.

Agriculture : The Gandhian plan aims at the reform of agriculture as the most important item in economic planning in India. The primary objective of agricultural development should be national self-sufficiency in foodstuffs and maximum regional self-sufficiency in food. This has to be achieved not only by larger and better inputs but also through land reforms — change in the system of tenure, abolition of the proprietary rights on land, consolidation of holdings, organisation of cooperative farms, etc. Money-lending should be abolished, and there should be increased credit facilities for the farmers. The Gandhian plan lays special emphasis on dairy farming as an occupation and as an auxiliary to agriculture.

Cottage Industries : The primary aim of the Gandhian plan is the attainment of maximum self-sufficiency in village communities. Hence, the plan discusses at length the problem of rehabilitation, development and expansion of cottage industries side by side with agriculture. Spinning and weaving are given the first place. The manufacturing of *Khadi* is important and it is almost on the same level as the production of rice and wheat. "Just as villagers cook their own *roti* (bread) and rice so must they make their own *khadi* for personal use. The surplus, if any, they may sell". At the same time, the Gandhian Plan wants the State to consider the revival and expansion of rural cottage industries as the main plank of its industrial planning. It should help the artisans by providing facilities for technical training regarding handicrafts, organise cooperative societies for the purchase of raw materials and for the sale of finished goods, protect cottage industries against unfair competition from large scale units, grant subsidies to those cottage industries which cannot develop otherwise and finally, provide cheap finance to the artisans and the cooperative societies.

Basic Industries : There is a general misconception about Gandhi being against the development of large scale industries. On the other hand, the Gandhian Plan recognises the need for and the importance of certain selected basic and key industries in India, especially defence industries, hydro-electric and thermal power generation, mining and metallurgy, machinery and machine-tools, heavy engineering, and heavy chemicals. The Gandhian Plan would like the development of basic industries not to interfere with or to hinder the growth of cottage industries. The most dynamic and scientific aspect of the Gandhian Plan is that the basic and key industries will be owned and managed by the State – they will be in the public sector.

There is much confusion about Gandhi's concept of machinery. Generally, people assume that Gandhi's emphasis on cottage industries and handicrafts is a clear indication of his opposition to modern machinery. This is wrong. Gandhi is not against all machinery, for the spinning-wheel itself is a piece of machinery. He protests, however, against the craze for machinery and its indiscriminate multiplication. He believes that the factory system using extensive machinery has become the source of exploitation of labour by a few capitalists. He welcomes machinery and modern amenities wherever they lighten the burden of the villagers without displacing human labour. Machinery is good when it operates in the interests of all, it is evil when it serves the interests of the few.

If we carefully analyse the Gandhian Plan, we will find that the aim is to develop agriculture and industries side by side and integrate them. The handicrafts and cottage industries are emphasised from the point of view of production and that of employment. At the time of independence, Nehru had come to dominate the Indian scene and Gandhi and his economic ideas were forgotten. Instead, Indian planning on the model of Russian experience was introduced soon after Independence. Only after a quarter of a century when the country was in the grip of an economic crisis between 1973 and 1975, people had come to think of the Gandhian Plan as a possible alternative to the Nehru model of growth. During the short period of the Janata rule, and in the Draft Sixth Plan some of these ideas were incorporated. Gandhian model of growth has relevance in the Indian context to some extent and has much to command itself. In concrete terms, the Gandhian model of growth calls for the following changes in the present system of planning:

(a) *Employment-oriented planning to replace production-oriented planning*: The basic premise here is that unemployment is our greatest enemy and that in its solution lies the key to the problems of poverty and inequalities. It would, therefore, be advisable to replace production-oriented planning with employment-oriented planning. This would necessitate demarcation of area of high employment potential which also ensures high and efficient products.

(b) *Agriculture and employment potential*: Agriculture offers great scope for enlarging employment in: (i) agriculture including animal husbandry, compost making, sanitation and gobar gas, (ii) rural works such as irrigation projects, soil conservation, land reclamation, afforestation etc. and (iii) rural or cottage industries. Under intensive cultivation, land can support a much larger number of workers. It has been estimated that in India 39 workers are employed per 100 acres in 1971 and as such India is classified as a low performance country but in Japan, South Korea, Taiwan and Egypt during 1965, the number of workmen employed per 100 acres was 87,79,79 and 71 respectively. These countries are high-performance nations with models of small farms and highly labour intensive pattern. The experience of these countries shows how another 50 to 60 million people can be employed in agriculture, and at the same time increase total output. The employment potential in the newly irrigated areas can be increased by 60 per cent provided there is only limited mechanisation i.e., the adoption of machines which supplement human effort and ease or lighten its burden rather than supplant it — "the Japanese style of farm machinery".

(c) *Large v/s Small Industries*: The Gandhian model of growth is in favour of small scale and cottage industries and it is against large-scale industries producing consumer goods, Charan Singh writes:

"No medium or large-scale enterprise shall be allowed to come into existence in future which will produce goods or services that cottage or small scale industry shall be allowed to be established which will produce goods or services that cottage enterprises can produce".

Charan Singh, an ardent advocate of Gandhian model was so much against large-scale units that he wanted them to export their entire production or close down. They should not be allowed to sell their output within the country. He also emphasised that public financial institutions should be debarred from providing finance to large-scale industry. They should generate internal resources for their expansion and development.

(d) *Equitable distribution*: Growing concentration of economic power in the hands of a few and inequality of income are the two major economic ills of the Indian economy despite professing Socialism. Gandhi conceived of the most natural solution to the problem of distribution. Accumulation of wealth and the concentration of economic power are directly due to centralisation of the means of production and centralised large-scale production. The natural solution is decentralised small scale production. This will cut at the very root of accumulation of wealth. And whenever large-scale production is inevitable (as in basic and key industries) it should be left to Government ownership and management. In the Gandhian model the problem of distribution is tackled at the production end and not at the consumption end.

The Gandhian model of growth hopes to achieve a national minimum level of living within the shortest possible time and aims at removal of concentration of income and wealth and growth with stability. In other words, it aims to avoid the weaknesses associated with the Nehru model of growth.

Reconciliation of the Nehru and Gandhian Models — the only solution.

While Nehru wanted to give prime importance to heavy industries, the Gandhian model attempts to give primacy to agriculture supported by handicrafts and cottage industries. Nehru model of growth based on heavy industry was the only suitable model in the 1950s and 1960s as the development of heavy industry was the instrument for making the country militarily strong to face external aggression, for laying the basis for further industrial expansion and for freeing the country from foreign dependence. Now that defence has been sufficiently developed and a strong foundation has been firmly laid for self sustained growth, it has now become possible to shift emphasis from heavy industries to capital light consumer goods industries of the small scale and cottage industries type. The implication is clear : The Gandhian model of growth is possible now since

Nehru's investment strategy had already laid a strong industrial base for economic growth.

True, small scale and cottage industries have a very useful role to play in India from the point of view of production and employment. But it would be unwise to neglect the development of heavy industry in future, in spite of the commendable progress made since 1951, India has not reached a fairly high level in the per capita output of steel and electric energy — both of which are also needed to expand small scale and cottage industries. In 1980, India produced only 15 kg of steel per capita as against 557 kg by the USSR and 446 kg by the USA. The scale of output of steel and electricity generation is too low to merit slowing down of investment in heavy industry. Besides the goals of self-reliance and defence preparedness are as important, if not more, as those of removing grinding poverty, mounting unemployment and widening disparities in wealth and income. In the name of the Gandhian model of growth, it would indeed be suicidal to neglect or slow down investment in heavy industry. But as emphasised earlier, Gandhi was not against the development of heavy and basic industries, in fact, Gandhian Plan (1944) recognised the need and importance of basic and heavy industries such as power, iron and steel, machinery and machine tools, heavy engineering and heavy chemicals.

A good case can, however, be made to shift investment from medium and large scale enterprises producing consumer goods to cottage and small scale industries. No more licences need be given to new medium and large scale units and this will be in the interests of both production and employment. In the Nehru model, importance was also given to cottage and small scale units. Even on the question of high costs, it was argued that with the extension of cheap electric power throughout the country, there was no reason why cost of production in small units should be higher as compared to larger units. But in the process of implementation of the Nehru model, small scale and cottage industries were given a step-motherly treatment and large scale and medium sized units were allowed to stifle small units. By the Industrial Policy Statement of 1977, the Janata Government wanted to rectify this mistake. The Janata Industrial Policy Statement asserted:

> "The emphasis of industrial policy so far has been mainly on large industries completely, relegating small industries to a minor

> role... The main thrust of the new industrial policy will be on effective promotion of cottage and small industries widely dispersed in rural areas and small towns. It is the policy of the Government that whatever can be produced by small and cottage industries must only be so produced."[2]

Active support and encouragement to cottage and small sector does not imply that the existing large and medium units in the consumer goods sector should either be closed down or should be permitted to continue only on the condition that the entire output would be exported. These are unwise and unrealistic suggestions. Units which have been set up and which have been producing for the market for many years — both domestic and international should not be closed down. But these units may be encouraged to diversify to new lines of production and increase exports as much as feasible. At the same time, the small sector should be helped to improve the quality of its products, reduce cost of production and make goods available at competitive rates. It is interesting to observe that the Gandhian Plan (1944) lays down a general policy of State control over the price of goods, profits and labour conditions in the privately-owned industries, checking the further expansion of private enterprises, purchase of foreign assets by the State and regulating competition between cottage industries and large scale industries.

Charan Singh has commended the Chinese model of growth because China is said to have followed the Gandhian path and that she has fed and clothed her people better than India has done. Charan Singh writes:

> "Various reports from unimpeachable sources indicate that not only had Mao Tse-tung given first priority to agriculture since 1962 but he had relied more on human labour and decentralised labour intensive enterprise in building country than on large-scale mechanised projects and industries."[3]

This is much too simplistic an analysis. It ignores the fact that before the year 1962, China gave first priority to heavy industry and not to agriculture. For example, in the First Five Year Plan (1953-57), China provided over 50 per cent of its investment allocation to heavy industries. Only later, she started developing agriculture and industry simultaneously — the Chinese called it "the theory of walking on two legs". Further, it is important to note that China did not neglect the importance of heavy industry even when she gave first priority to agriculture. Besides, China did not underplay the role of heavy industry for defence and infrastructural base. She has become a first rate military power to challenge the mightiest empires of the world, she had given up its dependence upon Russian aid and Russian technicians without any adverse effect on her growth process. The success of China is basically due to combining admirably the Soviet model with the Gandhian model. The weakness of the Indian planners was not in the formulation of Nehru Model of Growth but in the poor implementation of the same, viz., implementing the heavy industry base to a larger extent but failing to implement successfully the agricultural content of the plans and those relating to small-scale and cottage sector and agriculture.

At the present stage of development, there is every justification in focusing attention on the employment objective as much as on the need for accelerating the process of growth. There is a powerful case for an employment-oriented pattern of planning. It is, however, wrong to indict the Nehru model of growth on the ground that it had neglected agriculture and the small sector and that this had resulted in all the economic problems faced by the country, viz., inflationary rise in prices, acute shortages, industrial sickness, growing inequalities, mounting poverty etc. It would be wrong to ignore the development of heavy industry and put all the emphasis on agriculture and the small-scale sector. Let us not forget that it is inadequate investment in the power development programmes and the insufficient generation and distribution of power which has led to the failure in the agricultural sector. In fact, there is no conflict between the heavy industry and the agricultural sector in the use of human and material resources. Both can be developed simultaneously. If the approach of balanced growth was valid in 1950s, it is all the more so in 1980s.

Nehru was quite conscious about the development of agriculture. Speaking before the National Development Council on November 8, 1963, Nehru stated:

> "Agriculture is more important than industry for the simple reason that industry depends on agriculture. Industry, which is, no doubt, very important will not progress unless agriculture is sound and stable and progressive..... People seem to think that an in-

dustrial plant solves all the problems of poverty, which it does not. It has a long-term effect on the economy, no doubt. And I have no doubt in my mind that the problem of poverty will not be solved in India except through industrial progress, industrial progress of the latest type. This is the truth. However, at the present moment, whichever way you start in India, you come back to agriculture."[4]

Nehru further emphasized:

"One of our States which in comparison to others is more prosperous is Punjab where there is hardly any big plant, but there are plenty of small industries. Some States which are full of big plants are lower down in the scale of per capita income, in spite of the development of industry, because agriculture is not developing."[5]

Nehru after laying the foundation of heavy industry was convinced that agriculture had to be developed simultaneously with industry. He put it in unequivocal terms:

"If we fail in agriculture, then we fail inevitably in industry also." In other words, a shift in balanced growth of industry and agriculture was recognised by Nehru as the second stage in our process of development.

Sukhamoy Chakravarty, writing about the Indian Development Experience of the first three plans mentions:

"But probably more importantly, the inability to carry out effective land reforms in the early fifties when conditions had been reasonably opportune along with the maintenance of the largely unchanged input base of traditional agriculture, meant that the agrarian transition was left largely incomplete."[6]

Nehru did recognize the failure on land reform. But he had to compromise with landed aristocracy in view of the democratic political framework. S. Chakravarty in a footnote mentions:

"It is a reasonable conjecture that the compulsions of building up a post-colonial state based on consensus led Nehru to compromise to a much greater extent with rural vested interest than was necessary."[7]

To sum up, India has the experience of Nehru Model of Development being worked out. There was failure on several fronts and the model got distorted in a variety of ways during the process of implementation. The Gandhians accuse Nehru for neglect of agriculture and small scale industry. But the people of India provided them an opportunity to work out the Gandhian Model on the ground with emphasis on agriculture, land reform and small industry. Although much trumpeteering was done about giving a boost to small industry, but due to strong vested interests, no serious dent could be made. Rather Janata Party was defeated at the polls. During this short period, no concrete results could be achieved in the area of land reforms. The real problem is not the Nehru Model versus the Gandhian Model, because there is sufficient consensus on reconciliation of the two models, the real issue is implementation. Nehru himself lamented:

> "I think that, on the whole, we plan well. I think also that, on the whole, we do not implement, well. It is not good to have a theoretical plan and not implement it fully."

REFERENCES

Jawaharlal Nehru's Speeches.

Planning Commission, Draft Five Year Plan (1978-83).

Industrial Policy Statement (1956).

Industrial Policy Statement (1977).

Sukhamoy Chakravarty, *Development Planning the Indian Experience* (1987).

Sethi, J.D., *Gandhi Today*, 2nd Ed. 1979.

Ruddar Datt, India's Economic Policy: Nehru Vs. Charan Singh, Mainstream, February 11, 1978.

NOTES

1. Planning Commission, Draft Five Year Plan (1978-83) p.1.
2. Industrial Policy Statement, 1977 as presented to the Parliament in December 1977.
3. Charan Singh : *India's Economic Policy*, p.50.
4. Jawahar Lal Nehru's speeches, Vol. 5, 1963-64, pp.111-12.
5. Ibid p.110.
6. Chakravarti S., *Development Planning: The Indian Experience* (1987) Oxford p. 18.
7. Ibid p.93.

Hindustan Daily, India's Economic Policy: Nehru vs. Charan Singh, [illegible] February [illegible], 1980.

5. Ibid p.119.

7. Ibid p.23.

7

NEHRU: PLANNING AND DISPARITIES (A Study of Inter-District Disparities in Infrastructure Development of Madhya Pradesh)

A.D.N. BAJPAI

To ink the contribution of Pandit Jawaharlal Nehru to Indian economic planning is a very difficult task. Any objective approach based on collecting the excerpts of speeches or writings of Pt. Nehru and deriving any sense out of them, is not sufficient enough to comprehend the entire passion and concern which he had in his heart to develop our economy. This could only be felt by those who were fortunate enough to listen to Pt. Nehru face to face or had the privilege to converse with him on any issue of national and inter-national import. So, whatever tribute we are paying to Pt. Nehru in the centenary year, is millionth part of what he has contributed to our economic development, rather what our country owes to him. He was the main architect of modern India. His excellence in dovetailing the approach of planning in a democratic set-up, scientific and industrial growth with an objective of egalitarian society is rarely found in any statesman. Pt. Nehru had felt the pulse of Indian people and had a clear vision of the future-developments. That is why he was able to affect the psyche, the behaviour, the thinking of Indian nationals to such a great extent.

Nehru and Planning

Our commitment towards planning does not merely date back to year 1951, the year in which the First Five Year Plan was launched, but to the year 1938 when Netaji Subhash Chandra Bose was the President of Indian National Congress. At the conference of provincial ministers held at Delhi on 2nd and 3rd October, 1938 it was decided that the problems of poverty and of unemployment, of national defence or of economic regeneration in general, could not be solved except through large scale industrialisation. This conference for the first time in the history of Indian economics, recognised the need of a comprehensive scheme of national planning.[1] Further in order to implement the decisions of the conference, the conference appointed a Planning Committee under the dynamic and inspiring Chairmanship of Pt. Jawaharlal Nehru and with the veteran economist Prof. K.T. Shah as the General Secretary. The National Planning Committee opened a new chapter in the economic history of India.[2] Thus, Pt. Nehru was associated with the Planning since its inception in our country.

There were two significant points about the planning which Pt. Nehru had in his mind throughout. First, the planning without political power is meaningless. Hence, an essential prerequisite for planning is complete freedom and independence and removal of all outside control. This implies that the country possesses in itself full sovereign authority to take any measures, adopt any policies and form any other relations with other countries as may seem best to its government authority in the interests of the country and its people.[3] Second, planning in true sense could only be possible when country is committed to Socialism. He was of firm opinion that real planning is hardly possible under the ordinary capitalist structure of society where so many vested interests intervene. Planning is inevitably connected with a Socialist Society.[4] But he never wanted socialism imposed upon the country rather it should penetrate in our society in an evolutionary process. Nehru wanted to use the instrument of economic planning to attain national self-sufficiency or self-reliance.[5] He wanted planning to arrange happy wedding between large scale and small, cottage industries,[6] to increase the national income, to raise the minimum standard of living, liquidating, illiteracy, expanding health facilities and removing regional imbalances so that the national unity could be strengthened and divisive forces and elements kept away. Further, Nehru was of firm belief that for any successful and rational plan, its data-base should be adequate, accurate and up to date. But for the reliable and adequate data-base it is practically impossible to have projections for the future. For this purpose, he had included veteran mathematician Prof. P.C. Mahalanobis from the Indian Statistical Institute. It shows he wanted objectivity in planning. Another characteristic which he wanted was the feasibility of planning in terms of its implementation. Because the success of plan framed by economists and experts under given guidelines, objectives and ideology of political leadership, will depend upon two things, one the plan itself and two the people who are entrusted with its implementation. He opined the very best plan if run by wrong persons, will harm the country.[7] Thus, planning for Nehru, was not merely an academic exercise to formulate a plan but also its execution and efficacy to solve the problems of economy. Mahalanobis (1959) summarised the contribution of Nehru towards planning as follows:

> "He initiated thinking on planning in India. Through his speeches and through planning committees and the planning commission, he has exercised a profound educative influence and made India conscious of the need for national planning. Through the Congress party and the Government, he has made planning an instrument of national policy on the biggest scale outside the communist countries and has persuaded India to accept socialism as her goal. He has brought to Indian planning a full appreciation of the scientific revolution which is transforming the world a sensitive awareness of human values and cultural traditions, an inherent sense of democracy and an international outlook."[8]

Main Objectives of Planning

The main objectives of planning may be enumerated as rapid increase in national income and per capita income minimisation of income inequalities, removal of regional disparities and sectoral imbalances and stability. It means by planning the resources should be mobilised and allocated in different sectors in such a way which assures high growth rate in national income and per capita income on one hand and reduces inequalities of income, imbalances amongst different regions and sectors on the other hand. Besides, it is also one of the objectives of planning that it should help the economy in getting rid of the business cycle and provide stability in economic life. In sum, it can be said that planning in our country has been adopted to fulfil the trio objectives of growth, equity and stability. But how far these objectives have been fulfilled is a matter of investigation.

Theme of the Paper

The present paper has been prepared to highlight the impact of planning on regional disparities. Since 1951, we have witnessed 41 years of planned economic development. Seven Five Year Plans have been completed and the eighth is in operation. Therefore, it will be quite appropriate to evaluate the impact of planning in respect of its role in increasing the growth rates, reducing the income inequalities, regional disparities and sectoral imbalances. In this paper, the component of regional disparities have been selected for evaluation.

The Hypothesis

It is hypothesised that the planning has been instrumental in reducing the regional disparities. In other words it can be said that the development strategy has been planned in such a manner which has resulted in reduced disparities amongst different regions of the economy.

Methodology

To test the above hypothesis following methodology has been adopted:

(a) *Selection of Area:* For the purpose of studying the disparities, the State of Madhya Pradesh has been selected deliberately. Because the State is comparatively backward and its districts are spread over a vast area. The State was formed in 1956 by merging substantial part of the old Madhya Pradesh with the former part 'C' State of Bhopal, part 'C' State of Vindhya Pradesh and part 'B' State of Madhya Bharat.[9] The State has heterogeneous agro-climatic zones, and full of diversities. Hence, it becomes imperative to study whether the disparities which were existing at the time of merger of districts are decreasing or not.

(b) *Region and District:* In the present work the district has been taken as the unit for analysing the disparities. The district has been used as the proxy for regions. Though region is different from the concept of district. While former is natural outcome of certain natural or man-made forces based on similarities and homogeneity the later one is not. The district is an artificial demarcation forced by the problems of management and administration.[10] But in the present study emphasis has been laid on the 'district' only and inter-district disparities have been calculated.

(c) *The Scope of the Paper:* As stated earlier, the prime objective of this paper is to study the disparities amongst different districts of the State over time. The scope of study of these disparities has been confined to infrastructural facilities only which are existing in the district. The disparities can be studied in various ways like per capita income, agricultural development, industrial development, overall development etc. Actually, most of the work devoted to the study on disparities are based on overall development. But in the present paper, when efficacy of planning is being evaluated, it would not be appropriate to take up the overall development of the district because the total development depends upon so many factors as the natural and mineral resources available, the technology, the know-how and the skill, the expertise the enterprise and also the basic facilities provided by the State. Therefore, if the intention of the Government needs to be studied, it is preferable to highlight the disparities in infrastructural facilities. It is a well proved fact that without adequate and timely supply of basic facilities, the objectives of growth, equity or regional balances can never be realised. And these infrastructural facilities are mostly supplied by the State. Hence, it is expected that the development strategy of State should be sketched in a manner in which backward districts develop faster than the already developed ones.

(d) *The Infrastructure Facilities:* The infrastructure facilities include those basic services which have multipurpose uses and are required to sustain the economy in a long run. It requires huge investment to build-up and has long gestation period. It is not directly profitable but makes other activities profitable. The rationale of investment in this sector does not merely lie in the profitability of this sector only but its outside linkages with the economy. Bajpai (1989)[11] has made an attempt to define the concept of infrastructure in detail and trace out its history. The infrastructure of any economy is comprised of power, transportation, communication, banking, irrigation, education and health. Besides there are various non-economic factors also which work as infrastructure for economic development. Narottam Shah (1970)[12] classified these facilities in a detailed manner and incorporated various non-economic factors besides the main economic factor of infrastructure. Bajpai (1985)[13] also tried to associate some political attributes with economic development. In this context, it can be mentioned that main infrastructure facilities from purely an economic angle are those which are referred as above. As far as the contribution of infrastructure to raising national income or per capita income and reducing pressure of poverty is concerned no body can put doubt. The positivity of its favourable contribution has been empirically tested and found significant by Bajpai (1988).[14] In brief it can be stated that main infrastructure facilities are power, transportation and communication, banking, irrigation, education and health and they have a crucial role to play in developing any economy. Further, these are mainly provided by the Government. Therefore, if the regional or districtwise disparities are to be reduced, the Government should try to minimise the infrastructural imbalances. The Government has made huge investment in this sector but how far that investment has been successful in minimising the gap among the various districts of Madhya Pradesh, is a matter of investigation.

(e) *The Indicators of Infrastructure:* The infrastructure sub-sectors, as stated above, viz. power, transportation and communication, irrigation, education, health and banking are quite vague as far as analytical point of view is concerned. Therefore, these require to be defined in a clear manner so that any tool may be used to derive any result. These may be termed as indicators of infrastructure sub-sectors. The identified indicators incorporated in this paper are as following:

Infrastructure Sub-sector	Indicator
A. Power	1. Per Capita Consumption of Electricity.
	2. Percentage of Villages Electrified.
B. Irrigation	3. Percentage of Gross Irrigated area.
C. Transportation and Communication	4. Road Length in (km) per 100 sq. km of Area.
	5. Railway route in (km) per 100 sq. km of area.
	6. Number of Post-offices per Lakh population.
D. Education	7. Percentage of Literacy.
E. Health	8. Number of Hospital beds per lakh population.
F. Banking	9. Per Capita Deposits (Rs.)
	10. Per Capita Credit (Rs.)
	11. Number of Banks Per Lakh Population.

Thus eleven indicators of six major infrastructure facilities have been analysed in this paper to see whether the disparities amongst different districts are reducing or not.

(f) *Time Period:* The period for the analysis is selected as 1960-1987. As mentioned earlier, the State of Madhya Pradesh was formed in the year 1956. So, the year 1956 could have been best year for comparing the subsequent changes taking place in various districts. But due to reshuffling of statistical organisation, and non-availability of statistics for 1956, it is thought appropriate to keep the year 1960 as base year. Further, the points are selected between the period 1960-1987 to show the variations in disparities. These points are 1960, 1965, 1970, 1971, 1973, 1975, 1978, 1981, 1984, 1987. Any how, for percentage of literacy for which only census statistics were available the analysis has to be confined to 1961, 1971 and 1981 and for banking whose statistics were collected for post-nationalisation period only, the analysis has to be limited for the periods after 1971.

(g) *Source of Data:* The data pertaining to earlier-cited indicators are collected from secondary sources mainly the publication of the Directorate of Economics and Statistics, Government of Madhya Pradesh. Important among them are selected Economic Indicators, Pocket Compendiums, and Agricultural Statistics of Madhya Pradesh. It has been always kept in mind that the statistics must be called from the authentic and reliable sources so that the results to be obtained are also reliable.

(h) *Tool for Analysis :* The statistics so collected from different sources are analysed by simple method of co-efficient of variation. The co-efficient of variation explains the average degree of variability amongst different districts from the average of districts. In other words, it is the numerical product obtained by dividing the standard deviation from arithmetic means. It can be converted in percentages by simply multiplying this product by 100. In a form of formula, the same can be written as following:

$$C.V. = \frac{\sigma}{X} \times 100$$

Where C.V. - co-efficient of variation

σ - Standard deviation

X - Arithmetic Mean.

The co-efficient of variation is generally used to analyse the disparities amongst different districts or regions. Hence, the same has been used in the present paper.

Analysis and Finding

The original statistics related to different indicators of infrastructure development in Madhya Pradesh are not presented in the paper because of their voluminous size. The statistics of 45 districts for 11 indicators and 27 years become too heavy to be mentioned in the paper. These statistics can be referred in Bajpai (1989)[15], if needed. Here only results of the co-efficient of valuations are presented.

Table 7.1 contains the co-efficients of variations calculated for different years after taking the cross-sectional data of 45 districts for each variable. The results of these co-efficients have been depicted by a graph also (Fig. 7.1). The results can be discussed as follows:

1. The inter-district disparities in per capita consumption of electricity were of 173.3% in 1960 which have reduced to 102.7% in 1987. There has been found a decelerating trend throughout the period.
2. Disparities in the percentage of villages electrified have reduced from 92.7% in 1960 to 23.1% in 1987. It also had a diminishing trend throughout.
3. The co-efficients of variations in gross area irrigated also shows that the inter-district disparities are minimising. The co-efficient which was of the order of 122.9% in 1960 has reduced to 76.3% in 1987.
4. As far as road length per hundred sq. km of area is concerned, the co-efficient of variation is having the same decreasing trend. The co-efficient, which was 49.3% in 1960, has come down to 38.1% in 1987. It shows that the inter-district disparities in respect to road infrastructure and narrowing down during the same period.
5. The coefficient of variation in railway route shows a marginal change. It explains that there has not been much diversification done in respect to railway track expansion in the State. The disparities are almost constant throughout i.e. around 72%.
6. The disparities in respect to the number of post offices per lakh population also appear to be decreasing from 1960 (39.5%) to 1987 (30.7%).

7. Similarly, the inter-district disparities in percentage of literacy is also narrowing down. The coefficient of variation which was 37.6% in 1961 decreased to 33.9% in 1971 and 29.5% in 1981 census.
8. The coefficient of variations calculated on the basis of number of hospital beds per lakh population shows that inter-district disparities are minimising. In 1960 the coefficient of variation was 99.7% which came down to 79.4% in 1971 and 73.5% in 1987.
9. The statistics pertaining to banking infrastructure have been included from the year 1971 onwards. Therefore, the coefficient of variations for pre 1971 could not be calculated. The inter-district disparities as explained by coefficient of variations, are decreasing in respect to per capita deposit, per capita credit as well as to number of banks for one lakh population since 1971. The coefficient of variation in per capita deposit has come down from 270.9% in 1971 to 123.8% in 1987. Similarly the same in respect to per capita credit and number of banks has decreased from 229.2% and 79.6% to 117.5% and 28.8% respectively.

Conclusions

From the above discussion it can be derived that the inter-district disparities are decreasing in almost all infrastructure facilities. Thus, the hypothesis which was established earlier, can be accepted. But at the same time it must not be ignored that though the disparities are decreasing but still there are vast-disparities existing amongst the districts of the State. Maximum disparity is highlighted in per capita deposit (123.8%), followed by per capita credit (117.5%), per capita consumption of electricity (102.7%) and percentage of gross irrigated area (76.3%). Minimum disparity is found in percentage of villages electrified. Therefore, it can be suggested that the government should continue with its development strategy which is favourably planned towards backward or less developed districts. In this very context one thing must be remembered that mere creation of facilities does not solve the problem of unemployment and poverty. For generation of employment and income, it is to be seen how intensively these facilities are being utilised. So, quite possible the in equalities in income might increase even with decreasing infrastructural facilities. But the evaluation of intension of government to reduce disparities in a planned manner must be made at first stage in

TABLE 7.1: Co-efficient of Variations

Years	P/C Elec Consump.	% of Elec. Vill.	% of G.I. Area	Road Length	Raly. Route	No. of P.O.	% of Literacy	No. of Hos. Beds	P/C Deposit (Rs.)	P/C Credit (Rs.)	No. of Banks
1960	173.3	92.7	122.9	49.3	72.7	39.5	37.6*	99.7	—	—	—
1965	158.4	94.7	124.9	39.8	72.7	28.6	—	85.5	—	—	—
1970	142.2	59.5	102.0	36.3	72.7	26.1	—	80.3	—	—	—
1971	131.7	55.6	99.0	34.6	71.9	26.0	33.9	79.4	270.9	229.2	79.6
1973	136.1	54.3	99.3	34.8	71.9	25.9	—	79.1	228.7	200.6	64.7
1975	127.0	54.2	97.8	35.6	71.9	25.9	—	74.9	197.4	185.9	61.6
1978	113.6	50.41	89.6	32.1	71.9	27.6	—	81.2	148.6	144.1	45.6
1981	110.0	47.2	84.9	31.5	71.9	28.9	29.5	74.2	124.0	132.8	34.1
*1984	108.8	34.33	79.4	33.7	71.9	29.3	—	69.7	120.9	113.4	26.9
1987	102.7	23.1	76.3	38.1	71.9	30.7	—	73.5	123.8	117.5	28.8

*Figure relates to 1961.

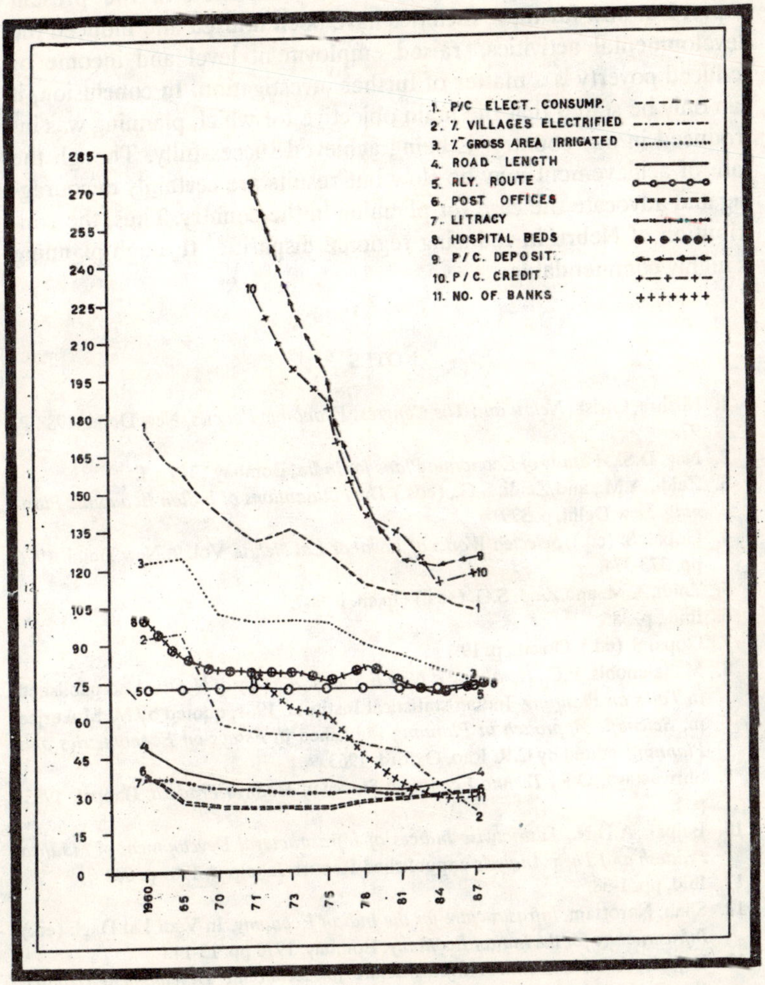

FIG. 7.1: Graph showing the Coefficient of Variations (1960-87)

minimising the gap of existing facilities and at the second stage in overall economic development. So, the government in the State of Madhya Pradesh has been successful in reducing the gap existing in infrastructure facilities which has been discussed in the present paper. But how far these facilities have been utilised and induced the developmental activities, raised employment level and income or reduced poverty is a matter of further investigation. In conclusion, it can only be stated that the main objective for which planning was introduced in our country, is being achieved successfully. Though the rate of achievement may be slow but results are certainly encouraging and advocate the case for planning in the country. Thus, the contribution of Nehru in reducing regional disparities through planning is highly commendable.

NOTES

1. Mishra, Girish, *Nehru and The Congress Economic Policies*, New Delhi, 1988 P. 97.
2. Nag, D.S., *A Study of Economic Plans for India*, Bombay 1949 p.1.
3. Zaidi, A.M., and Zaidi, S.G., (eds.) *The Foundations of Indian Economic Planning*, New Delhi, p. 379.
4. Gopal, S. (ed.), *Selected Works of Jawahar Lal Nehru*, Vol. 9, New Delhi. 1976 pp. 373-374.
5. Zaidi, A.M. and Zaidi S.G. (eds.) Op.cit. p. 387.
6. Ibid., p. 386.
7. Gopal,S. (ed.), Op.cit., p. 19.
8. Mahalanobis, P.C., *Heralding a New E Spoch: A Study of Nehru.* Also published in *Talks on Planning*, Indian statistical Institute, 1961, quoted by M. Mukerjee in, *Scientific Approach in Planning* Published in *Essays on Econometrics and Planning*, edited by C.R. Rao, Oxford, 1963.
9. Shrivastava, O.S., *Techno-Economic Survey of Madhya Pradesh*, Bhopal, 1985, p. 1.
10. Bajpai, A.D.N., *Districtwise Indices of Infrastructural Development of Madhya Pradesh and Their Analysis* unpublished Report, Jabalpur, 1989 p. 60.
11. Ibid, pp. 1-38.
12. Shah, Narottam, *Infrastructure for the Indian Economy*, In Vadi Lal Dagli (ed.) *Infrastructure for the Indian Economy*, Bombay, 1970 pp. 13-14.
13. Bajpai, A.D.N., *Political Infrastructure for Economic Development (Hindi)*, Kantily, Vol. 4, Ujjain 1985.
14. Bajpai, A.D.N., Vicious Circle of Infrastructure Development A Case Study of Indian Economy, *Southern Economist*, Bangalore, 1986 pp. 37-39.
15. Bajpai, A.D.N., op. cit., 1989, pp. 210-254.

SECTION II

INDUSTRY

8

NEHRU : SOCIALISM AND MIXED ECONOMY

A.K. SINGH

India was fortunate to have as its first Prime Minister a statesman and a leader of the stature of Jawaharlal Nehru, who had the vision and the capacity to lead the country on its march to progress on secular, socialist and democratic lines. Solid foundations were laid under his leadership for future progress. As the chief architect of modern India Nehru left an indelible mark in all spheres – be it science and technology, be it arts and culture, be it the creation of democratic institutions, be it the creation of economic infrastructure or be it the strategy of development.

Nehru gave us a number of new ideas and institutions to guide the economy and polity of the country – the concept of planning in a mixed economy, the concept of a secular state, the concept of democratic socialism, the principles of non-alignment and *panchsheel*, the need of a scientific temper and modern technology for removing the poverty of the nation. Each of these ideas and institutions is of enduring significance for the task of nation-building, which was Nehru's chief and all-pervasive concern.

We propose to discuss Nehru's idea of socialism and the instrument of socialism that he adopted, that is, mixed economy with a growing public sector in the context of a democratic system. Nehru had socialist leanings from the very beginning. In the early period he was influenced by Fabian socialism and that influence continued throughout his life. He had also read the writings of Lenin and Marx and was considerably influenced by them. In 1927 he visited Soviet Union and saw the work of socialist construction with his own eyes, which had a powerful impact on his thinking. During the next 35 years or so of his life he tried tirelessly to propagate the idea of socialism. The type of socialism, that Nehru pointed out time and again, had to be evolved in the Indian context, within the Indian idioms and could not be imported from a foreign soil.

The Socialistic Path

In 1929 in the *Lahore Session* of the Congress Nehru declared his socialistic ideas categorically when he said:

> The philosophy of socialism has gradually permeated the entire structure of the society the world over and the only point of dispute is the pace and methods of advance to its full realisation. India will have to go that way too if she seeks to end her poverty and inequality. Though she may evolve her own methods and may adopt the ideals to the genius of her race."

Again in 1930 in the famous *Karachi Session* he moved the resolution on fundamental rights and economic policy which laid down the foundation of the future economic policy of the country. Right from 1931 it was said that the key industries and services should be nationalised. Again, he made an important statement in the Lucknow Session of the Congress where he categorically stated:

> "I see no way of ending the poverty, unemployment, the degradation and the subjection of our people, except through socialism. That involves vast and revolutionary changes in our political and social structure, the ending of the vested interest in land and industry as well as the feudal and autocratic Indian state system. That means the ending of the private property except in a restricted sense and the replacement of the present profit system by higher ideals of the cooperative services."

The *National Planning Committee* was appointed in 1938 and Nehru was made its Chairman. After deliberations for several years during which phase he had to face imprisonment, the report of this committee came out in 1948. This report gives a charter of the economic transformation of the country and the line on which the country wanted to go ahead. It was a rather radical charter in which they talk of the collective agriculture and nationalised industry and control over private sector. Unfortunately when it came to the implementation of these policies we find that there were many compromises and many retreats which were forced by circumstances.

To continue the story further, these ideas were given a concrete shape in the *Avadi Conference* in 1954 when the famous resolution on socialistic pattern of society was adopted. In the Second Five Year Plan which followed a couple of years later the idea of socialistic pattern of society was spelt out in clear terms. It was a system in which the private profit will not be the guiding motive; it will be the social interest or social welfare which would guide all decision-making. This was the idea of socialistic pattern which Nehru was advocating in which monopolies will be restricted and there would be equality of opportunity and equality of development.

Till his very end he was struggling to implement these ideas. At the Bhubaneshwar Congress of 1964, the resolutions that were moved under his inspiration talked of restructuring of social and economic relations. So, whether before independence or when he was in power he continuously struggled to propagate these ideas and to implement them to the extent possible given the social and political context.

Democratic Means

The means were equally important to him as the goal because he had that fundamental faith in individualism, in individual liberty. The idea of violent means to communism or social development was anathema to him. He said and believed that socialism can be attained through democratic means also. The idea of democratic socialism is essential to Nehru's concept of social reconstruction in the country. He said: 'It is possible in theory to establish socialism by democratic means, provided of course, full democratic process is available. The rejection of democracy does not or should not come from the socialist side'. He further elaborated, 'We think that in the final analysis it promotes growth of human beings and of society because as we have said in our constitution we attach great value to individual freedom because we want the creative and adventurous spirit of the man to grow'. The totalitarian kind of structure was not the approach he wanted to adopt. The ideas of democratic socialism, the *Panchayati Raj* institutions, were propagated by him. Although there was a retreat in the 1960s, we are again talking of taking the planning process along the democratic lines to the village level.

Mixed Economy

The instrument that Nehru chose for the socialist transformation of the country was the instrument of a mixed economy because he was convinced that capitalist path was not suitable to India and totalitarian kind of communism was against the ethos of the country. So he tried to cut out a new path which is called a non-classical way of social transformation or a middle path for development which combine the virtues of individual freedom and liberty with that of equality, while avoiding the evils both of capitalism and socialism. The idea of a mixed economy was not something which was adopted after Independence. Rather it was the outcome of a gradual process of thinking that was evolving within the Congress Party and outside. The idea that certain key industries would be nationalised and public sector would expand was in the minds of our leaders even prior to Independence.[2]

Soon after Independence Nehru established two important institutions. One was the Planning Commission, which acquired a position of prominence under his patronage, which sadly is no longer there. The other important institution was needed because planning also requires a date-base, which was missing at that time. So the Central Statistical Organisation was created to collect systematic data on various aspects of the economy so that proper policies could be evolved.

Nehru was convinced that basic and heavy industries had to remain in the public sector. The idea was that public sector will gradually expand. The mixed economy of which Nehru was talking was a transitory phase in socialistic transformation. At that early stage he felt that the state or the Government did not have the means, the resources and technical and administrative manpower to run the whole gamut of economic activities. So certain key industries had to be within the Government control. There was scope for private sector too, but gradually their relative roles were to change. The public sector was expected to acquire the commanding heights of economy, from which the economy could be propelled in the directions – the socialistic directions - which he had in his mind.

The public sector was emphasised for two or three things. Firstly, basic and heavy industries and industries important from strategic view points had to be in public sector. Secondly, he considered public sector as a means of curbing monopolies because free play or private initiative is always likely to culminate into monopolistic or oligopolistic situations. The third point was the idea of taking over commanding heights – basic industries, trade, banking and so on and infrastructure from which the economy could be guided.

Essentially Nehru was a pragmatist. His approach was never a doctrinaire approach or a rigid approach. So private sector, he declared, would be given scope to expand and undertake activities for which it is suitable. He categorically stated that 'to take over the private industries already created is an infantile idea' because he felt that 'state should not block the resources, scarce capital in old industries for acquiring junk in the private sector', rather the state should concern itself with building up the new industries for the country's growth. He also felt 'when there is so vast scope of activity that you cannot take command of the whole area, it would be wrong to stop or curb the private sector all together'. The idea that was in his mind was that of the mixed economy, where the private sector will have its scope and area of operation but it would be within the overall guidance and the control of the state. Gradually the share of public sector will go on expanding so that ultimately we arrive at a stage from which the whole economy could be controlled. Thus we find the share of public sector investment increasing from about 40 per cent in the First Plan to above 60 per cent in the Third Plan, which were formulated during his life time.

Contribution of the Public Sector

Now let us talk of the contributions of the public sector which is much maligned these days. Indeed, if we go by the overall contributions to the national economy its achievements are undeniable. At the end of 1986-87 there were 214 public enterprises in the central sector with a total capital investment of Rs. 52,000 crores. The total sale proceeds of the public sector amounted to almost Rs.70,000 crores. Today the public sector in India is contributing about one-fifth of GNP and slightly more than one-third of the manufacturing output in the country. It has helped in building up basic and heavy industries which have not given only self-reliance in economic field but which have proved of utmost importance for our national defence. The public sector has helped us in moving towards the goal of a self-reliant economy as well as that of political self-reliance. In terms of employment also its contribution is very important. In the private organised sector employment is not increasing over the past ten years and even prior to that the increase in the organised private sector was quite low. The expansion in the employment opportunity is coming mainly through the public sector.

There is a good scope for increasing the efficiency in the public sector. But the question of efficiency is not confined to public sector. In the private sector also you can give ample examples of inefficiency and exploitation; so much so that more than 100 textiles mills, which were bled by the owners and the money was siphoned away to other lucrative areas, had to be taken over by the State. According to the *Economic Survey* for 1986-87 there were as many as 108 public enterprises which were making profits and in the case of ONGC the profit was above 1,000 crores. Half of the public sector enterprises were making profits and about half were running into losses. So it is not correct to say that public sector always makes losses. One has to see that is the charter that is given to public sector to fulfil. Usually the activities taken up in the public sector are such where the returns in economic terms are low. Then, there is the deliberate policy of providing certain cheap inputs by keeping the electricity rates low, or by subsidising the agricultural sector by keeping the interest rate low, in certain activities, by keeping the prices low through subsidy. Much of the gain or profit of the private sector is actually due to the initiative of public sector. Private sector agriculture as well as industries are getting subsidised inputs, which is reflected in higher private profit while the public sector may be suffering losses.

If we look at the overall contribution of the public sector to national economy in terms of taxes it has paid, in terms of depreciation funds, in terms of the investment that it has financed out of its own resources it turns out to be substantial and the gross rate of return then would be something around 19 per cent.

Distributive Justice

So much about the con' .ibution of public sector. Let us also examine whether the mixed economy model has been able to ensure some of the goals which Nehru and other policy-makers had assigned to it. In terms of employment and output we have traced that there has been an advancement but what about restriction of monopolies, monopolistic elements and the inequalities which have tended to perpetuate; rather they have increased over the years in spite of the policy pronouncements. Again, the problems of unemployment and poverty could not be solved through the strategy that was adopted. One can quote a number of authorities who have pointed out that the mixed economy model has failed to either achieve socialistic pattern of society or high rate of growth. Prof. V.K.R.V. Rao said in an article that this middle path has not resulted in an appreciable progress either towards socialistic transformation or towards economic development.[3] Again Prof. Sukhamoy Chakravorty has said, "the organisational framework devised to deal with the problem of growth accompanied by a better distribution of income have turned but to be inadequate in relation to our needs."[4] Thus in terms of the goals of social justice and equality the mixed economy model has not been very successful.

It would be worthwhile to pursue reasons of this failure – whether it could be said that the mixed economy model was not a suitable instrument for socialistic transformation and third path of economic development is not all together possible and so we have to revert to either of the classical paths – unbridled capitalism or complete communism – or whether this system of mixed economy is viable, which has certain shortcomings which can be removed. The present author would subscribe to the latter view. Prof. V.K.R.V. Rao has observed that the instrument of mixed economy was not basically wrong. He has pointed out two models of how the public sector can operate in the mixed economy.[5] One is where public sector is used in the interest of the private sector as it has largely happened in the country. The other path, which was desirable, was where the public sector could really take over the commanding heights of the economy.

An Assessment

Nehru had the right vision that gradually we should take over the commanding heights and control the private sector. But in practice his approach was not bold enough. Whatever may be, the Congress Party had become a weak instrument for the purpose.[6] The socialistic elements had parted company with the Congress. The other leaders paid only lip service to the socialistic pronouncement of Nehru. The administrative bureaucratic structure that he allowed to continue, which was engrained in the capitalist colonial tradition was also an inadequate instrument to realise the objectives of socialistic transformation. Had Nehru put more emphasis on changing these institutions the story would have been different.

NOTES

1. For a brief account of Nehru's economic thought see V.B. Singh, *From Naoroji to Nehru: Six Essays in Indian Economic Thought*, Macmillan Co. of India Ltd., Delhi, 1975.
2. For a discussion of the views on socialism and public sector of Nehru and others see G. Myrdal, *Asian Drama*, Vol. II, Ch. 17.
3. V.K.R.V Rao, "Some Fundamental Aspects of Socialist Change in India," *Indian Economic Journal*, Vol.21, NO.3, 1971, pp. 186-201.
4. S. Chakravarty, "Nehru's Concept of Planning,"in A.V. Bhuleshkar (ed.), *Growth of Indian Economy in Socialism,* Oxford & IBH Publishing Co., Bombay, 1975, p. 31.
5. V.K.R.V. Rao, *op cit.*
6. C.P. Bhambhri, "Nehru and Nation Building," in A.V. Bhuleshkar (ed.), *op cit.*, p. 4.

9

NEHRU AND PUBLIC SECTOR

JAGDISH PRAKASH

Pandit Jawaharlal Nehru, as the first Prime Minister of the country, laid the foundation for rapid industrialisation and development of the country and it is due to his thinking, vision and efforts, today, India is one of the few technically advanced nations of the world. His mind and heart were inexorably drawn to the plight of India and the appalling condition of millions of his countrymen held in the savage torment of alien subjugation. He was highly concerned about the amelioration of the lot of the masses and he chose the instruments of planning and public sector for bringing about necessary economic changes for their progress.

In fact, there was no option before us and we should realise the circumstances and compulsions under which our public sector policy was formulated by Pandit Jawaharlal Nehru. He pointed out very frankly that "In fact not because you think or I think or anybody thinks but inevitably the trend of events is to make the State more and more the organiser of constructive industry and not the private capitalist or any other person".

India was the first country to emerge from the colonial status into an independent sovereign country in 1947. At that time, he found that India was a very backward nation industrially. Being a predominantly agricultural country, millions lived in abject poverty. He foresaw that if we were to raise the standard of living of our countrymen and the status of our country in the map of the world, we must industrialise at a rapid rate. That is why his main thrust was to modernise India through industrialisation and he wanted to first concentrate on the building up of basic and heavy industries and necessary infrastructure so that India might develop the capacity of her own to produce the basic metals and also build up capacity to fabricate the equipments for various key, basic and strategic industries. He fully agreed with Hanson who stated that "whatever the ultimate perspective may be, the country anxious to develop economically has no alternative but to use public enterprise on a considerable scale, at the very least in order to get things going." At that time, it is notable, private industry was at a nascent state and it did not possess the capacity to undertake such gigantic task of building modern India. Thus, rapid expansion of public sector has not come about in an accidental manner, but it has behind it a definite social and economic philosophy of Nehruji.

Under his stewardship, when the first Industrial Policy Resolution was passed in 1948, several specific industries were allotted to the public sector and the rest were left to be developed by the private sector. Even then it was also resolved that in appropriate cases the public sector could enter into the area allotted to private enterprise. It is quite notable that he had thought about the public sector in the country as an instrument of its development even in the late thirties as Chairman of the National Planning Committee of the Congress and had strongly advocated that "profit motive" should be subordinated to "social motive".

Pandit Nehru did not rest with this and later got the resolution on Socialist pattern of society passed first in the Avadi Session of the Congress and later in the Parliament. On the eve of the Second Five Year Plan, the greater thrust was laid on heavy industrialisation and consequently in the Second Industrial Policy Resolution, passed in 1956, the public sector was given a predominant role to play in the development of the country so that it might become self-reliant, as soon as it was possible. Panditji very rightly thought that it was the public sector alone which could provide and strengthen the base and sinews of industrialisation of our large country, which at that time, had many milestones to cross and a long distance to cover to reach the level of industrialisation of countries, such as, France, U.K., U.S.A., Japan and U.S.S.R. In the Parliament in May 1956, he stated that "I want this House to realise how vast and unexploited a field lies there for the public sector to occupy, and the public sector is occupying. We do not mind if the private sector advances also, provided that in regard to the basic and strategic things the public sector holds the field." He further stated that "May I say here that while I am for the public sector growing, I do not understand or appreciate the condemnation of the private sector? The whole philosophy underlying this plan is to take advantage of every possible way of growth and not to do something which suits some doctrinaire or imagine we have satisfied some text-book maxim of a hundred years ago." Thus, it was the strong conviction and vision of Panditji of a just, self-reliant, technically advanced with scientific fervour and modern economy that placed public sector at the centre of India's development.

It was under his stewardship and with the help of T.T. Krishnamachari, K.D. Malviya, C. Subramaniam and other socialist thinkers, giant public sector enterprises were set up and almost all the basic, key, heavy, and strategic industrial units were set up in the country which have indeed changed the economic complexion and map of the country. It has been very rightly stated that "alongwith the small bands of dedicated colleagues, Nehru began the gigantic task of the reconstruction of India and the transformation of an ancient society into a modern state. For the next seventeen years, as First Servant of the Indian People, he worked tirelessly towards these ends." It has also been aptly observed that "never before in the history of man had such a revolution been attempted on so large a scale with democracy as the base, and with so little to begin with."

The giant public sector units and multipurpose projects were great temples of India for Nehru. While delivering a speech at the opening of the Nangal Canal (8th July, 1954), he stated that "As I walked round the site I thought that these days the biggest temple and mosque and gurudwara is the place where man works for the good of mankind. Which place can be greater than this — where thousands and lakhs of men have worked, have shed their blood and sweat . . . where can be a greater and holier place than this, which we can regard as higher?"

At this time and even today there has been a controversy regarding private *vs.* public sector. Nehru was very clear in his mind and always thought both are complimentary and must strive together in building the nation. Under his stewardship, in Avadi Resolution, it was stated that "the private sector has thus definite place in our economy at present and should be encouraged to play its part within the broad strategic controls of the plan."

He was of the clear view that "the distinction between the public and private sector was one of relative emphasis; private enterprise should have a public purpose and there is no such thing under present condition as completely unregulated and free private enterprise. The view that private enterprise can function only on the basis of unregulated profits is an anachronism. The private and public sectors cannot be looked upon as anything like two separate entities; they are, and must function as, parts of a single organism". In fact, he did not have any rigid doctrine or dogma about it. Speaking at the meeting of the AICC in 1957, he stated "so long as we feed, clothe, house, it will not matter whether we call ourselves capitalistic, socialistic, communist or any thing else".

While initiating the discussion on the Second Five Year Plan, Nehru made it clear that "while the Public Sector must obviously grow and even now it has grown, both absolutely and relatively — the private sector is not something unimportant. It will play an important role; though gradually and ultimately it will fade away. But the public sector will control and should control the strategic points in our economy."

Nehru had very rightly felt that the public sector would provide the economic foundation for increasing opportunities for gainful employment and improving living standards and working conditions for the masses. It would also reduce disparities in income and wealth, prevent monopoly and concentration of economic power in the hands of small number of individuals. What he thought and planned at that time, has proved to be true. It is quite true that had he not laid the foundation of development of the country through public sector, the country would not have advanced so much as it has today. As thought by Nehru, the public sector even today, is a strong instrument in the hands of people of India, and their government to help eradicate poverty and bring hope and cheer to the multitudes of our countrymen who have been dreaming for a long time of the day when tears of helplessness and misery will be wiped off from the sunken cheeks of billions of people in our motherland.

As Nehru envisioned, the public sector enterprises have grown in an unprecedented manner and have, undoubtedly, attained what the British socialist leader, Bevan called the "Commanding heights of the economy" of the country. We cannot think of our country without these enterprises. They have come up to his expectations in fulfilling their obligations and have permeated the socio-economic structure of the country and they have now acquired the necessary ability and capability to build the nation a very strong one. The investment in them has increased from mere Rs. 29 crores in 1951 to Rs. 71,299 crores in 1989. They, today, cover a very vast and varied range of activities and really dominate the economic scene providing economic and social justice to the people of the country.

They dominate the industrial infrastructure scene of Indian economy consisting of coal, steel, power, petroleum, non-ferrous metals, fertiliser, communication equipments etc. The overall scenario which one witnesses today is that apart from the entire core sector, most of the basic and strategic industries considered vital for economic security and national self-reliance are in the public sector. Equipment needs of sectors, like railways, telecommunication, nuclear power, defence etc. have also been entrusted to the public sector. They have also come to the rescue of several sick enterprises taken over from private sector mainly to sustain production and protect employment.

There has been a controversy over the grant of autonomy to the management of such enterprises. Nehruji had advocated that sufficient autonomy should be given to them. He was against the use of bureaucratic style of management for these enterprises. He stated very clearly that "I have no doubt that the normal governmental procedure applied to a public enterprise of this kind will lead to the failure of that public enterprise. Therefore, we have to evolve a system for working of public enterprises where, on the one hand, there are adequate checks and protection, and, on the other, enough freedom for that enterprise to work quickly and without delay". He was also not in favour of rigid Parliamentary control over them. He once reiterated that "we can not sit down in this house everyday and control public enterprises from here. It just cannot be done — but if we are too insistent we shall lose a great deal of money — and it will develop a kind of static atmosphere, which is very bad for growing industry." Thus, he wanted to establish proper balancing between control and autonomy.

Today, we often hear about the *privatisation* of these public sector enterprises and we have to remember Nehru in this connection. It would have been rather very painful for him to see this instrument of economic and social change being discarded as useless specially because they are not generating "profits". Have the various objectives which he advocated for their establishment not been achieved? Have they really lost their utility? Have they not made India a self-reliant country? Have they not been responsible for the nation to "take off"? Have they not been instrumental in planned development of the country with avowed objective of "growth with justice"?

If we have to pay homage to this great leader, thinker, historian and statesman of the country, we must see that not only public enterprises grow in the country but they also fulfil the objectives which Nehru advocated so strongly. This indeed throws a greater burden on the shoulders of those who are managing the affairs of these large and very giant units. Speaking in the Constituent Assembly on 7th April, 1948, he remarked that "I do hope that it (state enterprise) is not going to be run by people who have worked in the nuts of the departments but by persons of vision, push and drive, not by people who write on the files but who do the work." They should remember his words: "I look for — towards this our country. India, whose children we are. Where is she going? Where have we to lead her, which way we have to walk and what mighty tasks have we to undertake? Some of these will be completed by those who come after us. The work of a nation or a country is never completed. It goes on —".

10

INDUSTRIAL GROWTH : Policy Perspectives

LALLAN PRASAD

As an industrial power India has improved its ranking in market economy countries from 15th in 1970 to 12th in 1985 (Table 10.1). The value added in manufacturing has increased five times in India during this period as compared to 3 to 4 times of most developed countries. Japan and Brazil registered higher rate of growth in manufacturing sector than India. The growth rates in major sectors of industry in India varied from year to year. During 1960-80 industrial output increased at an annual average rate of 5.5 per cent. The growth rate was highest during 1961-65. During 1970s growth rate of 9 per cent was recorded only in 1976. The growth rate was below average in 1973-75 and 1980. In 1980's the growth rate was lowest in 1982-83 (3.2) and highest in 1988-89 (April-Aug.) (10.2). Shortage of power, wagons, poor performance in agricultural sector due to floods and droughts, labour troubles, low capacity utilisation and shortage in demand have contributed to low production in certain years. On the whole, however, the performance of industrial sector has been better than agricultural sector. The policy measures initiated by Panditji in early 1950s have paid rich dividends in course of time, helping India to emerge as an industrial giant.

The foundation of an industrial policy for free India was laid in 1948 with a lead role for public sector in key areas. A comprehensive Industrial Policy Resolution was however adopted in 1956 which aimed at accelerating rate of economic growth and speed up industrialisation, developing heavy and machine making industries, expanding public sector, building up large and growing cooperative sector, reducing disparities in income and wealth and preventing private monopolies. Other noticeable features of the resolution were emphasis on development of small and cottage industries, balanced growth of industry and agriculture, training of technical and managerial personnel and improvement of living and working conditions of labour etc. The resolution of 1956 is still the bible for planners in this country. The policy resolution of 1977 had limited impact. Its emphasis on small industries resulting into reservation of a number of industries for small scale sector was not acted upon for long. The 1980 resolution reiterated government's emphasis on large industries considering industrialisation as *sine quo non* of economic progress. It further emphasised on optimum utilisation of installed capacity, faster promotion of export-oriented and import substitution industries and correction of regional imbalances etc.

The capital goods and basic industries got the highest attention in our industrialisation scheme. A structural change took place due to planned intervention in course of time. Traditional industries like textiles, jute, rubber and food etc. were retrogated in background while engineering and metals, petroleum and recently electronic industries have become prominent. These structural changes are also reflected in our export trade, although the performance of export sector has been dismal compared to international standards. Small countries like Korea, and Singapore have done much better than India in this sector. India's total export in 1986 was of the order of 16269 million dollars as against 34517 million dollars of Korea and 22495 million dollars of Singapore.

Employment generation by large scale sector has also been grossly inadequate. This has been mainly due to the capital intensive nature of large industries. Public sector which has an investment of over 6000 crores of rupees today, provides direct employment to 22 lakh persons in all. This is also considered to be on higher side as many plants are overstaffed. With over 30 million unemployed and many more being added every day, large scale industries' capacity to provide employment at massive scale seems to be doubtful. There is a need to promote small and cottage industries, capacity expansion in private sector, trade liberalisation, promotion of consumer goods and export goods industries, knowledge intensive and service industries and above all to do away with the licence and quota raj which has done more harm than good to Indian economy in past. The demand for liberal industrial policy in recent years thus strews from the realities of economic life in this country.

The industrial licencing policy aimed at promoting industrialisation on the basis of effective utilisation of resources, reducing foreign exchange dominance, encouraging small scale sector, bringing about greater regional dispersal and preventing concentration of economic power. But it ultimately turned into a control mechanism for the sake of control. Narsimhan Committee which went into details of licensing system came to the conclusion that a heavy price had been exacted in terms of high cost structure and insufficient attention to the quality of product. The operation of array of controls on investment and production had resulted in presumption of a share of market by those fortunate to have been licenced to invest and produce. Resource utilisation has been in-efficient due to over protection. The Committee, therefore, suggested delicensing in case of industries producing mass consumption goods, items of high export possibilities, items which may be imported freely and also industries in which technology is changing fast. The Government accepted the recommendations of the Committee and announced delicensing of 25 broad categories of industries in March 1985. It was extended to 82 bulk drugs and drug formulations in 1985. MRTP and FERA companies were also allowed to invest in 22 industries delicensed. The facility of 'broad branding' was provided in Jan. 1986 enabling the companies to change their product mix without seeking licence. The policy aimed at full capacity utilisation by diversifying the products without loss of time. The cut-off limit for MRTP Act was also raised from Rs. 20 crores to Rs. 100 crores. Many of the industries which were opened for the entry of MRTP and FERA companies in which they were not allowed to invest earlier. The Government also allowed capacity increase on the basis of past performance and advanced technology and rationalisation.

The recent steps for policy liberalisation includes doing away with licensing of units with investment up to Rs. 50 crores and also where projects do not require foreign exchange, promotion of industrialisation of backward regions by setting up growth centres and removal of several industries from the negative list of licensing.

Fiscal measures are also directed towards liberalisation. New funding schemes for instance allow companies a reduction of profits up to 20 per cent if an equivalent amount is deposited with IDBI or utilised for plants and machinery in the same year. Depreciation is allowed now on block of assets instead of individual assets. Depreciation rates are also rationalised. Modified value Added Tax (MODVAT) has been introduced to reduce the cascading effect of multipoint excise taxes.

While it is too early to judge the impact of policy liberalisations introduced in recent years the performance of industrial sector in past five years has confirmed the belief that such measures were long due.

Public sector has reached the 'Commanding heights' due to industrial policy in past. Investment in public enterprises has gone up from Rs. 29 crores in 1951 to Rs. 61603 crores in 1987. While originally this sector was envisaged to build infrastructure for industrialisation by developing such industries as iron and steel, heavy engineering, machine tools, transport equipment, oil, mineral and metals and chemicals etc., it was allowed to go into distribution of consumer goods, operating hotels, insurance and banking business and consultancy services etc. Steel accounts for largest amount invested (Rs. 6913 crores) followed by minerals and metals (Rs. 6747 crores), coal (Rs. 6305 crores) petroleum (Rs. 5105 crores) (Table 10.2). Public sector has helped in providing a base for India's industrialisation by going into the areas in which private sector was shy to invest due to long gestation period and heavy investments. But public sector has not come up to the expectations of public in India.

The public criticism of public sector is growing for its dismal performance in some cases and inadequate performance in many cases. The top ten loss making enterprises in public sector which include DTC, FCI, HEC, IDPL etc. had incurred total losses worth Rs. 900 crores in 1986-87. Public sector units as a whole have shown a profit of Rs. 1769 crores in that year, bulk of which came from petroleum and power which are state monopolies. Efficiency of public enterprises can be increased, not by outright sale of these enterprises to private sector, but by relaxing controls and introducing competition in the areas in which these units have monopoly position. In U.K. for instance, British Oil Corporation competes in the production and sale of oil with a number of companies in private sector. Formation of more joint sector units to marry managerial talent of private entrepreneurs and the resources of state, encouraging public to invest in shares of public sector, contracting out services and promoting subsidiary companies for sale to private entrepreneurs by public sector companies are other measures which may help in improving the performance of this vital sector of our economy. There is a definite need of partial privatisation to induce a business culture in the public sector.

TABLE 10.1: Value Added 1-Manufacturing

(in millions of current dollars)

Country	1970	Rank	1985	Rank
India	**6960**	**15**	**35597**	**12**
China	28794	7	95103	6
Brazil	10433	9	58089	9
Mexico	8414	11	43613	11
Italy	29205	6	93973	7
U.K.	35954	5	101470	5
Belgium	8226	13	18570	16
Netherland	8652	10	23063	14
France	40502	4	124436	4
Australia	9495	14	30730	13
Germany	70888	3	201640	3
Japan	73339	2	395148	2
Sweden	8333	12	20878	15
Canada	16710	8	58862	8
U.S.A.	254115	1	803391	1
Spain			44891	10

Source: World Bank Report, 1988.

TABLE 10.2: Investment in Public Sector, 1986-87, Cognate Groups with Investment of more than Rs. 5,000 crores each

Cognate Group	Investment (in crores of rupees)
Steel	6913
Minerals and Metals	6747
Coal	6305
Power	7409
Petroleum	5105
Chemicals, Fertilizers & Pharmaceuticals	5818
Total investment in above groups	38297
Total investment in all public enterprises	61602
Percentage investment in the cognate groups given above	62%

Source: Public Enterprises Survey, 1986-87, Vol. 1.

11

PANDIT NEHRU : Mixed Economy, Industrialisation and Technology

S.C. MATHUR

In discussing and analysing Pandit Nehru's role in the industrialisation and economic development of India and bringing India on the industrial map of the world, it is necessary to point out how the emergence of Soviet power was welcomed by Indian patriotic opinion as a positive factor to the final liberation of the oppressed people. This is what India's two greatest sons wrote about the Great October Socialist Revolution of 1917: "There is no questioning the fact that the Bolshevik ideal has behind it the purest sacrifices of countless men and women who have given up their all for its sake; and the ideal that is sanctified by sacrifices of such master spirits as Lenin cannot go in vain; the noble example of their renunciation will be emblazoned for ever and quicker and purify the ideal as time passes. (Mahatma Gandhi, *Young India* 1928).

Jawaharlal Nehru was 'greatly inspired' by the Soviet Revolution and he wrote in *The Discovery of India* :

> "I have no doubt that Soviet Revolution had advanced human society by a great leap and had lit a bright flame which could not be smothered, and that it laid the foundations for that new civilization towards which the world could advance."

The great achievements of socialism in the reconstruction of Russia deeply impressed Jawaharlal Nehru and in his book *The Discovery of India* he wrote:

> "But most of all we had the example of the Soviet Union, which in two brief decades........had made tremendous progress".

After achieving its independence India has scored remarkable successes in developing and strengthening her national economy under the stewardship of Nehru. Her industrial output has grown several times and her agricultural production has more than doubled. An important contribution to this progress has been made by Soviet – Indian economic and technical cooperation in which Nehru had from the beginning evinced keen interest and which continued to grow in his time and solidly laid the foundation of India's economic progress and development. This cooperation was based on the principles of complete equality, respect for sovereignty and territorial integrity, non-interference in each other's internal affairs and mutual benefit. A distinguishing feature of this cooperation is that it is aimed at helping India to build an independent and comprehensively developed national economy. Its basic aim is to help India, develop its industries, above all heavy industry and expand and consolidate the public sector of the economy, which corresponds to the objective requirements of the country's economic progress and the economic policy of its government.

Even before the country became independent, Indian leaders recognised the fact that political independence without economic development is meaningless. At its Karachi Session in 1931 the Indian National Congress stated: "The state shall own and control key industries and services, mineral resources, railways, waterways, shipping and other means of public transport." The resolution called "Fundamental Rights and Economic Policy" supported by Nehru clearly showed the influence his visit to the Soviet Union in 1927 had on him. In his Autobiography, Nehru admitted that he had the sanction of Mahatma Gandhi in introducing the resolution at the Karachi session.

In his letters sent from prison to his daughter in 1930-34, Jawaharlal Nehru spoke highly of the possibilities and prospects of economic planning and the role of state in co-ordinating and controlling economic development in the interests of the people. In his letter dated July 9, 1933 entitled 'Russia's Five Year Plan', Nehru laid particular emphasis on the role of planning. "The Five-Year Plan has completely changed the face of Russia," Nehru wrote, "From a feudal country it has suddenly become an advanced industrial country. There has been amazing cultural advance and the social services, the system of public health and accident insurances are the most advanced in the world. The argument about the success of the Five-

Year Plan is rather a pointless one. The answer to it is really the present state of the Soviet Union. And a further answer is the fact that this plan has impressed itself on the imagination of the world. Everybody talks of 'planning' now and of five-year and ten-year plans. The Soviets have brought magic into the word". Such were the conclusions drawn by Nehru from his analysis of the results of the First Soviet Five-Year Plan.

Planning and planned economic development, therefore, had become deeply imbedded in the personality of Jawaharlal Nehru. The economic and social achievements of the Soviet Union based on its Five-Year Plans continued to influence Nehru. In 1938 he helped to set up a planning body—The National Planning Committee—which appointed him Chairman to prepare 'a blue-print for India's planned development'. Industrialisation was the primary objective, for it was clearly realised even then that poverty and unemployment, problems of national defence and economic regeneration could not be solved without it. Nehru took up Chairmanship, since it was, as he said "a work after my own heart and I could not keep out of it".

He recognised, however, that under the conditions prevailing in India it would be impossible to go over to full-fledged socialism and a completely planned economy. That is what gave rise to the concept of "mixed economy" in which both public and private sectors had to play a significant role.

Independent India chose the policy of non-alignment in its foreign relations. It implied a measure of economic independence. This was not possible without planning and therefore, the building of a public sector. If India had gone along the path of capitalism with a free-for-all economic growth, it would not have been possible to create even an autonomous private sector. India could not have followed an independent foreign policy in that circumstance. After India gained its independence, Nehru set up the National Planning Commission of India. Under his guidance the Commission worked out the First Five-Year Plan for national economic development. Nehru regarded economic planning as the starting point in the coordinated development of the key branches of industry, which would be directed by the government within the framework of a national programme and carried out through scientific utilisation of the material and manpower resources in the interests of the economic and social progress of the country.

After studying the experiences of economic development in a

number of countries, Nehru arrived at the conclusion that building modern national industry was India's top-priority work if it wanted to consolidate its hard-won national independence and lay the foundations of steady economic and social progress. When he spoke of national industry, Nehru had in mind above all heavy industry. This is borne out by his statement's to the National Development Council during the discussion of the Second Five-Year Plan. "If we want to develop India", he said "and that is our intention, then we must really industrialise India.....we must plant the roots and lay the foundation on which the structure of an industrial India can be erected. Priority, therefore, must be given to the development of heavy industry".

India chose "mixed economy" for historical reasons. But it assigned the leading role to the public sector. It was the hope of Jawaharlal Nehru and others that the public sector, in being able to move the economy in a desired direction would be able to influence the growth of the private sector. Nehru had said that "planning is a continuous movement towards desired goals." These goals were: growth, modernisation, self-reliance and social justice. Despite the fact that India's economic performance has not been "outstanding", it has impressive achievements to show. Its national income grew at the rate of 3 to 5 per cent (1st plan to the end of the 6th plan), while the average annual growth rate in the period of 1951-1986 has been nearly 4 per cent. In spite of a hostile international environment in the eighties, India is one of the few countries which have been able to maintain their growth rates. One of the significant achievements of planning was growth in the level of saving from 10 per cent (1950-51) to about 24-25 per cent (1985-86) which is indeed high for a developing country with a low per capita income. Indeed, India's saving rate is comparable to that of a middle income country.

The public sector of the Indian economy owes its origin to the conviction of Nehru and other Indian leaders that decisive role in the production and distribution of material of goods should be played by the state. The historic words of the first Prime Minister of independent India to the effect that the state should ever more actively become the organiser of industry spoken in 1948 have become a reality today.

The industrial policy of India especially with regard to the public sector, is regulated by two important policy statements of the government of India, those of April 1948 and April 1956, as well as by the Directive Principles of State Policy and the national Five-Year Plans.

The First Five-Year Plan gave a broad outline of thrust to these policies when it said: "whether one thinks of the problem of capital formation or of the introduction of new techniques or of the extension of social services or of the overall realignment of the productive forces and class relationship within society one inevitably comes to the conclusion that a rapid expansion of the economic and social responsibilities of the state will alone be capable of satisfying the legitimate expectations of the people. This need not involve complete nationalisation of the means of production or elimination of private agencies in agriculture or business and industry. It does mean, however, a progressive widening of the public sector and reorientation of the private sector to the needs of planned economy."

The April 1956 industrial policy statement further clarified the role of the state in economic development. It singled out 17 industries to be developed exclusively by the state. These were defence production, iron and steel, heavy castings and forgings, heavy plant machinery required for iron and steel production and mining, heavy electricals, coal and lignite, zinc, copper, lead, aircraft, ship-building, telecommunication equipment, distribution of electricity etc.

Twelve industries including fertilisers, aluminium, machine tools basic and intermediate products required by chemical industries, road and sea transport were to be progressively state-owned, though the private sector might also participate in these fields.

All the remaining industries were left to the initiative and enterprise of the private sector.

The statement also said that "it was always open to the state to undertake any type of industrial production." The role of the public sector has since been spelt out several times by the government. On December 21, 1954, for example, Jawaharlal told Parliament: "It is obvious in a country as under-developed as ours that we cannot progress except by state initiatives, except by enlarging the public sector, and except by controlling the private sector at important points. The important thing is that the strategic points must be controlled by the state........ if I may repeat, our policy must inevitably be one of realising production and increasing employment as rapidly as possible. In doing so it is essential that public sector grows as rapidly as possible.

In pursuance of the policy of her father, Jawaharlal Nehru, on June 14, 1966, Mrs. Indira Gandhi further clarified the position when she said: "we advocate the public sector for three reasons: to gain control of the commanding heights of the economy; to promote critical development in terms of social gain or strategic value rather than primarily on consideration of profit; and to provide commercial surpluses with which to finance further economic development."

Jawaharlal Nehru took special interest in the adoption and enlargement of the state sector and in its continuous growth with the result that from only five public sector enterprises in the country in 1951, their number had grown to over 200 by 1983, and 'their total investment reached more than Rs. 35,000 crore'. Massive allocations have been made to the public sector in the various plans of India, and today there is hardly any field—economic, commercial and financial—in which the public sector is not playing a significant role. The bulk of the investment has gone to the production of raw materials, and the investment in steel, petroleum, coal and minerals and metals has been phenomenal. Other important sectors of investment are chemicals, fertilisers, pharmaceuticals, engineering and power. Thus it is clear that the public sector has been a vital catalyst to the general industrial development of the country, something of which Jawaharlal Nehru had been greatly enamoured. India has achieved a great degree of self-sufficiency in the production of most manufactured products, and is capable of sustaining future growth in vital sectors primarily through domestic effort. This is reflected in the commodity composition of India's foreign trade, in which the share of imports of manufactured goods has steadily declined. On the other hand the share of industrial goods, particularly products of engineering, in the country's export has been growing. This has been accompanied by a corresponding growth in technological skills on which Jawaharlal Nehru laid great emphasis.

In Nehru's thinking, industrialisation, modernisation and technological competence were all interrelated concepts. Today the public sector is a reservoir of technological competence. It has mastered technologies in diverse fields so that it can provide consultancy to foreign countries as well as undertake turnkey projects. It has also mastered technologies in such "high-tech" areas as atomic power and space research. If today India is counted among the top ten industrialised nations of the world, the most significant contribution to this was made by the public sector. The Soviet Union has participated extensively in the development of India's technological competence and in training country's personnel. It was he who, as I have just said, laid the foundation of Soviet-Indian economic and technical cooperation, received Soviet aid without strings, and led the country towards realising the goal of planned economic development and the attainment of self-sufficiency and technological skills.

The public sector has naturally drawn criticism both from within and outside India. True, the public sector units have not always shown profitable operation. On a purely formal basis, the statistics may seem to bear this out. The point is that the expansion of the public sector launched by the Nehru government in the 1950s primarily affected the key branches of industry above all power and metal production, oil extraction, mining, engineering and chemical industries which require colossal capital investment and need a long period before repayment can start.

India has already carried out Six Five-Year Plans during the years of its independence and has already achieved considerable results. The Sixth Five-Year Plan ended in 1985 and the 7th plan began in the same year. As Nehru envisaged, the thrust of the plans has been the absorption of new technology, modernisation, reduction of costs and greater competition.

The Soviet Union has, since Nehru's time, offered India assistance in building 70 large industrial enterprises and other projects in the public sector. They form the nucleus of the national economy, the basis of stepping up the rate of extended reproduction. Jawaharlal Nehru said, "The Soviet Union has given as many precious gifts; the most precious gift of these is friendship". Jawaharlal Nehru showed great interest in the construction of the Bhilai Steel Plant. Despite the great demand on his precious time, he managed to visit the construction site several times to enquire how things were going and to take timely measures to deal with problems. On December 16, 1957, during the first visit to Bhilai, Nehru noted in the Visitor's Book: "Today I spent some hours in going round the Bhilai Project area and seeing what had already been done and how this great work was progressing. To record my impressions of this visit is not easy for Bhilai is one of those plans which have become imbedded in the national consciousness as significant symbols of a new age in India. Long before one comes to Bhilai, one is forcefully conscious of it. Still, the impact is great, and what was once a dream begins to take shape and come true — a symbol and portent of the India of future. Regarding power development, Nehru said, "if you tell me how much power, hydropower and thermal India has been producing, then I can immediately form an idea of its industrial development".

India, a country of continental dimensions had a power capacity of 1.2 million kW when it gained independence. "I should imagine that there are two sets of the progress of a nation: how much iron and steel and how much power it is producing". This was the thinking of Jawaharlal Nehru which defined the framework of the Five-Year Plans, which have put India on the industrial map of the world.

Nehru attached great importance to the development of oil, power and heavy industries. He has written in his *The Discovery of India* : "the importance of oil and petrol grows and affects imperialist policies". Indeed modern imperialism has sometimes been called "oil imperialism". On May 25, 1956 Nehru spoke in Parliament about the crucial importance of oil. Mr. K.D. Malaviya, the then Minister of Natural Resources, said, "There can be no freedom for the country's economy or its defence unless the oil industry is owned and controlled by the State".

The 1956 Industrial Policy Resolution of the Government of India was, therefore, a concrete expression of India's economic experience in the period 1947-1955 a crucial period when it became clear that India could not receive any substantial assistance from capitalist countries for its industrialisation, more so when their interests clashed with India's interests.

By 1955 the Government of India was already working on a plan of oil exploration. The Directorate of Oil and Natural Gas (later called Oil and Natural Gas Commission) was set up. This alarmed foreign oil cartels. Pressure was brought to bear on Nehru by various quarters to make him give up the project. But Nehru stood to his ground. He said: "The policy is dead clear and the policy is — I repeat — that oil is one of the major commodities in the public sector." It was the challenge of oil cartels that India had to meet and deal with successfully in the years after 1955 under the inspiring leadership of Prime Minister, Jawaharlal Nehru.

On May 13, 1960 oil was obtained from the first prospecting well at Ankleshwar. Jawaharlal Nehru, who paid great attention to the development of the national oil industry, visited the project several times. During one of his trips to an oil field where he wanted to see how oil was extracted a gusher began spouting oil, spattering his clothes, Indian and Soviet experts standing there were discomfited, but the Prime Minister was unperturbed: "I shall address the Parliament in this Sherwani", he said. "Let everybody know that we now have our own oil. And he named the well "Vasundhara" the source of prosperity which proved prophetic. Ankleshwar justified the hopes of the great son of India. Today it is one of India's major oil fields, accounting for a substantial part of the on-land oil output.

Jawaharlal Nehru also realised that India could not develop an oil industry without its own refineries. He took great interest in the setting up of oil refineries. The Koyali refinery was set up with Soviet assistance and its foundation was laid by Jawaharlal Nehru. Speaking at the ceremony, he said: Creating an oil refinery in Gujarat became possible due to the cooperation of our great friend the Soviet Union. That country has great technical achievements and we can learn a great deal from them. Jawaharlal Nehru wanted India to imbibe, absorb and make use of the latest technology in every field of economic and industrial life. This was his concept of modernisation.

During his visit to the U.S.S.R. in 1955, Jawaharlal Nehru visited the famous Urals Mechanical engineering plant in SVERLOVSK. He called it a plant of plants, and remarked that it was just what India wanted. He was greatly impressed with the Soviet technological innovations and Soviet technological competence and wanted that the Soviet Union should provide to India most up-to-date technology in every field, which it did willingly and ungrudgingly.

It was Jawaharlal Nehru who laid the foundation stone of the Heavy Machine — Building Plant (HMBP) in Ranchi in 1963, and the construction was completed in 1968. The basic objective of the plant was to serve the growth of steel industry — to produce steel equipment for a one-million tonne capacity steel plant per year.

Thus Nehru regarded planning as an uninterrupted process, as a necessary element and an important tool for bringing about industrialisation in the country with the help of modern advanced technology available in the world. In his thinking which he translated into practice during his Prime Ministership India's development meant the industrialisation of the country by which he mainly meant the development of heavy industry. "Choosing the path of mixed economy" which suited Indian conditions, the leading role had been assigned to the public sector.

SECTION III

AGRICULTURE

12

NEHRU AND PLANNING — Choices in Agriculture

G.S. BHALLA

Of all the national leaders in India, it was Pandit Nehru who had the greatest ideological commitment to the achievement of economic and social freedom as represented by socialism. And Nehru firmly believed that planning was essential to achieve this ideal, as planning would enable the harnessing of resources of investment in priority areas.

The achievements and failures of economic planning in India have been widely evaluated. This paper is not aimed to undertake yet another detailed review of economic development in India since Independence. The purpose of this paper is much more limited — it makes an attempt to critically analyse Nehru's ideas on role and importance of agriculture in the national economy and his contribution to agricultural planning in India.

The paper is divided into four sections. After the Introduction on Nehru and Indian Peasantry, Section 2 is devoted to a brief discussion of Implementation of agrarian policy after independence. This is followed by a detailed evaluation of agricultural planning and policies during Nehru's period in Section 3. This section contains a critical review of land reforms, agricultural policies and terms of trade between the agricultural and the non-agricultural sectors. Finally, Section 4 contains a brief summing up.

I

Introduction — Nehru and Indian Peasantry

To start with, the Indian National Congress was dominated by upper middle class intellectuals and eminent lawyers. However, the leadership soon realised that since agriculture constituted by far the most important activity of an overwhelming majority of working people in India, the Congress could not become a potent force without activity involving millions of peasants in the movement.

But involving peasantry in freedom struggle implied that the leadership should have some understanding of their living conditions, should understand the basic cause of their misery and should give them some hope for the future. It goes to the credit of leaders like Gandhi and Nehru along with innumerable peasant leaders that rural peasantry did become an integral part of the national movement. Gandhi and Nehru had a live contact and intimate knowledge of peasants' life which they had acquired by participating in and leading peasant struggles in various parts of the country. In the case of Nehru, it was casual circumstances that thrust him into the problems of the Indian peasantry during early 1920. But his involvement and leadership of Partapgarh peasants gave a new and permanent dimension to his outlook".[1] It may be underlined that both Gandhi and Nehru at that time strived for involvement of peasantry in the freedom movement without in any way playing up the contradictions between the peasants and the landlords. In order to avoid unnecessary rural tensions, they went to the extent of disapproving the activities of peasant leaders who advocated militant struggle against the landlords. Although sympathetic to the miserable lot of peasantry, Gandhi was averse to perpetuating class struggle in the countryside. His main interest was to involve the kisans into non-cooperative movement. In the early twenties, Nehru had no alternative ideology to that of Gandhi. Like Gandhi he also advised the kisans that they should "pay their rents and devote their full attention to non-violent struggle for *Swaraj*".[2] Although opposed to unauthorised excessive exactions by the landlords, in effect he preached kisan-zamindar unity. Even on the issue of ejectment of tenants his attitude was very ambivalent. At that time under the influence of Gandhi, Nehru was under no circumstances prepared to support much less to lead a radical kisan movement. Although Nehru's first contact with peasantry had a profound impact on him, according to Gopal "whether Nehru was aware of it or not, his attitude at this time implied informal collaboration with the government in the maintenance of law and order...".[3]

Nehru's ideas underwent a radical change during his stay in

Europe during 1926 and 1927. By the time he came back to India, he had developed a marxist outlook and had started advocating radical economic programme for the Congress. For example, in the area of agriculture he wanted complete abolition of landlordism (but with compensation) and creation of a co-operative village as a basic unit of agricultural production:

> "Any movement which seeks to become a mass movement must necessarily have an economic programme for the masses....
> Our ultimate ideal should be large nationalised farms, and peasant proprietors cultivating their own farms, but without right of alienation". Big estates have to be broken up. There should be no confiscation, but "land will be acquired on payment of compensation. A principle that must be borne in mind in fixing the land tax or rent is that of a living wage or income".[4]

Nehru's views about economic reorganisation became more radical with the passage of time. By 1944, National Planning Committee, of which Nehru was the Chairman, had already started talking about state control of agriculture and industry. It was no wonder, therefore, that soon after Independence in 1948 the Congress Agrarian Reforms Committee prepared one of the most radical documents on the agrarian relations. Their Report envisaged not only the abolition of intermediaries, ceiling on land-holding and security of tenure, it also advocated cooperative village management to enable small holdings to increase their output by making use of scientific methods of cultivation. Cooperative village management was to be combined with development of small and cottage industries to provide employment to rural people and relieve the pressure of workers on agriculture. This was perhaps one of the most comprehensive, clear headed and articulate statement of the Congress on agrarian changes under Nehru's influence.

II

Implementation of Agrarian Policy — the Planning Context

Soon after Independence the planning process was initiated in India under the leadership of Nehru with the avowed aim of accelerating the growth of the economy and uplifting the conditions of the poor. It may be recalled that the beginning of the thinking on planning process had been initiated by the National Planning Committee in the latethirties. This Committee and its sub-committees produced several important documents, some of which favoured socialism and at least state control of industry and agriculture. In fact, this was much to the chagrin of Gandhi who did not like the implied radicalism. However, the war had changed the entire scenario and by the mid-forties planning had become quite popular so much so that even the capitalists/industrialists in India had produced their own plan — the Bombay Plan. In addition People's Plan and Gandhian Plan had also been brought out.

At that time, Nehru's ideas on planning were quite radical. To him planning was inevitably connected with the establishment of socialist economy within a democratic structure. But Nehru had no wish to frighten away people by stressing the socialist aspect.[5]

Nehru's ideas about planning matured with the passing of time and also changed in response, therefore, to the changing economic and political situation in the country. For Nehru Planning was to be the mechanism for bringing about the economic transformation of India on socialist lines. Nehru was aware that only through rapid industrialisation could India enable its working population to have higher living standards. But he was also aware that since a large working population was dependent on agriculture, in the case of India, agricultural progress was a *sine qua non* for industrial and overall development. Immediately after Independence, the most important task of the government was rehabilitation of millions of displaced persons and of putting on even keel the disrupted economy. The First Five Year Plan that was formulated was in fact nothing but a collection of already existing schemes. This plan gave a high priority to agriculture and a large proportion of public investment was to be undertaken on agriculture, irrigation and power. Being the first attempt at planning, the First Plan enabled the policy-makers to clearly conceptualise on the process of planning. It was stressed, for example, that for accelerating the rate of growth of the economy and achieving the plan targets, it was essential that the rate of saving and investment be raised substantially. The planners calculated that in order to realise a targeted growth rate of five per cent per annum the saving rate in the Indian economy should be raised from existing five per cent of national income to 20 per cent. This could only be done through tightening of belts and through mobilising a large part of incremental incomes. Mobilisation of surplus labour for creation of physical assets could also indirectly contribute to the growth process. This conceptual framework, notwithstanding, the first plan was primarily an irrigation and agriculture plan that gave high priority to agriculture.

Nehru justified the priority to agriculture in the following way:

> "Apart from that, situation in the country today is such that, if our food front cracks up, everything else will crack up, too. Therefore, one must not weaken our food front. If our agriculture becomes strongly entrenched, as we hope it will, then it will be relatively easy for us to progress more rapidly on the industrial front, whereas if we concentrate only on industrial development and leave agriculture in a weak condition we shall ultimately be weakening industry. That is why primary attention has been given to agriculture and food and that, I think is essential in a country like India at the present moment".[6]

The First Five Year Plan turned out to be a success. Whereas the national income recorded a growth rate of 3.6 per cent, per capita income raise at an average annual rate of 1.7 per cent during the plan period. Agricultural output rose by 4.3 per cent and foodgrain output increased from 50.8 mn tonnes in 1950-51 to 66.9 mn tonnes in 1955-56. During the plan many hydro-electric and irrigation projects were initiated and some were completed. The performance, in other sectors was also good. Consequently, the actual growth rate of income turned out to be higher than the targeted growth rate.

By 1956, Nehru had acquired a great deal of confidence. On the economic front, the food situation had improved though temporarily and the plan turned out to be a success. On the political front with the death of Patel, Nehru had emerged as the undisputed leader and the right wing opposition to his ideas had sufficiently weakened. Therefore, in 1956 Nehru decided to launch an ambitious plan for industrialisation of the country. Nehru prepared the ground for it in the famous Avadi resolution in which he declared establishment of socialist pattern of society as the objective of planning in India. [illegible] he emphasised, was nothing but a reiteration of what was contained in the Preamble and Directive Principles of the Constitution that planning should take place with a view to establishment of a socialistic pattern of society.

The second plan gave high priority to the building up of basic and heavy industry in the public sector. It was argued that an emphasis on heavy industry by accelerating the rate of growth in the economy would reduce the dependence of the economy on import of capital goods and thus make it more self-reliant. It is sometime argued that the second plan neglected agriculture and employment. It is true that as compared with 31 per cent of total outlay on agriculture and irrigation during the first plan, the second plan allocated only 21 per cent to these two sub-sectors. But the outlay was much higher in absolute terms because the second plan was much bigger. Further the plan document itself gave great deal of emphasis to agriculture. Not only that, the plan underlined the need for generating more employment through developing agro-industries as also cottage and small scale industry in the rural and urban areas of India. These industries were assigned the task of not only providing large employment but also of meeting the increased demand for consumer goods and services.

As is well known the plan suffered several problems. Firstly, agricultural output did not increase substantially during the plan and recourse had to be made to import foodgrains on a large scale. The economic problems became more serious because of border war with China. Large imports of foodgrains undoubtedly helped the country to tide over the difficult food situation but once again brought home to the Indian leadership, the need for giving greater emphasis to agriculture.

By 1963, Nehru had accepted that agricultural production came first "I am all for industry, I am all for steel plants and this and that, but I do say agriculture is far more important than any industry".[7]

III

Agricultural Planning and Policies During Nehru's Period — An Evaluation

Nehru's strategy of agricultural planning consisted of two planks. First, it emphasised the need for removing the semi-feudal constraints to development — 'the medieval rubbish' as Marx called it through radical land reforms, not only for initiating the process of agricultural growth but also to lay the foundation of an egalitarian agrarian structure. The second plank of Nehru's strategy was to technologically modernise agriculture through large public investment in irrigation, power, research and extension and other rural infrastructure. Since land reforms included cooperativisation, the small farms were to be organised into bigger production units for enabling them to make use of modern scientific technology. This Nehru thought was essential for increasing productivity and income of a large number of small and marginal cultivators and thereby raising their living standards. Agricultural growth was to proceed simultaneously with rapid industrialisation for building a self-reliant prosperous economy.

The evaluation of agricultural policies during Nehru's period can be done in several ways. First, one should examine whether during Nehru's period the institutional structure was changed and made more equalitarian through land reforms as repeatedly professed by the Congress. Secondly, one should examine whether agriculture was given adequate attention. This can be done by looking at the priority given to agriculture in terms of investment in infrastructure. Other policies like terms of trade between agriculture and non-agriculture should also be analysed. Finally, the nature and pattern of growth of agriculture during Nehru's period ought to be critically reviewed. An attempt is made here to undertake a brief evaluation on the above lines.

A. *Nehru and Land Reforms*

Coming first to land reforms, there exists a great deal of evidence to suggest that the land reform legislations passed by various state legislatures were not very radical and suffered from several loopholes and secondly that even the envisaged land reforms were not properly implemented.

The main objectives of land reform legislation passed by the various State Governments in India during the mid-fifties were the abolition of intermediary interests, imposition of ceilings on land holdings, regularisations of land rent and provision of security of tenure and eventual ownership rights. It was also decided to consolidate land holdings in order to increase productivity.

An evaluation of the implementation of land reforms shows that the objectives were only partially realised. Land reforms were fairly successful with regard to the objective of abolition of intermediaries in most parts of India. As a result as many as 20 million tenants were brought in direct contact with the State and Rs. 6700 million worth of compensation was to be paid to the ex-intermediaries of which nearly half had been paid by the beginning of the Fifth Five Year Plan. It is, however, notable that in many parts of the country, the landlords with the connivance of the local bureaucracy were able to resume land for self cultivation by ejecting a large number of tenants. In States like Bihar, Orissa, Rajasthan, Madhya Pradesh and West Bengal, landlords managed to keep very large holdings because of their power and influence. In general, the level of success of zamindari abolition depended on the strength of the peasant movement. At the all India level, percentage of area under tenancy declined from 20.34 per cent in 1953-54 to 10.70 per cent in 1960-61.

The legislation regarding imposition of ceilings on land holdings failed miserably due to loopholes in law and large scale connivance of surplus farmers with revenue administration, lack of will power of policy-makers and relative weakness of the peasant movement. Consequently, the pattern of land distribution has remained extremely skewed and has not undergone any significant changes. Thus in early fifties (1953-54) marginal and small cultivators with less than 2 hectares constituted 60.00 per cent of all cultivating households, but accounted only for 15.44 per cent of operated area. By 1981-82. their proportion farmers had increased to 75.33 per cent although the area under their cultivation now constitutes 28.10 per cent of total area. The phenomenal increase in the proportion of marginal and small farmers along with landless labour in the emerging agrarian structure in India has very serious and significant implications.

The legislation regarding security to tenure and determination of their rents has also remained more or less on paper. In actual practice, tenants hardly enjoy any security and it is the market forces that have determined the terms of tenancy. But these inadequacies of land reforms notwithstanding, the large scale abolition of intermediaries has made self-cultivation, the dominant mode of production in most parts of India. This is turn has broken many of the semi-feudal institutional constraints and has created conditions for growth of agriculture albeit on capitalist lines. The unequal distribution of land and dominance of large farmers, along with the availability of new technology has also created the basis of capitalist development in many parts of India.

B. *Nehru's Neglect of Agriculture*

This brings us to the second point namely the priority given to agriculture in planning during Nehru's period. It is often alleged that Nehru neglected agriculture and favoured industry. Nehru's neglect of agriculture can be interpreted in two ways. The first, perhaps the vulgar one, is that being an aristocratic city dweller Nehru did not know the problems of peasantry. The second can be that Nehru did not give sufficient priority to agriculture in the planning process. Consequently agricultural growth was low and hence the poor peasants could not very much benefit from the planning process.

To any student of history, it would indeed be naive to accuse Nehru of not knowing the problems of Indian agriculture and the lot of the Indian peasantry. As discussed earlier, not only did he have an intimate knowledge of their misery, he also had given adequate thought about the method through which their living conditions could be improved. Infact in many ways his basic understanding of the problems of Indian agriculture remains valid even today despite important technological developments that have taken place in agriculture since the mid-sixties.

Nehru believed that the main reason for low income of large number of farmers was heavy population pressure on land and very small holdings. With very low income from these holdings, the tenant was incapable of undertaking investment and making use of fruits of new technology. Nehru's answer to the problem of small holdings as discussed earlier, was cooperativisation. But the cooperative movement had failed to make much headway. Nor had community development programmes been able to break the problem of agricultural stagnation. Nonetheless, he was aware of the urgent need to achieve higher foodgrains output. Having failed on the institutional front, he was not prepared to give up technological solutions. Therefore, the only second best solution was to undertake large investment in irrigation and other rural infrastructure. It was Nehru who called Bhakra and other hydro-electric projects as India's new temples. And Nehru gave big emphasis to the building up of scientific infrastructure. The Indian Council of Agricultural Research and Agricultural Universities were strengthened on the pattern of Land Grant Colleges in the USA. It is indeed ironical that the qualitative technological transformation in India — the green revolution that led to self-sufficiency in foodgrains by the mid-seventies came about not during his life time but soon after his death. But the foundations for the technological developments were laid during Nehru's time.

This brings us to the question of low priority to agriculture in various plans. We have already discussed some aspects of this question. It has to be appreciated that Nehru emphasised the basic fact that Indian people could not raise their living standards without rapid industrialisation. Further development of industry and basic and heavy industry was considered essential by him for achieving economic self-reliance. No doubt in this matter Nehru was influenced a great deal by soviet experience.

But favouring industry did not mean that Nehru did not realise the importance of agriculture. As noted earlier the First Five Year Plan was basically a plan for agriculture. In his plan, as much as 31.5 per cent of total plan outlay was allotted to agriculture and irrigation. It is true that the proportionate outlay on agriculture and irrigation declined from 31.5 per cent during the First to 20 per cent during the Second and 23 per cent during the Third Plans. But in absolute terms the allocation was larger. In terms of achievements also, the increase obtained in net irrigated area was about 2 mn hectares each in the first two and 1.7 mn hectares in the Third Plan.

These days, under the influence of liberalisation there is a general tendency to decry the achievements of the Second and the Third Plan. Whereas this is not the main focus of discussion in this paper, it can be underlined that the priority to heavy industry since the second plan was paid off in building an independent and self-reliant economy. Further keeping in view the intimate linkages between modern agriculture and heavy industry, particulary in the sphere of petro-chemicals (fertilizer) and agricultural machinery, much of the advances made recently in modernising agriculture would have not been possible through domestic resources.

C. *Adverse Terms of Trade for Agriculture*

There is a one area, however, where there was a serious lapse during Nehru's regime. This refers to adverse terms of trade for agriculture. The radical intellectual thinking during the 'fifties was that industrialisation could take place only through mobilisation of surpluses from agriculture. The extreme coercive example was Soviet experience. But in milder form several economists from Nurkse to Lewis advocated the use of surplus agricultural labour for capital formation — an euphemism for extracting surplus for industrialisation. The Chinese example was extolled by almost every economist and politician. Nehru himself was also quite impressed. India failed to mobilise surplus labour for capital formation — because of the inability of the grass root organisation to enthuse the peasantry and also because of unequal accrual of the benefits of such efforts due to skewed distribution of land holdings.

But resources were mobilised from agriculture by keeping terms of trade adverse to it. The food prices were kept deliberately low right up to the middle of the 'sixties. This was done with the explicit aim of avoiding the dangers of inflation. The theoretical argument was that making wage goods costlier would reduce industrial profits and thereby discourage private investment. Another sophisticated argument for keeping term of trade against agriculture was that such a policy would shift incomes to non-agricultural classes, who like the classical capitalists, were much better savers than the poor agriculturists who were likely to consume the entire additional incomes.

So much so that when during a long period of twenty years from 1950 to 1970, the terms of trade did move in favour of agriculture for a few years during 1964-65 to 1969-70, there was such a hue and cry decrying this development as the one that was bound to fatten the already overfed wheat producing Kulaks from the North-West India and was bound to lead to serious economic crisis.

The upshot of all this was that agricultural prices remained depressed — term of trade ranged between 72 to 94 from 1950-51 up to 1964-65. The prices were kept low, besides compulsory procurement and rationing, through large scale import of foodgrains. The policy-makers failed to appreciate the positive role that remunerative prices would have in conjunction with technology to achieve a high growth of agricultural production through increases in yield levels. The terms of trade remained substantially against agriculture till the mid-sixties. It was only with the institution of Agricultural Prices Commission during 1965 that the need to give remunerative price to farmers was appreciated for the first time.

D. *Nature and Pattern of Agricultural Growth*

In order to have a balanced view, the above critical aspects of agrarian change and development in India should be counterpoised against the actual performance of agricultural sector during Nehru's period. Seen historically, in this respect the record seems quite creditable.

That the post-Independence Nehru period marks a turning point in the history of Indian agriculture is clear from the fact that compared with a growth rate of less than 0.5 per cent per annum during 1904-05 to 1944-45, the agricultural sector recorded a growth rate of 3.1 per cent during 1949-50 to 1964-65. This growth rate was achieved primarily through large public investment in irrigation, power, extension and research and other rural infrastructure although the abolition of intermediaries also helped in removing some barriers to growth.

But although creditable, the growth performance fell fare short of the needs of the economy and the targets set by the planners. This is because population growth rate accelerated to 2.25 per cent after independence compared with less than one per cent during the first half of the century. Further, with rise in per capita income the demand for foodgrains started outstripping the supply in most of the years.

Thirdly agricultural production was characterised by wide year to year fluctuations. During the first plan (1950-51 to 1955-56), food production hovered between 51 to 58 mn tonnes and 12 mn tonnes of foodgrains had to be imported to meet the domestic demand. Although the need for imports had been reduced considerably by 1955 and 1956, these rose sharply afterwards. Thus as much as 19.4 mn tonnes had to be imported during the second and 32.2 mn tonnes during the third plan period under PL 480. Such large scale imports no doubt helped in overcoming the acute food problem. Simultaneously these resulted in loss of self-confidence. Further these imports had a deflationary impact on agricultural prices and thereby tended to have a salutary effect on domestic food production.

Further despite these imports, the per capita availability of foodgrains did not show much rise during the entire period. Finally, most of the increase in agricultural output was confined to the irrigated regions comprising of North-Western States and coastal areas of India.

Thus the picture about the performance of agricultural sector during Nehru's period is quite mixed. The aggregate growth was no doubt, creditable, but it was highly inequitious. Further, the growth and its benefits were not widespread to millions of small and marginal farmers and landless labourers, but were mainly monopolised by middle and rich capitalist farmers. It was the latter — the capitalist farmers who became the chosèn agents and main beneficiaries of agricultural growth in India.

IV

Summing Up

Whatsoever might have been the predilections of Nehru, the agrarian structure that emerged in India during his regime and has continued since is highly inequitious among various sections of peasants and highly differentiated over several regions of India. This is primary because an attempt has been made to find solutions through application of technology without having brought about structural changes in land relations.

Nehru rightly understood the role of technology in improving agricultural incomes. Over the years concerted efforts were made to introduce better technology. The approach had started becoming selective during Nehru's period. By the later 'fifties the emphasis had shifted away from widespread community development to Intensive Area Development Programmes under the advice of Ford Foundation team of experts. Since area increases had ceased to be the main source of growth of output, intensive efforts had to be made to increase yield — the only alternative for achieving higher growth of output. For practical reasons, efforts to increase yields had to be concentrated only in selected highly irrigated areas. Further, even within these areas the main agents of growth and the main leaders could only be the progressive (rich) farmers. Yields started increasing in the beginning of 'sixties. These yields recorded phenomenal increase in irrigated regions after the introduction of new seed-fertilizer technology during the mid-sixties. Given the highly skewed regional distribution of irrigation and of land ownership in all the regions, it was but natural that the irrigated regions and middle and big surplus farmers should have been the main beneficiaries of massive public investment and technological upgradation in agriculture. All these were a natural consequence of failure of land reforms.

Different interpretations have been given for the failure of land reforms in India. Nehru's admirers believe that in the absence of committed cadre based party, Nehru was not strong enough to bring about revolutionary changes in land relations. His position, it is stated, was further weakened as the left forces instead of giving him critical support, were in fact opposing him. The alternative interpretation is that Nehru's talk about radical land reforms were only a rhetoric and that he was intentionally building a capitalist agriculture in India.

These controversies could perhaps, best be left to the historians. However, whatever may have been the subjective predilections of Nehru, it is clear that it was during his regime that firm foundations were laid for the development of agriculture in India on capitalist lines.

NOTES

1. S. Gopal: *Jawaharlal Nehru — A Biography.* OUP 1984. Vol 1, p.46.
2. Ibid p.57.
3. Ibid p.54.
4. Extracts from Prison Diary with Letters 19 October 1930 — 26 January, 1931. Quoted by Gopal Nehru An Anthology. OUP 1980, p. 138-141.
5. Gopal, op. cit. Volume 1, p.245, 246.
6. A Speech in Lok Sabha, 15 December, 1952, Gopal Anthology op. cit. p.310.
7. (Addressd to two houses of Andhra Pradesh on 22nd July, 1963.) The new strategy of economic development was 'first and essentially agriculture, with foundation of an industrial structure being laid at the same time. (Lok Sabha debate 22nd August, 1963.

13

RURAL INFRASTRUCTURE AND AGRICULTURAL DEVELOPMENT IN A BACKWARD ECONOMY

B.B. SINGH and RAJPATI RAM

Conceptual Framework

The importance of agriculture in the economic development of under-developed countries has been realised in recent years for a number of reasons. The rapid growth in population has been the obvious cause for emphasizing the urgent need for developing agriculture. India is a glaring example of it, where the problem of adequate food availability, at least in quantitative if not qualitative, terms specially in rural areas has remained the primary concern during the whole of plan periods. Rural development is undoubtedly linked with the development of agricultural sector. The recent emphasis in India on the creation of employment opportunities mainly through improvements in agriculture, supplemented by agro-based industries and related occupations, is programmed with the objective of achieving betterment in the quality of material life in the countryside. The importance of agriculture is thus, reinforced because of the shifts of strategy of economic development from urban and industry to rural and agriculture. For the purpose, government has launched a number of programmes from time to time during the plan periods.

The region of Eastern Uttar Pradesh has been proverbial for its backwardness, although the impact of the so-called Green Revolution has brought about significant transformation in the rural areas in general and agricultural sector in particular. But still, the situation is said to have been worsened. The HYV technology was spread extensively throughout the geographical contours of the country. The farmers were benefited to a great extent, by neutral-to-scale technology but were deprived of non-neutral-to-scale institutional factors. Hence, there have been few successful beneficiaries. The expectations are far behind from the real consequences of 20 years Green Revolution today.

Objectives

It has been assumed that the rural infrastructure acts as a catalytic force in boosting up the levels of agricultural development. It becomes, therefore, necessary to see as how far rural infrastructural development in the region of Eastern Uttar Pradesh is involved in controlling the level of agricultural development. The development of a combination of the two aspects would certainly provide a better ground for the rural socio-economic development. On the basis of inferences drawn out of the analysis, certain remedial measures can be suggested for improving the qualitative status of both rural infrastructural and agricultural development. Hence, the present study aims at explaining the regional variations in infrastructural variables as well as the variables of agricultural development and establishing causal relationship with each other.

Methodology and Data-base

The infrastructural variables considered in the present study consist of (i) electrified villages as percentage to total inhabited villages, (ii) percentage of villages up to 3 km from market *(mandi)* centres, (iii) percentage of villages up to 3 km from pucca road, and (iv) percentage of villages up to 3 km from senior basic boys and girls schools. The variables related to agricultural development include (i) percentage of area under HYV to gross cropped area, (ii) intensity of cropping, and (iii) percentage of area under commercial crops to gross cropped area. Composite indices for overall infrastructural and agricultural development have been prepared by assuming the corresponding means of each variables equal to 1. The whole region has been classified into four groups in the context of each variable, by incorporating the respective mean and 1/2 standard deviation. Ultimately, curvilinear trends at the second degree polynomials have been attempted for the three variables of agricultural development (Y) separately with respect to four infrastructural variables (X).

Based on 1980-81 data available from *Sankhikiya Patrika* of the 15 districts, the study has been carried out at tehsil level for 67 tehsils in Eastern Uttar Pradesh.

Relationships

It is apparent from Table 13.1 that the highest co-efficient of correlation (0.397) has occurred between cropping intensity and area under commercial crops indicating towards the fact that wherever the cropping intensity is more, the area under commercial crops is also high and *vice versa*. The second highest coefficient (0.391) can be noticed between *pucca* road and boys schools. It implies that higher the accessibility of *pucca* roads in rural areas, more is the availability of schooling facilities. The third highest positive coefficient is 0.309 between cropping intensity and area under HYV crops.

TABLE 13.1: Correlation Matrix

	HYV area	Cropping Intensity	Area Commercial Crops	Villages electrified	Market Centres	Pucca Road	SB Boys Schools
1. HYV Area	1.000						
2. Cropping Intensity	0.309	1.000					
3 Area Commercial Crops	-0.069	0.397	1.000				
4. Villages Electrified	0.201	0.103	0.017	1.000			
5. Market Centres	0.138	0.135	0.165	-0.139	1.000		
6. *Pucca* Road	0.103	0.108	0.154	0.221	0.219	1.000	
7. S.B. Boys Schools	0.190	0.249	0.196	0.126	0.120	0.391	1.000

Other important relationships can be mentioned as between cropping intensity and schooling facilities (r=0.249); rural electrification and *pucca* road (r=0.221); market centres and pucca road (r=0.219); and rural electrification and area under HYV crops (r=0.201). To be summarily stated that the HYV area is positively related, in priority order, with cropping intensity, rural electrification and boys schools; the cropping intensity with area under commercial crops, boys schools and market centres; and the area under commercial crops with boys schools, market centres and *pucca* roads.

Since, the agricultural development variables are associated with varying degrees of relationship with infrastructural variables, the analysis of intra-regional variations in both types of variable is highly needed and has been given as follows:

Rural Infrastructural Development

Infrastructure plays an important role in agricultural development. In fact, the farmers of a region with adequate infrastructural facilities may be in a better position to utilize their limited land resources than those of region where necessary infrastructure is inadequate. The increasing role of infrastructure in agricultural development specially after the introduction of High-Yielding Varieties technology in 1966 deserves special attention (Bajpai, 1984).

Figure 13.1 reveals that the level of infrastructural development is high in the eastern part of Eastern U.P. where the enhanced level has occured in the tehsils of Salempur, Padrauna, Rasra, Chosi, Azamgarh and Mohammadabad (Azh.). Other tehsils of equal importance are Faizabad, Kunda and Handia. High concentration of electrified villages can be seen in the central and centrally western parts of the region. Exceptionally high amount of electrified villages ($\bar{X}$ + S.D.), i.e., more than 49.57 per cent of the total villages, have been found in the tehsils of Sagri, Mohammadabad (Azh.), Lalganj, Faizabad, Bikapur, Handia and Phoolpur (All). The northern and southern parts of the region are characterized by poor electrification. However, the tehsils of Bhinga, Naugarh and Robertsganj accounted for less than 10 per cent as electrified villages to their total number of villages. The variation ranged from 1.09 per cent in Bhinga tehsil to 88.85 per cent in Handia tehsil. A better marketing facility has again concentrated in the eastern part of Eastern U.P. As many as 9 tehsils namely Naugarh, Salempur, Padrauna, Rasra, Azamgarh, Faizabad, Kunda, Chakia and Chunar, have accounted for more than 10 per cent villages up to 3 km from market centres. Southern, western and

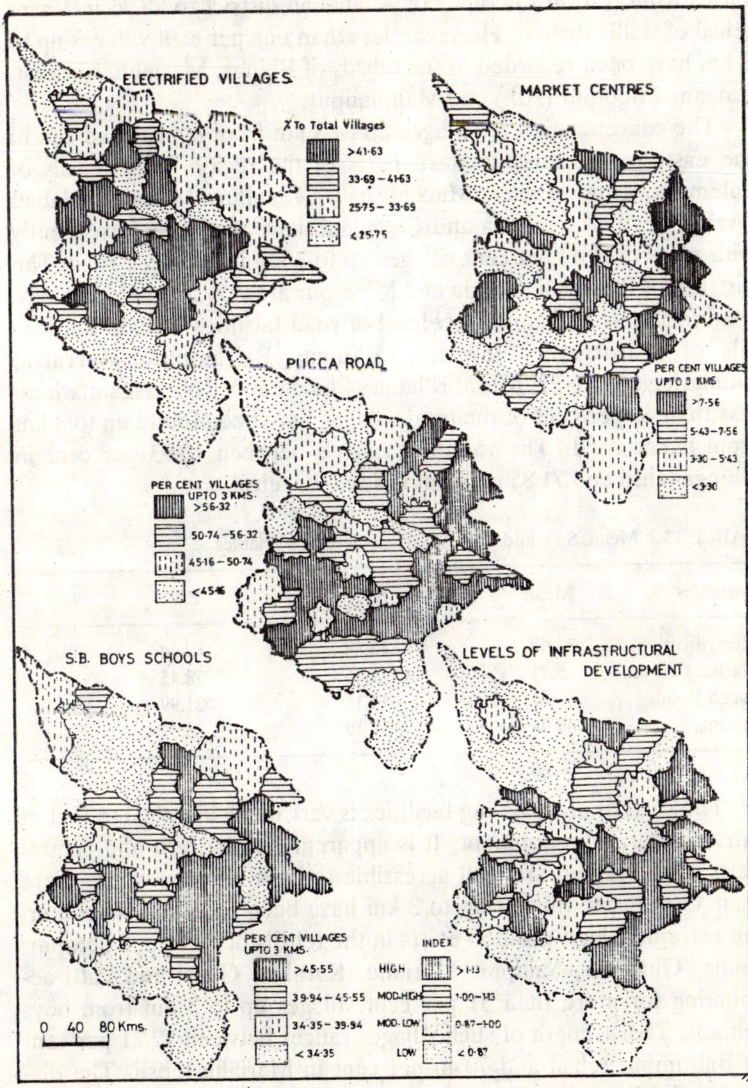

FIG. 13.1: Indicators of Infrastructural Development, 1981 (Eastern Uttar Pradesh)

north-western areas were found poorly endowed with marketing facilities. The percentage of villages up to 3 km from market centres varies from 0.20 in Phoolpur of Allahabad district to 22.36 in Rasra tehsil of Ballia district. However, less than one per cent villages up to 3 km have been recorded in the tehsils of Bhinga, Mariahu, Kerakat, Lalganj, Phoolpur (All.) and Manjhanpur.

The concentration of villages up to 3 km from *pucca* road lies in the eastern and south-western parts of the region. The tehsils of Salempur, Hata, Ballia, Machhlishahr, Jaunpur, Mohammadabad (Azh.), Patti, Karchhana and Chandauli have performed excellently with more than 62 per cent villages up to 3 km from *pucca* road. The districts of Bahraich, Gonda and Mirzapur are very much deprived of road facilities. Extremely low level of road facilities include the tehsils of Kaisarganj, Nanpara, Bhinga, Balrampur, Harraiya, Domariaganj, Sagri, Musafirkhana, Chakia and Robertsganj where less than 40 per cent of the total villages have been found up to 3 km from *pucca* road. The variation ranged between 10.93 per cent in Bhinga tehsil and 71.85 per cent in Jaunpur tehsil.

TABLE 13.2: Mean, S.D. and C.V. of Infrastructural Variables

Variables	Mean	S.D.	C.V.
Electrification	33.69	15.88	47.14
Market Centres	5.43	4.26	78.45
Pucca Road	50.74	11.16	21.99
Schools	39.94	11.19	28.02

The pattern of schooling facilities is very much identical to that of infrastructural development. It is apparent that eastern and central parts of the region are well accessible to boys schools, where more than 45 per cent villages up to 3 km have been recorded. However, the extremely high position exists in the tehsils of Deoria, Salempur, Ballia, Ghazipur, Saidpur, Mariahu, Kerakat, Ghosi and Patti accounting for more than 51 per cent villages up to 3 km from boys schools. The strength of such villages ranges between 12.21 per cent in Balrampur tehsil and 70.40 per cent in Mariahu tehsil. The districts of Mirzapur, Basti and Gonda have got poor schooling facilities. The exceptionally high deprivation (less than 25 per cent) has been noticed in the tehsils of Gonda (16.88 per cent), Utraula (24.52 per cent), Tarabganj (21.88 per cent), Balrampur (12.21 per cent), Domariaganj (24.58 per cent) and Robertsganj (23.19 per cent).

Agricultural Development

The primary concern of agricultural development especially in an undeveloped economy like Eastern U.P. where agriculture is the main sector of the over-all economy, is to get maximum return. Agricultural under-development can be regarded as the root cause of over-all under-development and the transformation of agriculture should, therefore, be given priority. The basic components of transformation of agriculture can be well understood by incorporating three types of development – (i) the expansion of HYV area in the total cropping pattern, (ii) extensive and intensive use of acreage under crops and (iii) shifting of sizeable acreage towards more remunerative crops. Thus, the agricultural development variables considered in the present study are the best suited to satisfy the requisite qualifications of development and the spatial variations their of have been analysed as follows:

It can be seen from Fig. 13.2 that the vast area of Trans-Ghaghra Plain has accounted for more than 40 per cent of cropped area under HYV. However, the western part of Trans-Ghaghra Plain including the districts of Bahraich and Gonda; and the southern uplands and Ganga Basin including the districts of Mirzapur, Allahabad and Varanasi have occupied less than 24 per cent area under HYV. As a matter of fact, the Ganga-Ghaghra Doab has also occupied smaller extent of HYV area, i.e., 24 per cent to 40 per cent. Among the areas of high level performance, the tehsils of Khalilabad (66.58%), Bansi (70.88%), Harraiya (71.18%), Domariaganj (85.69%) and Naugarh (60.97%) have occupied excellent acreage under HYV. Among the areas of poor performance, the tehsils of Gonda, Balrampur, Chail, Manjhanpur, Meja, Chakia, Chandauli, Mirzapur, Robertsganj and Dudhi have registered extremely low percentage (less than 15%) of area under HYV. However, the variation ranged between 1.18 per cent in Robertsganj tehsil and 85.69 per cent in Domariaganj tehsil.

The second constituent of agricultural development is the cropping intensity varying from 109 in Dudhi tehsil to 179 in Chandauli tehsil. Exceptionally high index of cropping intensity (more than 150) has been recorded in the tehsils of Basti, Mahrajganj, Ghazipur, Jaunpur, Kerakat, Faizabad, Chakia and Chandauli. On

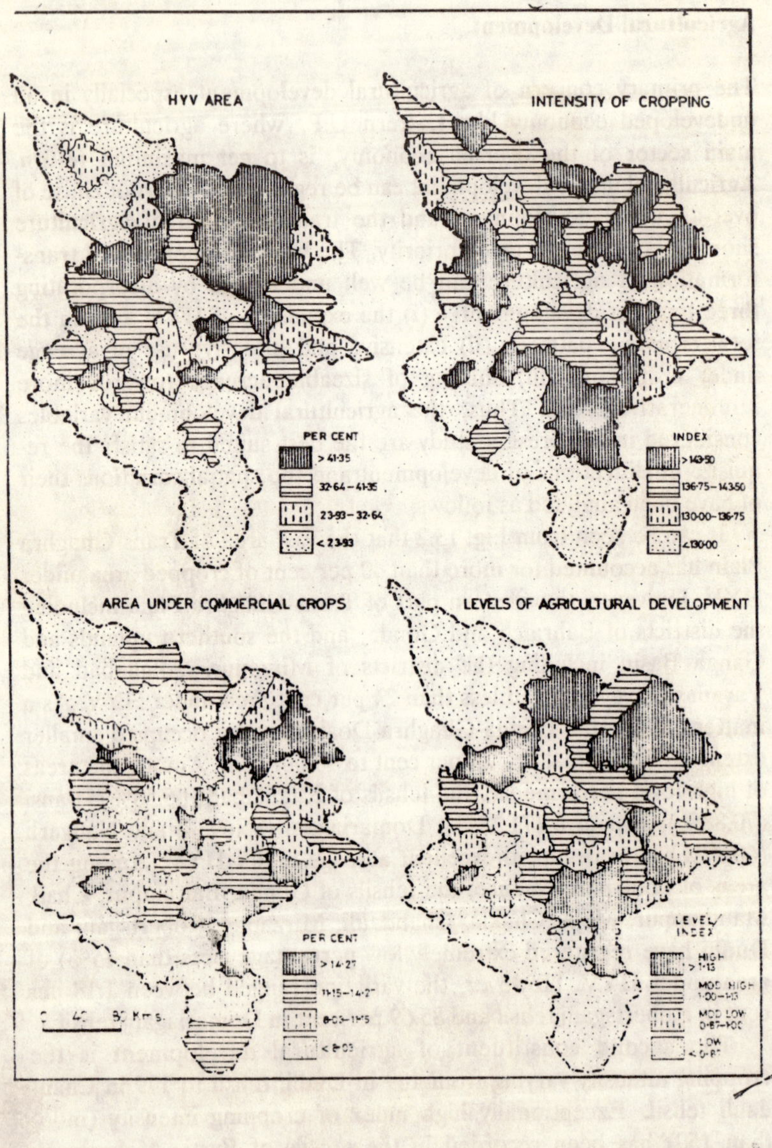

FIG. 13.2: Eastern Uttar Pradesh: Indicators of Agricultural Development, 1981.

the other hand, southern and south-western parts (the districts of Pratapgarh, Allahabad and Mirzapur) of the region have accounted for less than 130 as the index of cropping intensity. However, distinctly low index (less than 120) has been marked in the tehsils of Gonda, Bansgaon, Amethi, Patti, Gyanpur, Mirzapur, Robertsganj and Dudhi.

TABLE 13.3: Mean, S.D. and C.V. of Agricultural Development Variables

Variables	Mean	S.D.	C.V.
HYV Area	32.64	17.42	53.37
Cropping Intensity	136.75	13.50	9.87
Commercial Crops	11.15	6.24	55.96

The third component of agricultural development constitutes the extent of area under commercial crops. The region as a whole is highly deprived of commercial cropping and present wide variation over space. It varies from 0.05 per cent in Domariaganj tehsil to 38.56 per cent in Gorakhpur tehsil. More than 20 per cent area under commercial crops has been found in the tehsils of Gorakhpur, Hata, Padrauna, Phoolpur (Azh.), Chakia, Chandauli and Varanasi. Less than 10 per cent area devoted to commercial crops comprises the district of Bahraich, Gonda, Basti, Allahabad and Mirzapur. Out of these, the highly depressed situation has occurred in the tehsils of Khalilabad, Domariaganj and Sirathu where the extent of area under commercial crops was less than 5 per cent.

From the view point of over-all agricultural development, the vast area of the region remains under-developed. It can be seen from Fig. 13.2 that the agricultural development is highly pronounced in the districts of Basti, Gorakhpur, Deoria, Jaunpur and Varanasi. The high level of agricultural development in the tehsils of Gorakhpur and Hata can be attributed to HYV area and area under commercial crops. The major attributes of development in the tehsils of Chakia and Chandauli were cropping intensity and area under commercial crops. In all, the tehsils of Bansi, Harraiya, Naugarh, Gorakhpur, Hata, Padrauna, Faizabad, Soraon and Chandauli have attained enhanced level of agricultural development. The extent of HYV area has significantly contributed in the development of north-eastern part whereas the cropping intensity in the central part of the region. Special attention is needed for the development of north-western and southern parts of the region where both infrastructural as well as agricultural development components are highly lacking. In this respect, the tehsils of Nanpara, Bhinga, Gonda, Tanda, Chail, Manjhanpur, Sirathu, Karchhana, Mirzapur, Robertsganj and Dudhi are highly backward.

Rural Electrification and Agricultural Development

The programmes of rural electrification were not given much importance in the first three plans. Rural electrification then meant only an extension of electricity to villages. In the year 1966, in the wake of the drought and the sharp decline in agricultural production, the National Development Council reviewed the role of rural electrification and directed that the rural electrification programmes should be oriented towards providing electric power to pumpsets with a view to assisting the overall programmes for augmenting agricultural production. (Daya Krishna, 1971). Since then, the electrification has been acting as a catalyst in helping the farmer adopt more and more HYV, intensify his cropping pattern and also shift towards remunerating crops.

The causal relationship between rural infrastructure and agricultural development components has been shown in Fig. 13.3. It can be noticed that the role of rural electrification is a highly powerful agent for accelerating the area under HYV. The HYV area in the region has increased from 19.80 per cent in 1970-71 to 33.30 per cent in 1980-81, increasing at the rate of 5.34 per cent per annum. The regression coefficient of electrification (0.2164) implies that 1 per cent increase in the electrified villages would bring the resultant increase by 0.22 per cent in the HYV area. Almost similar pattern has been brought up with intensity of cropping also. It is interesting to note that the electrification coefficient is only 0.0728 indicating that 1 per cent in village electrification is bringing additional growth by 0.07 per cent in area under commercial crops. It is, hence, apparent that the electrification is a highly sensitive factor in remunerative foodgrain crops than commercial. This may be because of the fact that the region of Eastern U.P. has not got the impact of market forces. The region still occupies 88.85 per cent area under foodgrain crops, which is significantly higher than 73.92 per cent in the country as a whole. The impact of electrification on the production of commercial crops is tending to increase at the diminishing rate.

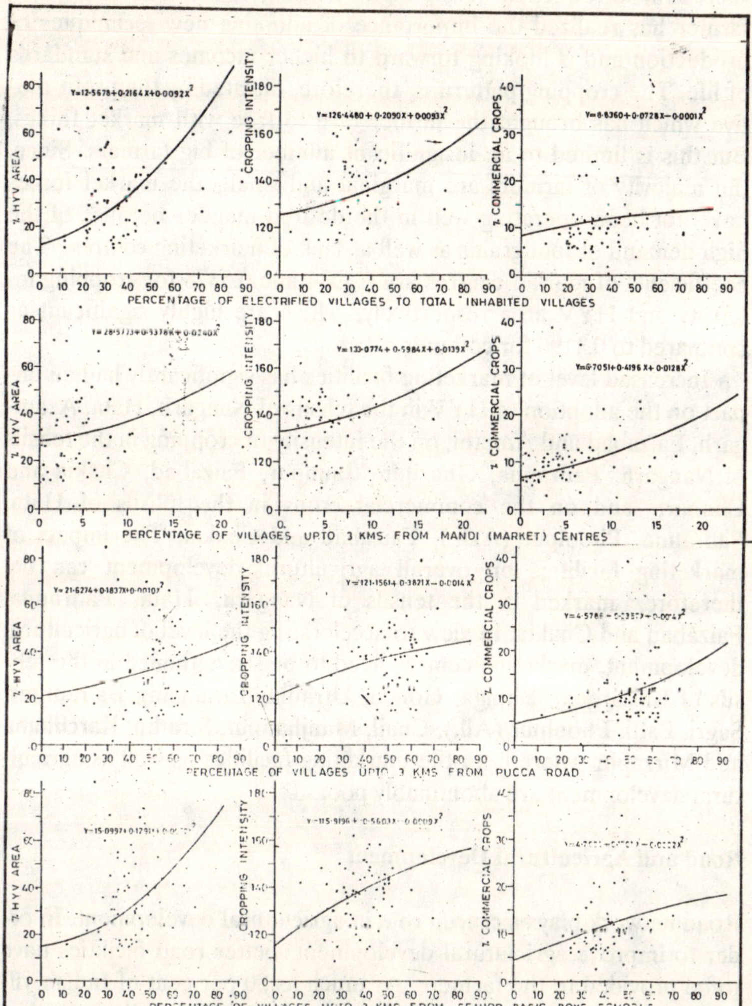

FIG. 13.3: Relationship between Rural Infrastructure and Agriculture Development

Market and Agricultural Development

The development of marketing facilities for the agricultural produce is an important constituent of the agricultural infrastructure. With successful introduction of the high yielding varieties of seeds, the farmer has realized the importance of adopting new techniques of production and is looking forward to higher incomes and standards of life. The cropping pattern is, therefore, dictated by the profit motive which has brought the farmer face to face with market forces. But this is limited to an insignificant number of big farmers. Since, the majority of farmers are marginal and small, the market forces have not been operating well in the desired manner because of the high demand of foodgrains as well as lack of marketing centres. The coefficients of market centres are 0.5984 and 0.5378 for cropping intensity and HYV area respectively, which are highly significant as compared to 0.4196 for commercial crops.

Increased level of marketing facilities has significantly had an impact on the adoption of HYV in the tehsils of Nangarh, Hata, Azamgarh, Faizabad and Amethi; on the intensity of cropping in the tehsils of Nangarh, Padrauna, Ghazipur, Jaunpur, Faizabad, Chakia and Chunar; and on the commercial crops in the tehsils of Hata, Padrauna, Phoolpur (Azh.), Faizabad and Chakia. The impact of marketing facilities on overall agricultural development can be, therefore, marked in the tehsils of Nangarh, Hata, Padrauna, Faizabad and Chakia. In view to accelerating the level of agricultural development, marketing centres need to be strengthened in the tehsils of Kaisarganj, Bhinga, Gonda, Utraula, Tarabganj, Balrampur, Sagri, Patti, Phoolpur (All.), Chail, Manjhanpur, Sirathu, Karchhana and Mirzapur where both the marketing facilities as well as agricultural development are abominably poor.

Road and Agricultural Development

Road network plays a crucial role in agricultural development. In order to improve agricultural development, better road facilities have to be provided to the farmers. As much as 80 per cent of Indian villages are not connected with any market by *pucca* all – weather roads. The farmer naturally cannot take his produce for sale to remunerative markets due to the absence of road and transport facilities (Shenoi, 1975). The relationship between transport and agriculture is highly positive. The major rather primary concern of agricultural development is to develop the road facilities so that the farmers can carry their inputs and outputs when required. Absence of roads is responsible to a large extent for the reluctance of the farmer to bring his produce to the markets (Prasad, 1979).

Pucca road is playing a significantly role in agricultural development. It is apparent from Fig. 13.3 that the roads coefficients are 0.3821, 0.2357 and 0.1837 for cropping intensity, commercial crops and HYV area respectively. However, the increase in cropping intensity is slightly diminishing because of the increase of *pucca* road. It has highly positive rate of addition to the extent of commercial cropped area, which is more than that of HYV area. The consequence of *pucca* road has been significantly marked in the development of agriculture in the tehsils of Hata, Padrauna, Saidpur, Mohammadabad (Gha.), Ghosi and Chandauli. In view of the positive relationship the agricultural development is highly suffering from the lack of pucca roads in the tehsils of Bahraich, Kaisarganj, Nanpara, Bhinga, Balrampur, Sagri, Tanda, Robertsganj and Dudhi. Therefore, the road facilities must be increased in order to increase the level of agricultural development.

Schooling Facilities and Agricultural Development

Education plays a very important role in the understanding of social problems. It enhances our ability to develop solutions for these problems. The economic growth depends to a large extent upon changes in human thinking which plays the catalytic role in productive process through organisational and managerial ability. Education also plays a key role in the production because it supplies physical and mental labour of higher order and thus helps in making right decisions for the development of the country (Phillips, 1971).

Schooling facilities in the region of Eastern U.P. have direct bearing on agricultural development. It is apparent from Fig. 13.3 that the regression coefficient of boys schooling facilities (0.5603) for cropping intensity is higher than that for commercial crops (0.1701) and HYV area (0.1291). It implies that the schooling facility is not an important infrastructural variable in the adoption of HYV and for the production of commercial crops. The impact of schooling facilities on cropping intensity and commercial crops is increasing at the diminishing rate whereas on the adoption of HYV, it is increasing at the increasing rate. In one of his studies, Ahmed (1972) found that education has played a key role in the strategy of agricultural development. The marginal impact of education on agricultural development has been found from the study of Punjab Agriculture (Chadha, 1970). It may be due to the fact that the education that the farmer has is not farm oriented or purposive (In a Marajakshri, 1969).

Schooling facilities have been directly associated with agricultural development in the tehsils of Bansi, Saidpur, Kerakat, Ghosi, Chakia, Chandauli and Varanasi. Similarly there are certain areas where lower level of agricultural development is accompanied by poor schooling facilities. Such areas include the tehsils of Bahraich, Gonda, Utraula, Tarabganj, Balrampur, Sagri, Tanda, Manjhanpur, Meja, Mirzapur, Robertsganj and Dudhi. These areas need immediate action for the sake of betterment of agricultural status.

Conclusion

The region under study represents the underdeveloped economy where land is scarce but labour abundant. Owing to predominance of marginal landholdings, the agricultural business is limited up to the production of foodgrains. It is a type of subsistence nature of agriculture which involves labour intensive operations. Owing to low investment capacity, the agricultural development has remained stagnant although some impact of Green Revolution has been marked, that is, shift of low productivity crops to high productivity crops but very insignificantly from foodgrains to non-foodgrains. The underdevelopment of the region has presented a vicious circle with low income, low savings, low investment and low labour productivity. As a result, the cropping intensity has not increased at the desired level. Ultimately, the responsibility for developing agriculture in the region lies on the development of infrastructure which is again blocked in view of the increased stagnation in the overall rural economy. In order to overcome these handicaps, the development of secondary and tertiary sectors are to be given the highest priority in the initial stages so that some structural changes in the economy can be thought of. In the later stages, some significant transformations in the agricultural sector would take place automatically.

REFERENCES

Ahmed, Manzoor (1972) : "Afghanistan, Education is an Integrated Agricultural Problem", in Manzoor Ahmed and Phillip H. (ed.), *Education for Rural Development*, New York, p. 365.

Bajpai, Brijesh K. (1984): "Regional Disparities in Agricultural Productivity, An Outcome Biased Infrastructure – A Case Study", *Agricultural Situation in India*, XXXIX (2), pp. 79-82.

Chadha, G.K. (1970): "Production Efficiency by farm size: A Study of Punjab Agriculture at 1960-70 level of Technology", unpublished Ph.D. Thesis, Punjab University, Chandigarh.

Daya Krishna (1971): "The New Agricultural Strategy", *New Heights*, Delhi, p. 141.

In-amarajakshri, R. (1969): "Social Factors and Pleasant Behaviour in a South India Village", *Agricultural Situation in India*, Vol. XXV, pp. 338-390.

Phillips (1971): "Science and Technology", in Lengyel Retev (ed.), *Approaches to the Science of Socio-economic Development*, Paris, p. 162.

Prasad, Ishwari (1979) – "Transport and Agricultural Development", in Ali Mohammad (ed.) – 'Dynamics of Agricultural Development in India', Concept, Delhi, 1-15.

Shenoi, P.G. (1975): "Agricultural Development in India – A New Strategy in Management", Vikas Publishing House, Delhi, p. 113.

14

NEHRU'S ECONOMIC POLICY AND ITS SUITABILITY TO INDIA : An Appraisal

R.C. GUPTA

Nehru was the sole architect of the Indian economic structure. He was well-acquainted with the poor living conditions in the villages of the country. People lacking barest necessities of life cannot work for the success of democracy. So he realised that in the absence of economic freedom, political freedom has no meaning. He formulated his concept of economic democracy for the economic march of the country based on three basic principles — equality to all, well-being of masses, and co-operative spirit. Nehru did not like prevailing economic inequalities in society and wanted to reduce the gap between rich and poor, offer equal opportunities to every citizen for many-fold development and uplift the rural and down-trodden people with co-operative spirit.

Socialism

Nehru during his extensive tours found very wide socio-economic gaps among various sectors of society. Zamindars brought untold miseries on the labourers and capitalists did not give fair deal to the workers. Thus in order to bridge the gap and provide equal opportunities to all, Nehru tilted towards socialism. In 1936, he as President of Indian National Congress said, "I should like the congress to become a socialist organization and to join hands with other forces in the world, who are working for the new civilization". But he opposed socialism of that extreme in which the state is all powerful and governs all activities.

Planning

To transform the existing socio-economic structure having wide gaps among various sectors of society and mal distribution of wealth and power to an equitable socio-economic order, requires systematic and pre-thought ways which we term planning. Nehru fully adhered to this dictum and made planning an effective instrument for rapid progress.

Agrarian Economy

Agriculture provided livelihood to 77.4% of the total population in 1951. Keeping this fact in mind he, for agrarian development, asked for the abolition of Zamindari System and redistribution of land to the tenants to increase production. He pleaded for co-operative farming as small land holding was the basic problem in the way of agricultural development. He introduced Community Development Programme on October 2, 1952, to increase agricultural production, income and employment and provide all necessary amenities to the village people.

Industrial Economy

Nehru gave top priority to the industries and chose Mixed Economy which in his opinion was best suited to India:

(i) *Private Sector* — He realized the importance of Private Sector but curtailed its scope as he believed that private enterprise on big scale inevitably leads to private monopolies. So he assigned them agriculture and small scale industries.

(ii) *Public Sector* — Big industry is an essential feature of progress of a modern nation. He said, "No modern nation can retain its freedom without the help of large scale industries which should be state owned. If nationalization adds to production we should use it but it is not a magic remedy for all the ills.

(iii) *Cottage Industries* — In mixed economy small scale and cottage industries play an important role by helping in accelerating production and providing employment to the people.

Nehru's overemphasis on industrialization, planning and utilization of latest technology shows his intention for making the country materially advanced and prosperous like western countries. He spent more on industries and placed agriculture to the second grade which is the life and blood of Indian economy. During First plan the expenditure on agricultural development was 14.94% which went down to 11.44% in Second plan. From Third plan onward 7% amount was allocated for irrigation and flood control and 2% for small scale and cottage industries besides marginal rise in allocation for agriculture. Nehru realized his mistake during his last days and admitted in Lok Sabha on December 11, 1963, but his successors blindly continued his policy without evaluating its suitability to the country.

Effects

Economic policy of Nehru and its implementation caused following adverse effects on our socio-economic system —

(1) *Foreign Loans* — Big industries required huge capital investment which the country could not afford at its own and it had to seek loans from western countries. In 1947, India had deposits worth about Rs. 3453 crore which it spent lavishly and had debt worth Rs. 32 crore.

Afterwards the loans increased enormously and reached Rs. 17,654.6 crore in 1975-76. Besides the government had also taken loans from own citizens on high rate of interest for investment but the return is very low and deficit continues to enhance. Huge amount of Rs. 54205.6 crore was paid as interest and service charges on loans to the foreign countries by 1976. We are under heavy debt which is above Rs. 100000 crore and the position is so disappointing that we have to seek loans for repayment. In 1989-90, Central budget shows that 16% of our revenue will come from internal borrowing and 18% of our expenditure — maximum on any single item will be on payment of interest in 1951.

(2) *Inadequate Growth of Agriculture* — Agriculture in spite of its being main occupation was not given due place and funds allocated for it were far below its requirements. No proper attention was paid to increase production by providing quality seeds, fertilizers and adequate irrigation facilities, financial help and lucrative prices of agricultural produce. Agricultural growth has been 2-3% per annum.

It resulted into heavy imports of foodgrains to feed our people, which is shameful to an agricultural country like India. Now the position has slightly improved.

(3) *Increase in Unemployment* — Big industries involved huge investment but did not provide proportionate employment. Besides, the use of machines curtailed the need for human labour and made the labour surplus. It contributed to the rapid increase of unemployment.

(4) *Dominance of Corruption* — Neglect of moral values and prominence of material progress after independence attracted the people towards money but the misdeeds of high-ups in post-Nehru era encouraged people to grab money more and more by hook or by crook and raise their economic standard for securing high status in the society. This thinking made corruption omni present and rampant here.

(5) *Inequality Increase* — Nehru basically wanted to remove disparity between rich and poor but the inequality among the people increased out of all reasonable proportions. Nearly 40% of the people are living at poverty line, whereas a few families have acquired major part of nations wealth.

(6) *Dwindling Economy* — Owing to adverse effects of this economic policy, agricultural as well as industrial production could not cope with the increasing demand of the country. The ratio of import over export is rising. This trend hindered the growth rate and increase in the Gross National Income. Our per capita income, when compared with other countries, shows that it is gradually going down to the lowest level except some African and mountainous countries.

Appraisal

A fair appraisal reveals that Nehru accorded top priority to big industries for rapid economic development, that required huge investment, which India could not afford and had to seek loans. But this industrialisation did not yield anticipated results and harmed our economy. This fact was realized by Nehru before Third Five Year Plan and was confessed by him in Lok Sabha on December 11, 1963. Had he not expired then, he would have changed the track. In Third Plan he slightly increased the allocation for agriculture and for the first time allotted funds for irrigation and flood control and small scale and cottage industries. But his successors did not take note of his changed mind, blindly followed the old policy and caused great harm to our economy.

At the time of Independence Mahatma Gandhi and Nehruji had two different view points for the development of the country. Gandhiji suggested to give top priority to agriculture and primary importance to small scale and cottage industries but Nehru differed and implemented his own views. When we compare the economic ideologies of Gandhi and Nehru, we find Gandhiji's concept far better and best suited for the country as India is an agricultural country with vast population. Increasing use of machines making the labour surplus may suit countries with lesser population but not the overcrowded countries like India.

Most advanced countries of the western world i.e. U.S.A., Russia, Germany, France etc. have developed fast by fully exploiting their ample natural resources but Japan on the contrary has developed by adequately utilizing her human resources and due to nationalism and strong will power of its people to make their country great. We treat our vast population as the root of all socio-economic ills whereas Japan considers it as the most significant resource. So it is high time for our government, leaving aside her ideological differences, to learn from Japan to fully utilize our human resources and looking into our resources and problems to change priorities as advocated by Gandhiji and put the wheels of economy on right track for making rapid march on the road of economic progress.

[illegible] changed mind, blindly followed the old philosophy [illegible] harm to our economy.

At the time of Independence Mahatma Gandhi and Nehru had two different view points for the development of the country. Gandhiji suggested to give top priority to agriculture and primary importance to small scale and cottage industries. [illegible] and implemented his own views. When we compare the [illegible] ideologies of Gandhi and Nehru, we find Gandhiji's concept far better and best suited for the country as India is an agricultural country with vast population. Increasing use of machines [illegible] the labour surplus may suit countries with lesser population but not the over-crowded countries like India.

Most advanced countries of the western world i.e. U.S.A., Russia, Germany, France etc. have developed fast by fully exploiting their ample natural resources but Japan on the contrary has developed by adequately utilizing her human resources and due to [illegible] and strong will power of its people to make their lives [illegible]. While [illegible] our vast population is the root of all socio-economic ills, whereas Japan considers it as the most significant [illegible] so it is high time for our government, leaving aside her [illegible] to learn from Japan to fully utilize our human resources and looking into the resources and problems to change priorities as advocated by Gandhiji and put the wheels of economy on right track for its [illegible] rapid march on the road of economic progress.

SECTION IV

NEHRU : PANCHSHEEL AND SECULARISM

15

NEHRU AND PANCHSHEEL

INDIRA PRIYADARSHINI

Except a few die-hards no person will ever deny the contribution of Mr. Nehru to the cause of international brotherhood and world peace. History records with pride the benevolent contributions which he made towards understanding among world leaders dealing with international problems. Mr. Nehru sought to apply to the relations between nations the ethical and moral principles that should govern the daily life of individuals. At a time when it appeared that there would be no co-existence as far as the communists and the free worlds were concerned, and the very future of mankind appeared dark, Mr. Nehru raised his lone voice in favour of co-existence, and if mankind is to name one man who with conviction and hope worked for the lessening of international tensions and greatly succeeded in achieving this, it is Mr. Nehru and none else.

It is the spirit of 'Live and let live' which is an accepted principle in international relations. What was just a cold axiom has been made a living reality in human relations by Nehru's efforts through his Panchsheel. For this, nations will gratefully remember him in times to come.

Twenty-five centuries ago two men in India rose above the din and disasters of war and gave a call for peaceful family – the Buddha and Ashoka. History had to wait long to see the rise and fulfilment of two other men – Gandhi and Nehru to take up the unfinished work of Budha and Ashoka.

Ashoka's edicts are the basis of Indian culture and Panchsheel flew from it. The message of Buddha, his suggestion of Eight-Fold Path has illuminated not only India but the whole world. That message was inscribed by the Great Ashoka on rock and stone which stand today to the truth that has guided India through the ages. Nehru knew well that it is only by recognition of this great truth India and the world will prosper. Unfortunately if the world denies and repudiates it and goes along its violent courses it will perish. So, to India and to most of the newly independent countries of Asia peace is a vital factor. Without peace it is not possible to have political freedom and economic contentment. As Frank Moraes puts it "the choice for pre-war Europe lay between guns and butter. The choice for post-war Asia lies between guns and bread". Unless Asia's economic conditions were improved and its standard of living stepped up, there will be no meaning of Independence in reality. That is how India and many Asian countries viewed the international scene. Progress to them meant peace which means strength which in turn "spells plenty and prosperity".

Under such circumstances the idealist Prime Minister of India declared a foreign policy for India based on the principles of non-alignment, anti-colonialism, racial equality and non-violence. To maintain a sound relation with the neighbouring countries, Nehru suggested five principles as a code of ethics for promotion of global peace. They are known as the Panchsheel. The five principles were first enunciated in the preamble to the Sino-Indian agreement on trade with Tibet in April 1954. Later in June 1954 when the Chinese Premier Chou-En-Lai visited New Delhi both the Prime Ministers signed joint statement where these five principles appeared. The five principles were:

1. Mutual respect for each other's territorial integrity and sovereignty;
2. Non-aggression;
3. Non-interference in each other's internal affairs;
4. Equality and mutual advantage and;
5. Peaceful co-existence and economic co-operation.

The statement said "If these principles are applied not only between various countries but also in international relations, generally they would form a solid foundation for peace and security and the fears and apprehensions that exist today would give place to a feeling of confidence".

Panchsheel with its underlying faith in human goodness and moral values was Nehru's answer to the doctrines of security pacts and arrangements. Subsequently these principles were accepted by Burma and Yugoslavia and Soviet Union had also expressed its approval of the Panchsheel. At the Bandung Conference these principles were elaborated into ten and embodied in a declaration on world peace and cooperation. Thus, over thirty countries accepted the Panchsheel.

Nehru ardently believed in these principles and said "I have no doubt that these principles of international behaviour if accepted and acted upon by all countries of the world would go a long way to put an end to fears and apprehensions which cast dark shadows over the world". In a speech on March 20, 1956 Nehru had made an offer to the Prime Minister of Pakistan to accept Panchsheel and expressed faith that if they base their dealing with one another on these five principles, "The nightmare of fear and suspicion will fade away".

Nehru had succeeded in convincing our neighbours that by following the Panchsheel we may secure ourselves, help others to be secure in their own homes and keep in check the improper ambitions of powerful nations wanting to dominate the world, physically or ideologically. However, the critics have not failed to criticise Mr. Nehru for his Panchsheel.

Signing the Panchsheel with China, then, meant India's recognition of China's suzerainty over Tibet. When there was friction between China and India over the question of Tibet, China hurled most wounding provocations against India . J.B. Kripalani, a stern critic of Nehru said, "Panchsheel was born in sin, for it was initiated to put our seal of approval on the destruction of an ancient nation which was associated with us culturally and spiritually and who had every right to enjoy autonomy and independence. The rest of the world especially the Africans believed that India, a large and populous country was behaving indecently and lacked the sufficient fighting spirit against imperialism while China was the real champion of the underdog everywhere. As a result, the image of India and Nehru was tarnished.

Moreover, from a treaty the partners should be equally benefited but here China got the lion's share. We sought security by a written treaty and believed that we were guaranteed against an invasion. We failed to demand any reciprocal benefit in insisting on a final border agreement which at that time was the only possible source of friction.

Nehru, on the other hand said that signing of such a treaty does not mean that India is afraid of China. There is no doubt that after the last war the rise of the United China is a major event in the middle of the 20th century and China has become a great power, united and strong. But India does not have to submit to China or draw up its policies in deference to China, not at all.

The Panchsheel is the code of International Ethics. It is a mistake to reduce it to the level of a preamble, to the treaty between India and China signed in 1954. This treaty from Nehru's point of view was a by-product of Panchsheel and not *vice versa*.

A man with love, concern and sincerity for all the countries of the world, Jawaharlal Nehru, received a rude shock when in 1962 China, violated Panchsheel and attacked India. Nehru was prompt in answering to the call of the situation but the blow was too much to endure. The idealism, the spirit of universal brotherhood and non-violence in him had received a mortal blow and he broke down both physically and mentally. At home his friends, colleagues even the countrymen were loud in criticism of Nehru, his foreign policy and the Panchsheel. It is believed that Nehru met his untimely death because of this.

Whether Panchsheel is a success or failure that is a separate issue, but one cannot doubt the sincerity of intention as well as emotion of the man who initiated this code. In his own words "The idea of Panchsheel lays down the very important truth that each people must ultimately fend for itself, striving intellectually, morally, spiritually — opening out all our windows to ideas from others, and learning from the experience of others. Each country should look upon an endeavour on the part of the other with sympathy and friendly understanding and without any interference on imposition". This is the role India has played through Panchsheel with the best of its ability and has been progressively recognised in other countries. Certainly the whole world has not accepted it, some countries have disagreed with it but there has been a belief in the integrity of the policy of India. "There has been recognition that it is a sincere policy based essentially on goodwill and fellowship with other countries, with no ill-will for any country".

Nations need the memory of unique personalities in their history and Nehru's greatest achievements, the ability to bridge differences will remain for future generations the guiding star of co-existence and global peace. In times to come man-kind will accept the Panchsheel as a sacred commandment to redeem the international politics that has been polluted with distrust, suspicion, greed, war and hunger of power.

16

PEACEFUL CO-EXISTENCE OR PANCHSHEEL

B. GHOUSIA

Introduction

Jawaharlal Nehru was one of the key figures of the twentieth century. He symbolised some of the major forces which have transformed our age. His activities in the year of India's struggle for freedom made him not only an intense nationalist, but one of the best leaders of humanism. He was intensely involved with the problems of the poor and the oppressed in all lands. In doing so, Jawaharlal Nehru gave articulation and leadership to millions of people in his own country and in Asia and Africa.

As a leader of free India, Jawaharlal Nehru recognised that his country could neither stay out of the world nor divest itself of its own interests in world affairs. But to the extent that it was possible, Jawaharlal Nehru sought to speak objectively and to be a voice of sanity in the shrill phrases of the 'Cold War'. Whether his influence helped on certain occasions to maintain peace is for the future historian to assess. What we do know is that for a long stretch of time, he commanded an international audience reaching far beyond governments, that he spoke for ordinary, sensitive, thinking men and women around the globe and that his was a constituency which extended far beyond India. He was a man who evolved, who grew in storm and stress till he became the representative of much that was noble in his time. His achievement, by its very nature and setting, was greater than that of a Prime Minister. His primary and overmuch riding goal had always been the maintenance of peace and promotion of international peace and security. According to him, 'Peace to us is not just a fervent hope, it is an emergent necessity.' He has further added that 'Peace can only come if we endeavour to establish the climate of peace.'

Peaceful Co-existence or Panchsheel

The concept of co-existence is a familiar old term in literature on communism which once upon a time had a different and specific meaning of its own; the term 'Panchsheel' (now used to describe the Five Principles stated in the preamble to the Indo-China agreement) is of ancient lineage in Buddhist literature and refers to the five principles of individual good conduct.

The chief positive means by which India sought to achieve the goals of her foreign policy is by following the concept and principle of peaceful co-existence of nations of diverse ideologies and interests. The idea that peoples of different religions and systems of philosophy could live and work together is as old as the Indian civilization. Free India has sought to apply this concept and principle in the realm of foreign relations in the context of rival economic and social systems and ideologies. Ever since recognizing the Government of the People's Republic of China in December 1949, it has been a dominant feature of India's foreign policy to promote very cordial and close relations with New China. The friendly Indian attitude was greatly reinforced by the agreement concluded between India and China on trade and intercourse between the Tibet Region of China effectively exercising sovereignty over Tibet since 1950 (for the first time after centuries of merely claiming sovereignty), there was a need to reconsider the basis of India's historic position in respect of Tibet (inherited from British rule) and place it on a new basis in the light of the changed context. Discussions, therefore, started between the two governments in Peking from December 1953 onwards which resulted in the above agreement. Early in 1954 the concept and principle of peaceful co-existence was given certain precision and formal recognition in what later came to be known as the 'Panchsheel', or Five Principles. That agreement stated in the preamble that it was based on the following principles: (i) mutual respect for each other's territorial integrity and sovereignty, (ii) mutual non-aggression, (iii) mutual non-interference in each other's internal affairs (iv) equality and mutual benefit, and (v) peaceful co-existence. The novelty of India's contribution lies in seeking to make these principles the basis of practical state policy and conduct in international relations. These principles were also incorporated in the Declaration of World Peace and Cooperation adopted by the Asian-African Conference at Bandung on the 30th April, 1955 as well as in a resolution on principles of co-existence adopted by the Inter-Parliamentary Union at its Helsinki Session in August 1955.

The most important decision of the Asian-African conference and historic in significance was the 'Declaration on the Promotion of World Peace and Cooperation' which asserted that the nations of the world should regulate their relations with each other on the basis of ten specified principles. The following were the ten principles:

(i) Respect for fundamental human rights and for the purposes and principles of the Charter of the United Nations;
(ii) Respect for the sovereignty and territorial integrity of all nations;
(iii) Recognition of the equality of all races and of the equality of all nations, large and small;
(iv) Abstention from intervention or interference in the internal affairs of another country;
(v) Respect for the right of each nation to defend itself, singly or collectively, in conformity with the Charter of the United Nations;
(vi-a) Abstention from the use of arrangements of collective defence to serve the particular interest of any of the Big Powers;
(vi-b) Abstention by any country from exerting pressures on other countries;
(vii) Refraining from acts or threats of aggression or the use of force against the territorial integrity or political independence of any country;
(viii) Settlement of all international disputes by peaceful means, such as negotiation, conciliation, arbitration or judicial settlement as well as other peaceful means of the parties' own choice, in conformity with the Charter of the United Nations;
(ix) Promotion of mutual interests and cooperation; and
(x) Respect for justice and international obligations.

Jawaharlal Nehru has observed that the 'major thing' about the agreement was its preamble, and added that if these principles were adopted in the relations of various countries with each other, a great deal of the trouble of present-day world would probably disappear.

During the visit to New Delhi of the Chinese Prime Minister, Chou En-lai, the Prime Ministers of the two countries reaffirmed these principles in their joint statement of 28th June, 1954 'and felt that they should be applied in their relations with other countries in Asia as well as in other parts of the world. If these principles are applied not only between various countries but also in international relations generally, they would form a solid foundation for peace and security, and the fears and apprehensions that exist today would give place to a feeling of confidence.' For the first time, these principles were termed as 'Panchsheel' by Prime Minister Jawaharlal Nehru at a State banquet given by him to the Indonesian Prime Minister on 23rd September, 1954. He also conceded that the Five Principles (Panchsheel) were not a magic formula which would prevent all the ills of the world; it sought to lessen tension and did not harm, criticize or condemn anybody. It was something which met the needs of today, while the opposing posture of military pacts and alliances had no relevance to the realistic conditions of the atomic and nuclear age. During the next few months, the term 'Panchsheel' became, as Jawaharlal Nehru put it, 'international coin' and the following countries (in addition to India and China) expressly affirmed their adherence to it before the end of 1956: Afghanistan, Burma, Cambodia, Egypt, Indonesia, Laos, People's Republic of Mangolia, Nepal, Poland, Saudi Arabia, the Soviet Union, Democratic Republic of Vietnam and Yugoslavia.

In the atomic and nuclear age, the alternative to co-existence is, as Jawaharlal Nehru put it, 'Co-destruction'. Belief in peaceful co-existence did not also mean putting up with a present evil as some critics sought to imply like colonialism and racialism. In practice, it would mean willingness to live and work with other nations and the desire and attempt to effect a peaceful change with a friendly approach – with no fear, hatred or aggressive intent.

In the context of the ideological struggle or 'cold war' in which the concept of peaceful co-existence has come to be used in post-war international relations, it means that it is both possible and necessary that countries with different political, economic or other systems should exist side by side and work together peacefully; it also means that every nation has a right to its political and social order and to develop along its own lines. Co-existence of nations of diverse ideologies is not a 'misfortune to be endured, but a fact which enriches the diversity of human society.' Peaceful co-existence of nations of diverse ideologies or ways of life (which is the core of Panchsheel) is the essential consequence of a democratic outlook. 'The person who rejects the idea of co-existence rejects basically the democratic outlook.' One could not live in compartments and be democratic inside a country and not so out side internationally. In putting their faith and reliance on these principles, the Government and the people of India were certainly not naive, as Western spokesman and the Press said they were, with pretentious monopoly of wisdom. When once these principles were accepted by other countries too, then, an atmosphere would be created in which a country which had subscribed to the principles and broke it, would get into 'hot waters' much more so than if it had not subscribed to it. Therefore, according to Jawaharlal Nehru, one had either to accept Panchsheel and Co-existence or conflict and Co-destruction. Jawaharlal Nehru told the Prime Minister of Pakistan that a declaration of adherence to Panchsheel 'gives far greater assurance of security and friendly relations than military pacts or military preparations'. To agree to any such declaration does not mean that we should not try to solve our problems. It means that we should solve them in a better and more friendly atmosphere, having ruled out the possibility of a recourse to war.

India posed these Five Principles as a challenge to all countries of the world, even though some countries had ridiculed or criticized it. Jawaharlal Nehru wanted of every country to say whether or not it agreed to it. 'The Panchsheel are a challenge of Asia to the rest of the world. And each country will have to give a straight answer to this question.....' He went to the extent of asserting that if the world honestly accepted the Five Principles, especially the principle of non-interference in internal affairs of other countries, then 90 per cent of the present-day problems of the world would certainly be solved. He had no doubt about it. As far as India was concerned, she sought to follow the principles of Panchsheel towards all countries of the world, whether or not these other countries had expressed formal adherence to them. Thus, India is 'endeavouring to develop the broadest possible measure of co-operation with the widest number of states'—in the words of Marshal Tito.

And finally, it is interesting to note that up to 1954 India had, on her part, sought to observe in her role in world affairs the principles of what later came to be known as 'Panchsheel'. But from 1954 onwards, more especially during the period 1954-55, she also sought to recommend these principles to the other states as well as for their observance, not only as between India and those states, but also among third-party states. This is a most significant development in her foreign policy during this period. Indeed, it is for this reason, apart from our natural bent, that our Prime Minister Shri Rajiv Gandhi was also giving first place to this striving for peace and to follow the Panchsheel.

17

NEHRU AND PANCHSHEEL

SUPRIYA DESHPANDE

India is singularly lucky in having three outstanding personalities whose thoughts have not only influenced our own people but the entire globe. Gandhi, Tagore and Nehru were leaders of world class. 'Gandhi applied the homilies of the Sermon on the Mount, especially the injunction to return good for evil', says Louis Untermayer. Prof. J.L. Kachroo notes that the poet in Tagore made him humanist, universalist and Nehru, the patriot, believed in Independence as the first step to progress. 'Yet he knew that political independence is a means and not an end and only through dedicated effort, education, and respect for the rights and opinions of others can a people become truly free' (Chester Bowles). Nehru's finest contribution is in his handling of the foreign affairs by evolving new concept – Panchsheel.

In evolving this policy Pandit Nehru drew from India's age old principles of non-violence and tolerance. As history records it, Nehru has been very loyal to the principle of Panchsheel, in spite of the spate of criticism it attracted in India. But many countries in the world have accepted it.

Against the background mentioned in the opening paragraphs it would be apt to understand the concept of Panchsheel as enunciated by Pandit Nehru. In a speech made in Lok Sabha on 17th September, 1955 Nehru propounded his concept in the following words:

'What are the five principles? Panchsheel. They are very simple:

> The first one is, the recognition by countries of their independence and each other's independence, sovereignty and territorial integrity. The second one is non-aggression; the third is non-interference with each other; and the fourth is mutual respect and equality and the fifth is co-existence, non-interference – political,

economic or ideological'.

He elaborated further,

> "The concept of Panchsheel means that there may be different ways of progress, possibly different outlooks, but that, broadly the ultimate objectives may be the same. If I may use another type of analogy, truth is not confined to one country or one people; it has too many aspects for any one to presume that he knows all and each country and each people, if they are true to themselves, have to find out their path themselves through trial and error, through suffering and experiences. Only then do they grow. If they merely copy others, the result is likely to be that they will not grow. And even though the copy may be completely good, perfectly good, it is something imposed upon them or something undertaken by them without that normal growth of the mind which makes it an organic part of themselves."

When Chou En-lai, the Chinese Prime Minister visited India, Nehru and Chou En-lai made a joint declaration that they would abide by the five principles. They had great faith in Panchsheel and its utility in international relationship. Panchsheel dominated Afro-Asian Conference held in Bandung in 1955. It was expanded into ten principles. These principles found favour with 29 representatives of Asia and Africa. Nehru and Chou En-lai took keen interest in propagating the concept of Panchsheel. Truly, it was a feather in Nehru's cap. The next destination was Moscow. Nehru visited the Soviet Union in 1955. A joint declaration was issued by Nehru and Bulganin on 22nd June, 1955, reiterating the determination of both the governments to adhere to the Panchsheel.

The world was slowly but surely appreciating the value of Panchsheel in international affairs. The U.S.A. too started viewing Nehru's ideas on international affairs with respect and understanding. Nehru told U.S. Senators that India will not be neutral where there is danger to freedom or democracy is threatened. Nehru's concept of Panchsheel brought India friends in Agro-Asian countries. Nehru became spokesman for Asia. Panchsheel generated goodwill among many nations of the world – big and small.

Nehru's non-alignment policy in foreign affairs has been criticised. One critic has said that it has championed international communism. This critic looks at the policy from only one side. The Panchsheel has a wider perspective. Dr. V.K.R.V. Rao, an eminent economist and former Education Minister has correctly assessed the merit of Nehru's policy of non-alignment in the following words:

> 'Above all Nehru was responsible for the policy of non-alignment which resulted in keeping an even distance between the two super forces or powers and taking every opportunity of bringing them round the conference table at the United Nations. In fact, in my opinion Nehru played an important role in averting a third World War by the policy of non-alignment and talking to the super powers without aligning himself with either of them.'

The policy of non-alignment has been able to reduce the tensions in Asia.

Perhaps Nehru's judgement of foreign affairs was hundred per cent correct when he perceived that foreign affairs is nothing but co-existence. He did not believe in military pact/agreements. He had taken lot of pains and used his communication skill to explain to the world that India's neutral policy is not being passive but based on the sincere desire to bring peace to the troubled world by cold war tactics. Nehru was sad when China did not adhere to Panchsheel in certain matters but he never toyed with the idea of giving it up. He continued to have faith in the concept of Panchsheel. Radhakrishnan aptly says that Nehru has sought to bridge the chasms that separate races, nations and systems. Pandit Nehru's policy of non-alignment won the approval of Russel who said that Nehru who stood for sanity and peace will lead us out of the dark night of fear into a happier day.

There was a thinking in India and some other countries that how a poor nation can economically grow without the economic help of the two super powers representing different blocs. Nehru, the great visionary had better ideas of linking economic planning and non-alignment. The basic industries he set up as the chief architect of Indian planning is a tribute to Nehru's pragmatism.

The leaders of India who succeeded Nehru have seen the advantage of Panchsheel and they have been adhering to them in one form or the other. India has gone to the help of the countries where democracy was in danger. The role Nehru played in making UN a really international forum is to his credit side.

Hiren Mukerjee in his book *The Gentle Colossus* says,

> "There is no need to think of any casual link, but it is interesting to recall that certain concepts of Buddhist thought which Jawaharlal admired very much, have left their mark on free India's foreign policy. The expression Panchsheel is of Buddhist origin; in expounding the Eightfold path which, the Buddha taught, one should seek to tread, if one wishes to find the reply to the problem of suffering, five principles of conduct were enumerated which in a different garb have formed the staple of treaties entered into India with several countries in pursuit of her policy of peace, the object being the elimination of the woes of a world affrighted by the dangers of war and all the evil it connotes."

The fact that in spite of many pressures to see Panchsheel become a failure Nehru stood steadfast in favour of it and made it as an effective model to follow for all those who have thoughts of love towards peace in the World.

The best feedback on Panchsheel has been given by Jawaharlal Nehru himself:

> "The development of India under Mahatma Gandhi's leadership was organic. It was something which filled in with the spirit and thinking of India. Yet it was not isolated from the modern world. This process of adaptation will go on. . . . This ideas of Panchsheel lays down the very important truth that each people must fend for itself. This is the role India has played. However little has been this role, during these past few years the general policy which we have sought to follow to the best of our ability has been progressively recognised in other countries. It may not have been accepted by all, certainly not; some have disagreed with some parts of it or even the whole of it. But progressively there has been a belief in the integrity of the policy of India. There has been recognition that it is a sincere policy based essentially on goodwill and fellowship with other countries, with no ill-will for any country."

Somewhere Shri K.P.S. Menon, has written that some critics are of the view that Nehru's idea of peace was exaggerated. But to them Shri Menon replies that they do not realise how close mankind was to a world war in the fifties on more than one occasions. The relevance of Panchsheel was all the more important at that time in particular.

The appreciation of Nehru's foreign policy has been a dominant factor all through the Asian and African countries. The Western World too has admired the value of Panchsheel.

Nehru himself has said in a speech at the closing session of the Asian-African Conference at Bandung, on 22 April, 1955 that the five principles not a magic formula which will prevent all the ills of the world. But it is something which meets the needs of the day. It lessens tension; it does not harm anybody, criticise anybody. The World is much to gain by appreciating Panchsheel and creating an atmosphere of peace for humanity.

18

NEHRU AND SOVIET UNION

V.K. PARKHOMENKO

Just in a few months from now we shall celebrate the Birth Centenary of the great son of India, the ardent fighter for freedom, the first Prime Minister of independent India and sincere friend of the Soviet people — Pandit Jawaharlal Nehru. The entire life of this outstanding state and political figure of contemporary India is the great deed of sacrifices to his people. His name is connected with the creation and realization of the main principles in internal and external policy of independent India, with her first steps towards the social and economic development.

> I will touch upon only one, but rather striking aspect of versatile activity of your great compatriot — his valuable contribution to the consolidation of Indo-Soviet friendship. Jawaharlal Nehru was the man of great learning, infinitely devoted to his people, sincerely anxious to the benefit and prosperity of his country. He was not only at the sources of friendship between our two countries and peoples, but also made a great contribution to this process as well as to the development of mutually advantageous Soviet-Indian cooperation.

Jawaharlal Nehru visited the Soviet Union three times and every time he was deeply impressed by the feelings of profound interest and sympathy of the Soviet people towards your great country, her past and present life. At the same time the deep and thorough interest and sincere respect which Jawaharlal Nehru felt for the motherland of the Great October Revolution and to Lenin as its leader had been strengthening even during his first visit to the Soviet Union in 1927. All these events had a profound influence, on the man who took the leadership of the whole Indian nation and who after achieving independence led the Indian people to create the democratic society. He had taken part in the celebration of the 10th anniversary of the Great October Socialist Revolution and was impressed by the progress achieved by the Soviet Union in different fields. It was that period of time when the United States and some other capitalist countries tried to treat the Soviet Union as if it was "untouchable".

However Jawaharlal Nehru stressed the necessity to develop the friendly relations between India and the USSR. In the book of essays on his trip to the USSR, published in 1928, and titled "Soviet Russia", he made an attempt to convince the Indian people to treat her northern neighbour not as enemy but as a friend of India. Jawaharlal Nehru could form a correct estimate of the importance of Soviet experience in creation of stable development of national economy and culture as if he might have foreseen the friendly assistance of the Soviet Union to independent India.

His deep confidence that the experience of the Soviet Union might provide an assistance to his motherland in solving most of social, political and economic problems, became an integrated part of his policy as the first Prime Minister of Independent India.

In his opening address to the Congress of the Indian National Congress in 1936 Jawaharlal Nehru stated: "If the future is full of hope, it is largely because of Soviet Russia and what it has done".

Jawaharlal Nehru considered making friendly relations with the Soviet Union and other socialist countries as one of the main tasks of Independent India. Just before the formal declaration of Independence of India in September 1946, in his speech in radio message to welcome the Soviet people, he said "They are our neighbours in Asia and inevitably we shall undertake many common tasks and have much to do with each other".

We all know that these words were not only formal statement. During subsequent years, the mutual relations between our countries have developed and strengthened without changing its nature — to reach the mutual understanding regarding most important contemporary problems — to secure the everlasting peace in the world.

The first Indian foreign policy has shown that its main direction, the struggle for peace, against imperialism and colonialism, for seeking an extensive international cooperation, has been absolutely in time with the fundamental principles of the USSR policy.

In his struggle for peace Jawaharlal Nehru has been perfectly against the principles of inevitable world disasters and war and preparation of war.

His belief and hopes in strengthening of peace were based not only on his humanistic outlook but he was confident that in nuclear age the world war has lost its sense and can lead to fatal madness.

The deep social conditions of international tension and the necessity of just solution of conflicts for strengthening peace was obvious to Nehru. He considered non-alignment as the policy which ensures the national interests in the best way and at the same time the strengthening of international peace both for India and other developing countries.

The anti-imperialist significance of non-alignment was fully shown in Nehru's distinctly negative attitude towards military blocks, knocked together by Western powers, with the participation of some Asian countries, and a military penetration of imperialism into Asia.

Considering the policy of non-alignment as the position in the struggle for peace and against colonialism Nehru identified it not as neutral policy. He never conceived non-alignment as a balance between socialist and capitalist worlds, and he reserved for himself the right to choose. At the same time the interests of the struggle for independence peace and progress brought Nehru more often closer to the USSR and the socialist concord. For its side the Soviet government estimated at their true worth, the progressive changes made by Nehru inside the country, and actively supported India's peaceful foreign policy.

The practical interaction of the Soviet Union and India, which had begun to form since the late 40s, on the concrete problems of international life, such as, the principle of unanimity of the great powers in the UNO, the withdrawal of the British troops from Greece, the membership in the UNO, etc. was marked in the 50s and 60s by a new stage in the history of the Soviet-Indian foreign policy cooperation and by strengthening the Soviet-Indian relations in all directions. During this period the first bilateral agreements on economic, scientific and cultural cooperation between our countries were signed, with the active participation of Nehru, and the construction of the first Indian industrial units with the help of the USSR which Nehru called "the temples of the new India", was started.

The most complicated problems that the Indian government had been facing since the moment India got independence — overcoming the economic backwardness, liquidating the dependence of the country on imperialist monopolies, turning it into a developed industrial state — got solution, due to Nehru's perception by way of creating the main branches of the nation's heavy industry in the public sector.

Realizing that the Western countries were unlikely to willingly comply with his government in solving the problems facing India in the sphere of economic development, and even in case of their consent to render aid in the industrialization of India, they would stipulate this help for the renunciation of the independent foreign policy pursued by the Indian Government and involvement of the country in the orbit of the Military strategic clans of the international imperialism, Nehru again and again followed suit the Soviet Union. Nehru's conviction that only the Soviet Union could render an effective and disinterested aid to India in creating the national industry, impelled him to take a firm decision not only to reach the agreement with the USSR on the construction of a metallurgic plant in Bhilai, but to firmly follow the course of constructing other big plants in India in the public sector in future.

Nehru considered that the Agreement signed on February 2, 1955, on construction of a complex metallurgical plant in Bhilai with Soviet assistance, to be the first serious step of the Indian Government on way to the creation of independent national economy and the Soviet-Indian Trade Agreement signed on December 2, 1953, those two agreements, laid down reliable foundations for future economic cooperation.

The 1955 visit of Jawaharlal Nehru and Indira Gandhi to the USSR was of great historic importance not only for the further strengthening the friendly relations between the USSR and India, but for easing the international tension as well.

Ambassador of India to the USSR K.P.S. Menon, who accompanied Jawaharlal Nehru is his trip to the Soviet Union, wrote that the Soviet people welcomed the first Prime Minister of Independent India "Not only as a great leader of India, but also as a friend of the Soviet Union and the envoy of peace..."

Prime Minister Nehru's visit to the USSR and the return visit of Soviet statesmen to India in 1955, laid down the beginning of a good tradition in the relations between our countries — regular exchange of visits of Soviet and Indian leaders, the coordination, common stands or similar positions of our countries in the struggle for universal peace.

A fresh, bright example of it are recent Indo-Soviet summits,

CPSU General Secretary Mikhail Gorbachev's talks with Prime Minister Rajiv Gandhi in Moscow and Delhi and the Delhi Declaration on Principles of Non-violent and Nuclear-Free World, signed during the first visit of Soviet leader to India in November 1986.

The basis of Indo-Soviet friendship laid down by Jawaharlal Nehru, due to the consecutive policy of his successors, are on the steady foundation: the Treaty of Peace, Friendship and Cooperation signed between the USSR and India in 1971. This Treaty is vivid realization of high level ties and traditional friendship between our countries and peoples. Being the logical result of the purposeful course of Jawaharlal Nehru for developing relations with the USSR in all spheres of human endeavour, this Treaty is an important factor of peace and stability in Asia and in the whole world.

The dynamic, multilateral relations between the USSR and India have stood the test of time and proved the fact that they may not be influenced by the vicissitudes, of political situation and momentary factors.

The ardent patriot of India, a great friend of the Soviet people Jawaharlal Nehru, dreamt about such relations between our countries and made a lot of efforts to achieve this lofty goal.

19

COMMUNAL POLITY MUST END!

I.K. GUJRAL

The politics of expediency and a distorted view of secularism are primarily responsible for the prevailing environment of virulent communalism and the fundamentalist separatism.

There were times when even the rabid communalists and the arch revivalists did not like to be branded as such. And even the practitioners of obscurantist rituals wanted to hide their pursuits behind the thick veils.

A large part of our contemporary value system has been determined by the Gandhian era. Very often, though erroneously, the Mahatma's role is viewed only in terms of our gaining independence. His most important contribution was what he had done for the nation's character and capacities. He repaired our wounded self-esteem and restored in us the courage and potency and transformed our outlook.

He recruited a new brand of leaders from varied parts of society giving a new coherence and meaning to the national life.

Though there was a high component of traditionality in his philosophy, he did not permit this to lead him into any obscurantist frame or outmoded faiths. On the contrary he was the biggest moderniser of our times. No one ever heard of Gandhiji going to the places of worship for the ritualistic *poojas*, or meeting with the God-men, *Tantriks* or astrologers or attending any exclusive caste or communal meetings. His ideology constructed intimate relationships between national identity, secularism and a non-communal polity.

For himself Gandhiji wanted to be judged simultaneously as a private and public person and that was the norm that he prescribed for all those who occupied various positions of leadership. His concept of the 'Satyagrah' was a comprehensive culture — a total way of life. The initiated ones experienced a sea of change in their traditional beliefs regarding ritualism, the caste system, communal alliances, status of women, the rural poor and so on.

On mass levels the Gandhian miracle transformed the psyche of the entire nation—even the non-participants were affected. The country learnt relevances of unifying the cultural diversities to mould a vibrant nation. He did not try to build a dogma or sponsor a religion, but he introduced a way of life that could raise an entire people to a new experience of self-realisation. He sponsored various movements to dissolve social stagnation and age-old degeneration prospering in the name of religion and tradition. There were always some sceptics who fell by the side but the Indian masses accepted the potency of his vision and brought forth fresh entrants to further his ideas.

Although the vast ranks of the Congressmen devoted their energies to combating the imperial rule, the dedicated bands of the constructive workers gave their whole time attention to the Harijan uplift, rural health and industry and to harmonise the communal divisiveness that the colonial rulers and their cronies were using to defeat the upsurge.

Even though the machinations of alien rule sometimes succeeded in making the Hindus and the Muslims fight each other, yet the mighty sweep of a cultural revolution was kindling a unifying self-esteem in the peasantry that revived our cultural unity.

Unfortunately, the national struggle ended in partial success. The colonial machination succeeded in breaking this cultural unity and split the country on the basis of religion.

Even in the tormenting environment of partition, Gandhiji did not give up. He continued his *'padyatras'* in the riot-infested regions to restore sanity and unity. It is not a mean compliment to his legacy that even in the midst of bloody communal riots the nation adopted a constitution that enshrined 'secularism' as the foundation of the Indian nationhood.

Nehru and his leading colleagues were fire-tested patriots and men of outstanding merit. They architectured institutions and policies that would consolidate the nation. His sense of history and vision induced him to emphasise an attitudinal change that would be scientific and unifying.

He knew fully well that our nation-state could stabilise only if the secular polity divorced itself from all communal pulls and fanatic revivalism. A pluralistic and liberal society could survive by unifying the large cultural diversities. He understood that chauvinistic call for 'uniformity' was in reality a slogan that sought to erase the minority cultures and their ways of life.

Neither Gandhiji nor was Nehru averse to the lofty spirituality of the *'Dharmas'* but it was obvious that the fanatics and the fundamentalists were causing confusion by distorting the purpose of religious beliefs.

Nehru was once asked, ". . . are you religious?" He replied, ". . . yes, but not of the temple-going type".

Even while the new Indian state was struggling to consolidate, the pristine determination of the Congress culture was weakening both in resolve and in its ideological commitment. The new power centres were opportunistic in outlook. They made alliances and coalitions with all types of persons and ideologies that would keep them in power and satisfy their greed. This was a major turning point in socio-political life of the country. A totally new pattern of 'Tomny Hall' style of leaderships emerged not only in the Congress but also in other smaller parties whose main merit earlier was their transparent commitment to secular, socialist ideology.

Politics of manipulations could not be value-oriented; it perceived benefit in aligning with the communalists and relying on the casteists.

As the grassroots base of the parties shrank and as the main political party was re-organised on the basis of loyalties to the individuals, the divisive revivalists captured the open field. The old Congress culture-wallas neither had the time for nor the commitment to any social change programme, if it hurt personal sectional interests of their new friends and allies.

Unfortunately, the tragedy did not befall the Congress alone that was now in the midst of a series of purges and fragmentations, it affected even parties of the left as well. They blotted their fair name by coalitioning with the branched communal groups and parties.

Making and breaking of the government made the small communal parties relevant and respectable. With impunity they could make alliance with any party of their choice.

This eroded the entire national edifice of the modern secular society. Even definition of secularism has been revised to mean equal 'flirtation with all religions'. Heads of administration and the states spend a good deal of their time visiting shrines, paying obeisance to the godmen and determine dates for swearing in of the ministries on the advice of *tantriks* and the shady astrologers.

Secularism is no more looked upon as an instrument for modernisation of the society and for induction of scientific outlook. The official audio-visual media goes out of its way to show a governor sweeping the floor of a temple or a minister touching the feet of some fake miracle-maker!

These activities cannot be viewed only as private pursuits. The ignorant masses view these as models of social behaviour. The revivalists thus acquire social respect and the obscure rituals breed fundamentals that, in turn, mothers communalism,. It is no use trying to fight the end result while nourishing roots all the times.

There is much talk of a-new education policy; a new cultural-cum-information policy. While paying lip service to secularism and national unity, there is no evidence of a concerted effort to attack frontly communalism in these spheres.

Why, for instance, the government does not remove stranglehold of the communalists from the educational institutions? When budget of the schools and colleges are financed by the government, the tender minds are exposed to all types of obscurantist teachings. In the name of religion, foundations are laid for communal divisiveness. The text-books that are prescribed and the way history is interpreted—these all have done immense harm. While chauvinism of the majority community is dangerous, it is no use overlooking the fact that the institutions managed and run by the minority communities are hotbeds of revivalism and separatist psyche. Major challenges to secularism are emerging from both sides. While the "Hindu Rashtra" wallas emphasise "uniformity" (called by the lofty name of Indianisation) of all diversities, the Sikh and the Muslim fundamentalists are insisting on inseparability of their religions from politics—a total negation of secular policy.

The Indian reality is diverse but not divisive. We have a large variety of languages, cultures and ways of life, but these all have contributed in building a unified civilisation. All along in our history we have been conscious of Indian nationhood that facilitated our struggle for freedom. Of course, it is only for the last forty years or so that a nation-state is being built; that seeks to encourage all cultural expressions, linguistic developments. It also seeks to emphasise the unity of our civilisation and the ennobling traditions. At the same time it must keep administration and political life at a respectable distance from the narrow affiliations of a caste or a community to enable it to hand our equitable social justice to all.

A secular state, particularly in a developing society, cannot be indifferent to social, cultural or economic backwardness. While modernising attitudes, it has to hasten slowly but it must ensure that there is distinct differentiation between modernity and westernisation particularly because of our traditional structures and value system.

Value-based Politics

Gandhiji understood this. He used some elements of traditions to serve modern functions. In the process he gave new meanings to old dicta. The *'Ram Rajya'* symbolised social justice while his devotion to truth manifested itself as the *'Dharma'* of the *'Satyagrah'* — "the truth force". Similarly he rejected fatalism and ritualistic orientations that had kept the Harijans in social bondage for centuries.

He taught us how to manufacture a new socio-political environment to serve the national objectives. When Gandhiji said, ". . . for me there is no distinction between religion and politics. . .", he was assigning a true meaning to the concept of *"Dharma"* that was not an institutionalised religion. He merely emphasised human virtues and personal ethics. His concept of *'Dharma'* transcended all bigotry and divisiveness. And this has to be re-emphasised in our value-based politics and public conduct. This concept would ensure insulation of the state from machinations of the merchants of religion who trade in its name. It is time we understood, if it is needed, distinction between *"Dharma"* and communalism. We must know that communalists are not religious people. They only use religions for personal and political objectives. There may be some who are both religious and communal but they usually act as communalists in politics by emphasising that only their religion is a complete code of life that enjoins on them not to segregate their faith from the civic affairs.

Such pleas inevitably breed dogmas of bigotry and intolerance of others. The communalist psyche emanates from ignorance of the moral teachings and universal humanism of even their own religion, leave alone a similar framework of the other.

The communalist organisations are, in reality, interested in using religion — not for any religious, spiritual or humanistic purpose. On the contrary, they use it for 'secular' (in the sense of state affairs) purposes, i.e., the non-religious and aimed at aggrandisement of power, position and wealth.

In this sense, therefore, communalism perverts religion and converts it into a political constituency. Soon an ethic-based code of conduct is replaced by aggressive politics that seeks to achieve that may not be possible otherwise. While it may be useful to define communalism, we must not get lost in this debate.

We must remember that communalism is a recent phenomenon that was originated by the clever British who wanted to use it as a checkmate to contain the emergence of an anti-imperialist intelligentsia who understood the implication of the unifying Indian culture.

When Macaulay — in the 19th century, contemptuously dismissed all Indian languages as unsuitable vehicles of modern thoughts he was, in his own way, fracturing the unifying civilisation. No alien ruler in the past had done this. On the contrary, the languages and the cultures that came from the north mingled freely with the existing ones and thus gave birth to new languages like Hindi and Urdu and the composite culture.

After the mutiny of 1857 — the British worked out a far-reaching political methodology that aimed at breaking the Pan-Indian ideality that had the inherent capacity to cut across cultural diversities and build an anti-imperialist united front.

The alien rulers emphasised the religion, caste, sects, *jatis* and languages in public services and later in the electorate. This indeed was their major anti-unity ploy. In the system of separate electorate and in the communal quota services, the people were perceived as members of a religious community or caste and not as Indians. And as the limited municipal and provincial autonomy came, divisive psyche played havoc with nationalist efforts of unification. The separate electorate laid the base for linking politics and communalism. In turn it led to clash of interests and even to inter-se riots. The colonial regime detested the Gandhian politics. So it encouraged and reinforced all types of communal polity.

This psyche continues to plague us. There should be no doubt in our minds that the British had effectively used communal organisations and parties as the main bulwark against the national movement. This disruptive role of communalism, traded as religion, continues its pursuits to harm our national objectives.

The British had legitimised communal politics with a purpose. Its continuity now is highly damaging and must end.

20

NEHRU AND NAM

G.N. SRIVASTAVA

Nehru was a genius diplomat and a conscientious politician of his age. He acquired these qualities during his struggle for independence of India. Various internal and external factors influenced his ideas and thoughts during his political career. After India's independence he became the Prime Minister of India. He also held the office of Foreign Affairs. Hence India's foreign policy was very much influenced by Nehru's political experience and his understanding of international conditions.

As an architect of Indian foreign policy, Nehru from the very beginning tried to follow a non-aligned foreign policy. He had a distinct idea of India's geopolitical conditions and its national aims against the warring big power interests in international arena. He stated once the nature of his foreign policy: "If you like a straight forward, honest policy, an independent policy is the best. Even in accepting economic help or in getting political help, it is not a wise policy to put all our eggs in one basket. Nor should we get help at the cost of our self-respect". To keep safe India's independence in the field of foreign policy and to get enough economic and military help from both East and West, Nehru found that the policy of non-alignment was the best means to achieve the goals. Therefore he introduced the policy of non-alignment in foreign affairs vigorously.

It has been claimed that the policy of non-alignment has its origin in India's traditional background and in the nature of national movement for India's independence. In an interview Nehru elaborated the policy and said, "We in India have evolved a foreign policy in keeping with the traditional background and temper of the country which also stands up to the needs of contemporary history. This provides it with strength and power beyond our economic or military potential". Moreover during the independence struggle, the Indian leaders like

Mahatma Gandhi and Jawaharlal Nehru keenly observed the role of Western countries and the Soviet Union in international arena. Their conflicting interests in world politics have led the Indian foreign policy-makers to follow an independent foreign policy from the very beginning. Nehru once stated, "We have tried to develop a certain attitude to the world called non-alignment or whatever you may call it. I should like you to remember that this policy has not suddenly come out of a hat. It had developed years before independence. It was natural, inevitable thing, both because of our thinking and because of our geography". Nehru vividly understood the international trend in late forties and said, 'I can understand some of the smaller countries of Europe or some of the smaller countries of Asia being forced by the circumstances to bow down before some of the greater powers and becoming practically satellites of those powers because they cannot help it. The power opposed to them is so great that they have nowhere to turn. But I do not think that consideration applies to India. During the later period Nehru came up with more distinct views regarding the origin of the policy and said, "I have not originated it. It is a policy inherent in the circumstances of India, inherent in the past thinking of India, inherent in the conditioning of the Indian mind during our struggle for freedom and inherent in the circumstances of the world today. I come in by the mere accidental fact that during these years I have represented that policy as foreign minister."

In 1947, when India got her independence and Nehru became its first Prime Minister, the cold war tensions between the West and the East were clearly visible. Therefore, in his first broadcast on foreign policy, Nehru carefully stated, "We propose, as far as possible, to keep away from the power politics of groups, aligned against one another, which have led in the past two world wars and which may lead again to disasters on an even vaster scale....." The contemporary international conditions led Nehru to vigorously defend and justify his policy of non-alignment. Nehru was against any type of exploitation and division of world into blocs. He made it clear, when he stated the aim of Indian foreign policy and said that India would work for "one world", a world in which there would be free cooperation of free peoples, and no class or groups would exploit another.

Nehru could realise that under the prevailing international conditions, India could not join hands with any one of the two big powers. This was essential not only for international peace, but also for socio-economic development of India. In 1947, India won her independence after the colonial rule of about 200 years. Naturally, during the late forties, it was a backward country, in need of aid to modernise its economy and defence. West was the main source of aid to India. But the lessons of national movement had taught the Indian leaders not to overlook the importance of the Soviet Union and the other socialist countries which could help the developing countries like India in their developmental process. Moreover, the policy of non-alignment was followed by India with an aim at avoiding another world war. Indian leaders had an experience of two world wars in the twentieth century. It was believed that the formation of conflicting power blocs had caused those world wars. Hence, the foreign policy makers in India carefully avoided the repetition of the process and discarded the military pacts like North Atlantic Treaty Organization (NATO), which was formed in 1949 under the US initiative.

As a theory the non-aligned policy was an ideal thought. But Nehru, as the first Prime Minister of India, faced many odds to implement the policy. In the beginning his non-aligned policy was not positively accepted by any of the big powers. He could not prove himself a reliable ally of the big powers and was severely criticised for not joining any side. Even the newly independent countries could not accept the justification of following a non-aligned policy, which was so staunchly put forward by Jawaharlal Nehru.

The first problem which Nehru faced as a Prime Minister of independent India was Indo-Pakistan conflict on Kashmir in 1947, when Pakistani tanks invaded Kashmir. India was virtually left a friendless country in the international forum. Western countries supported Pakistan, directly or indirectly and the Soviet Union did not participate in the United Nations' debate on Kashmir. But, in spite of these disadvantages and adverse international circumstances, Nehru did not give up his non-aligned policy. This strong posture during the crisis period helped him later in the fifties, when the non-aligned policy gradually got recognition by a few big powers and many developing countries.

In the fifties Nehru gradually broadened the scope of non-aligned policy. 'Peace' and 'Cooperation' were assumed as two important factors for the success of non-alignment. Under Nehru's leadership, India established friendly relations with the neighbouring countries and the leaders from big powers like Soviet Union and China visited India. Nehru also paid return visits. It is to be mentioned here that India was severely criticized in some quarters for its membership of

Commonwealth. But Nehru did not agree to withdraw India's membership from Commonwealth though he reserved India's right to take independent decisions suiting her national interests.

China is an important neighbour of India and a friendly relation with it has been India's basic policy. Though their relations were strained due to Tibet's incorporation with China in 1950, in 1954 both India and China signed Panchsheel, the five principles of peaceful cooperation — (1) Mutual respect for each other's territorial integrity and sovereignty; (2) Non-aggression; (3) Non-intervention in another's domestic affairs; (4) Mutual benefit and equality; and (5) Peaceful co-existence. Signing of Panchsheel was a remarkable achievement of non-aligned policy. China was a socialist country and was till then a member of monolithic socialist camp. Indeed, India's non-aligned role in Korean war only facilitated India's improved relations with the socialist group of countries. The Soviet leaders also visited India in 1955-56. Thus Nehru's non-aligned policy attracted international attention.

The success of the policy of non-alignment culminated in Bandung Conference of 1955. Along with Asian and African countries, socialist country — China and NATO member — Turkey, also attended it. The ten principles, which were adopted in this conference laid the foundation stone of non-aligned summit at Belgrade in 1961. The conference demanded freedom for all colonial people and condemned the policy of racialism. It appealed to the big powers to protect international peace and security. The other decisions and discussions of the Bandung Conference brought the Asian and African countries closer.

In 1961 the policy of non-alignment was institutionalised. About 25 Asian, African and Latin American countries met at Belgrade and confirmed their commitment to non-alignment, peace and security. They opposed colonialism, neo-colonialism, racism and arms race between the big powers. Nehru was one of the founding fathers of the non-aligned movement (NAM), but he made it clear that non-aligned countries did not aim at forming another bloc; rather they would prefer to be recognised as a third force.

Nehru's non-aligned policy was brought to a test in 1962 and faced a severe criticism within the country and outside during India-China border conflict of 1962. During the conflict India was practically left alone without a reliable supporting power in international arena. India's non-aligned policy could not guard it against being a victim of aggression. On the other hand the Western countries also tried to take advantage of the crisis. But Nehru did not agree to bow down either to Western or Eastern pressures. To strengthen his country he took economic and military help from both the blocs. He said once, "When there is crisis involving the possibility of war, the very fact that we are non-aligned should stir as to feel that more than ever it is up to us to do whatever we can to prevent such a calamity coming upon us." Thus Nehru's decisions during the crisis explain the flexible character of non-aligned policy.

The above discussion emphasises Nehru's understanding of non-aligned policy and his methods to practise it. To conclude, we can say that Pandit Nehru put forward a novel idea in international relations to find out a way in between the two conflicting blocs. His novel idea gave the world a new dimension and no one can question its relevance even today. Rather today the non-aligned movement has been strengthened with 102 developing countries of Asia, Africa, Latin America and Europe. Nehru's policy has turned into a movement today and the Ninth Summit of NAM at Belgrade has proved it and has given a new impetus, direction and life to the movement.

21

NEHRU AND SECULARISM

H.M. JAUHARI

We should remember that the British India was composed of India, Burma and Ceylon. Burma was first separated and thereafter Ceylon. However, the Britishers spread the communal virus all over India from the very first day, that means 1757, that unfortunate day when Sirajuddaulah, the Nawab of Bengal was defeated by Clive. If we look into the pages of history, we find how the East India Company started playing one community against the other. For a short period in 1857, the Britishers were overawed by the massive demonstration of Hindu-Muslim unity in 1857, during the First War of independence which the British historians, much to the chagrin of Indian revolutionaries and honest students of history depict as Sepoy Mutiny. The Viceroys, thereafter, watered the small plants of communal hatred which resulted in the partition of Bengal in 1905 on communal lines by Lord Curzon. But the great Lord had to swallow a humble pie soon thereafter and the united movement of Hindus and Muslims again got Bengal United — unfortunately the final division came in 1947. India was divided on religious basis — Pakistan representing the Muslims and India, the Britishers felt, representing the Hindus. But the machinations of the Britishers could not succeed primarily because of the two great stalwarts of secularism — Mahatma Gandhi and Pandit Jawaharlal Nehru. They strongly felt the need for the establishment of a secular state where religion could not be allowed to creep in the matters of administration and the running of the government. The word 'secularism', according to dictionary meaning, is an ideal where politics is completely separated from religion. Nehru himself says, 'the need of the moment is to secularise the intelligentsia at least and to proceed on secular lines in politics. . . how long that will take I cannot say. But religion in India will kill the country and its people, if it is not subdued'. In another speech he asks, "What is communalism itself? You may well have described Hindu communalism as Hindu nationalism and you would have been correct they came into conflict with each other". He concludes, "It is a strong sight with a moral that none can miss to see the Christian rulers of India pretending to become the bulworks of Hinduism and Islam".

Hence after assuming the Prime Ministership in 1947, Pandit Nehru laid a great emphasis on the secular aspect of the Government. Inside his own party there were various leaders who had communal ideals and who spoke many a time on religious strains. Nehru was very much against them. He writes to Kidwai in 1951, "We have to think outside our narrow grooves of thought and action and face the situation squarely. History has cast a role upon us and we cannot escape from it". He writes, to Dr. B.C. Roy on August 17, 1951, "If any person raises his hand to strike down another on the ground of religion, I shall fight him till the last breath of my life, both as the head of the Government and from outside".

In his fight against communalism, in his tireless endeavour to build a real secular state, Pandit Nehru finds himself a lonely man after the death of the Mahatma. The members of the Congress High Command were largely and inherently communal in their outlook, though they would seldom come out in the open. There came a critical moment in 1951, it is not known to many – Nehru wanted to resign. He said, "I regret to say that the President attaches more importance to his astrologers than to the advice of his Cabinet on some matters. I have no intention of submitting to the astrologers", (Nehru to N.G. Iyenger, September 22, 1951). Nehru wanted to have the Hindu Code Bill passed and to see that a Code Bill for Muslims should also be passed. But he failed to get the second one passed and here is one instance where he capitulated to the Muslim fundamentalists. M.C. Chagla in his autobiography writes, "Jawaharlal showed great strength and courage in getting the Hindu Reform Bill passed, but he accepted the policy of Laissez faire where the Muslims and other minorities were concerned. Jawaharlal deeply sympathised with the unfortunate conditions and situations of Muslim women and always spoke to his intimate ones his failures to do something positive for them."

Pandit Nehru always held that there would be no official religion in free India. He emphasised that belief was a private matter for each individual. He wanted secularism to be the cement of a new social contract binding together the multi-religious inhabitants of India into one political community – the integrated Indian — with religious faith having no bearing on civil, political or administrative rights.

contract binding together the multi-religious inhabitants of India into one political community — the integrated Indian — with religious faith having no bearing on civil, political or administrative rights.

22

NEHRU'S SOCIALISM — A Balanced Approach

N.K. GUPTA

Nehru was one of the chief figures who brought the independence struggle to a successful termination. He was onc of the indomitable fighters of Indian freedom who pioneered the concepts of complete independence, Indian Constituent Assembly and Socialism. His preeminent political position and power gave him the opportunity to put into execution some of his principal notions. In power for an unbroken period of eighteen years, he attempted to build the foundations of a strong democratic secular and socialist India.

Jawaharlal's short visit to Soviet Russia in November 1927 revealed to him the great achievements of that country in the field of education, female emancipation, the betterment of the conditions of peasants, workers etc. But in his book, *Soviet Russia*, written in 1928, Nehru refused to take any categorical attitude towards Russia. He considered what had happened and was taking place there, nevertheless, was an elemental and dramatic manifestation of human energy. Russia could be of interest in helping to find some solutions to the problems facing the World. Nehru was initially inspired by the Marxist approach to the cosmos and history. In his Autobiography he confessed that the communist philosophy of life gave him comfort and hope. It attempted to explain the past and offered hope for the future. Marxist ideas of freedom from religious dogma won the intellectual appreciation of the agnostic Nehru. The Marxist canon of historical interpretation, with its view of a developing pattern and its apocalyptic belief in the inevitable realization of a classless society appealed to Nehru. As a front rank nationalist leader and as a socialist intellectual he did of course swear by the idea of casteless and classless society but in his writings and speeches one misses the noble and crusading zeal of Kabir, Vivekanand, Gandhi and Lohia for removing this great evil. Marxism interested him, influenced him, but he never became a thoroughly convinced Marxist. Although in his Autobiography he confessed that Marxist attitudes to action deeply impressed him, it is doubtful if he would have felt delighted in the company of red military generals posing as the vanguard for an armed proletarian seizure of social and political power. He could never agree with authoritarian techniques of communism in action. He did not show much interest in the labour theory of value and the surplus value theory. Nehru agreed with Lenin's thesis that modern imperialism 'is the consequence of capitalist accumulation and its tendency to expansion.'

Gradually Nehru became disenchanted with communism when he found Russian aggressive expansion in Finland in 1939, the ghastly purges and bloody liquidations of triumphant Stalinism. In 1952, Nehru drove the communists almost mad with fury when he made the declaration that hundred years of development in the fields of philosophy, science and economic thought had rendered Marxism out of date. The growth of adult suffrage and trade union movement have brought to focus the democratic methods of social change and economic transformation. Even the capitalist systems of economy which Marx denounced have undergone transformations and hence the application of Marxist revolutionary ideas had to be carefully reconsidered in the light of transformation, in world politics and economics.

In his speeches in Singapore in June 1950, Nehru denounced the communist movement in Asia to be an enemy of Nationalism.

In the context of the Indian situation, Nehru had renounced his adherence to the sociology of class antagonism and struggle and, in the Gandhian manner, had stated that class struggle could be peacefully solved. Thus with the advance of years with the assumption of administrative responsibility and with the revelation of the devastating techniques of International Communism, Nehru's emotional leanings towards communism which were partly bred on account of his reactions against British Imperialism had considerably toned down if not absolutely withered away.

Nehru's socialism is an improvised and modified approach to suit the tenets of democracy and to solve the socio-economic problems inherent in a traditional society aspiring for rapid economic growth and modernization. He was a great visionary and planner. In May

1929 he resolved that in order to remove the poverty and misery of the Indian people and to ameliorate the conditions of the masses, it is essential to make revolutionary changes in the present economic and social structure of society and remove gross inequalities. This was not fully an acceptance of socialism but indicated an approval of the socialist approach.

In March, 1931, the Congress at its Karachi session passed an important resolution on fundamental rights and its economic programme in which among other things a clear statement was made to the effect that the state shall own or control key industries and services, mineral resources, railways, waterways, shipping and other means of transport. Nehru supported the *Swadeshi* movement and gave emphasis on agrarian reforms and improvement of the condition of industrial workers.

Rapid changes in international events deeply influenced Nehru in shaping his brand of socialism. Economic planning at a national level had already started in the USSR in 1927. A Fascist government had been established in Italy in the middle twenties and a Nazi government in Germany in the early thirties. It was a time of conflicting movements which found expression in the civil war in Spain. These developments reflected in the emergence of an influential group of socialists even within the Congress. Jawaharlal Nehru was deeply conscious of the dangers of following the path of fascism, notwithstanding its transitory game and it was his constant endeavour to direct political and economic thinking in India along the channels of integrated national planning on socialist lines as suited to the needs and gains of the Indian people. Nehru as chairman of the National Planning Committee set up in October 1938 gave a decisive turn to thinking on economic problems in India. He believed that the organisation of economic life must conform to the principles of justice to the end that it might secure a decent standard of living.

His aim was to build a free and democratic state in which the fundamental rights of the individual and the group – political, economic, social and cultural would be guaranteed. The state would be progressive and would utilize the scientific and other knowledge for the advancement of the people as a whole and for the promotion of their happiness and their material as well as cultural and spiritual well being. It would not permit the exploitation of the community by individuals or groups to the disadvantage of the former and to the injury of the nation as a whole. To realise the social objectives the state must plan and coordinate the various activities of the nation so as to avoid waste and conflict and attain the maximum results.

The principle of state ownership or control over key industries and services, minerals, public transport and defence industries was clearly accepted with possibility of extension of all public utilities and large scale industries. The cottage industries were to be encouraged and protected and competition prevented for large scale industries. Planning was to deal with production, distribution, consumption, trade, social services, income and investment and other forms of national activity which act and react on each other. These were the big decisions on which Nehru built his edifice of socialistic pattern of society and got the same enforced in the post independence era. The aim was to lay sound foundations for a continuing increase in the level of national income and the level of living to get rid of the fear of unemployment and to bring about increasing equality of opportunities and the lessening of great disparities of income and wealth. He emphasized on the rapid development of heavy machine building, heavy electricals, steel and non-ferrous metals and energy to supply a sound foundation for economic self-reliance.

He wanted close inter-locking of progress in industry and agriculture. Industrial development was essential to provide an increasing supply of fertilizers, pesticides, machinery and equipment for agriculture, irrigation, drainage and land improvement. An increase in agricultural production was essential to supply additional food and raw materials for industrial progress.

To him there was always a need for increasing the supply of scientific and technical personnel and expanding facilities for training them. He always took a keen interest in science and technology in general. It was due to his personal interest that a large number of national laboratories were established and large resources were made available for the development of atomic energy and the exploration and exploitation of oils and minerals in one public sector. He created the infrastructure conducive to the training and expansion of scientific and technical manpower.

His attitude to foreign aid was favourable so far as it did not mean alien influence in economic affairs. He had no objection to foreign loans and aids provided these were intended to assist economic development and were given in the form which would not give rise to any foreign influence in Indian affairs.

On the agrarian side too ever since 1947 a revolution has been under way. The basis of all India land reform is one simple slogan "All land to the tiller". The cooperative movement and several other schemes initiated by the govt. helped to eliminate the middleman – exploitation of the money-lender and gave hope to the small farmer and landless labourer. Democratic decentralization or the Panchayati Raj was innovated to make the villagers self-reliant and self-sufficient. 'Planning from below has strengthened the democracy at the grass root level'.

Nehru had unflinching faith in democratic institutions and constitutional methods. He wholeheartedly subscribed to the idea of welfare state accepted by Pigou. He was committed to the theory and practice of mixed economy. The concept has been operationalised by the Five Year Plans.

In short I firmly believe that Nehru's socialism which can be termed as 'Nehruist' will always provide the rest of the underdeveloped world with a pattern of development which will make communism or state socialism look both old fashioned and barbarian by comparison. It is rather a special form of socialism whose emphasis is on equality rather than on state ownership of the means of production, distribution and exchange. It attaches more importance to people's consent and cooperation than to anything else.

SECTION V

FREEDOM MOVEMENT AND THE PERSONALITY OF NEHRU

23

FORTIETH ANNIVERSARY OF INDIAN INDEPENDENCE

N.B. DAS GUPTA

Here we attend a seminar on a day — May 8, 1989 that happily coincides with the 128th birthday of our great poet Rabindranath Tagore who has always been a constant source of inspiration to our freedom fighters through his stories, novels, essays, poems and songs. We take this opportunity to honour him and pay him our humble homage.

I specially remember and honour to-day the millions of patriots who sacrificed themselves silently for the cause of their motherland, and who are to-day unsung and unheard of.

In this connection I may remember to-day one essay by Rabindranath, History of India, written in 1909. Rabindranath refers to certain limitations of our study of history. History, he says, is often the record of leaders and heroes, their achievements, successes and glories. It is seldom the record of the people; it is seldom the record of the suffering humanity. At the same time he draws our attention to the spirit of India — the spirit that unites us — the spirit that has united the Aryans, the Shakas, the Huns, the Pathans, the Mangols and the Dravidians. Here is also a definite pointer to the fact that this spirit of unity has failed to have its impact on the Britishers—a fact to which our attention has been drawn by Marx.

Herein lie the limitations of the various histories of our freedom movement; herein lie the areas either ignored or merely touched upon, which require special study and herein lies the need of a new and bold perspective. What is happening to-day is that our young students go through some distorted and sometimes scissored pages of freedom movement. The history that is presented to us is through an elitist approach, and we are made to believe that our freedom struggle was the struggle of the English educated 'middle class', set to create a renaissance with the ideals of patriotism, nationalism and democracy for liberty from the foreign yoke. The masses—the common people, the peasant, the working-class—are thus either ignored or just referred to; whereas the fact is that no freedom-movement can be successful unless it goes beyond the elite-intellectual barriers and confines. The historian is called upon to study the entire society; the social history must be enquired into — the various classes are to be looked into. Naturally the economic history becomes of vital importance. Unless we know the eighteenth and nineteenth century trade, finance, labour, revenue and land policies, and the various stratas of agrarian relationships, how can we analyse satisfactorily the various peasant and tribal movements like those of Birsa Munda, Phadke, Moplas and others. Again, in order to understand the various shades of communal and caste problems, we must have a thorough study of the social relationships of our country and the various social and religious movements during the last 250 years. Lastly we must refer to the most neglected part of our freedom struggle — the revolutionaries — starting from Mangal Pande and down to the R.I.N. heroes — without whose sacrifices, the freedom that we enjoy to-day, could have hardly been possible.

The Europeans came to India to fleece the golden bird. The Portuguese, the Dutch, the French and the English fought against one another to gain supremacy. India was in a state of disintegration. The trading-class wanted to have peace with the East India Company and its representatives Raja Raj Ballabh, Umichand, Jagat Seth and others, remained as silent spectators when Lord Clive defeated Nawab Sirajuddaula in the Battle of Plassey in 1757 and installed Mirjafar as the Nawab of Bengal. The government of Clive spread its tentacles far and wide and let loose unbridled exploitation. Indian textiles which had a high market in foreign lands, were banned for export, the Indian artisans were mercilessly persecuted and Indian market was flooded with cheap Manchester Cotton. Indigo plantation was developed; opium was exported to China — very rapid expansion of export trade started — of Punjab wheat, Bengal jute, Assam tea, oilseeds, hides and skin. There was open and merciless loot and exploitations. Marx very beautifully and correctly pointed out the three successive phases of British exploitation of India. Direct plunder of Indian masses marked the first phase — the period ranging from 1757 to 1813 — the period of the Company's monopoly trade. Indian finished goods were purchased at a very low price and exported to Europe. The English Merchant obtained the required money for the purchase from public revenues. The Second phase started with the Industrial Revolution and the consequent capitalist exploitation — 'the homeland of cotton was inundated with cotton'. The third phase started after 1858 when British Business Houses, export-import firms and banks began to operate. This is the phase of finance-imperialism. Thus the wealth of India systematically drained out. Agriculture was impoverished. The Britishers helped the *mahajans* and the landlords — the princes, Nawabs and Zamindars. It has been very aptly pointed out by Danial Thorner, "In no other period of Indian history, can we find so large, so well-established, and so secure a group of landholders as that which grew up and flourished between the 1790s and 1940s".

Here, we must also remember the rise of the Indian Capitalist: The Indian capitalist mainly consisted of Parsis in Bombay, Vanias in Gujarat and Marwaries in Bengal and Chattairs in the South. Some new collaborations could also be seen — Goenkas and Ralli Brothers, Jhujhunwalla and Grahams, Ghanashyamdas and Shaw Wallace, Jatia and Andrew Yule and others. The rise of capitalism naturally brought in the existence of the working-class, that played such vital role in the freedom-struggle-though that positive role is often minimised by the interested class-historians. How many of us are aware of the fact that the first working-class strike took place on May 12, 1827, when the palanquin bearers in Calcutta staged a successful strike for the improvement of their rates? The boatsmen and *mallahs* and the cab-drivers of Calcutta also staged a solidarity strike and in the afternoon, a long procession of all met at the *maidan* under the presidentship of a palanquin-bearer. The second recorded strike was organised by the Railway Coolies of Howrah Station with the dual demand of eight-hour work and regulated rate of payment.

When the summit of British exploitation was reached, people—not the well educated elite—but the common people started revolting. The Great Revolt of 1857 was engineered by the Indian soldiers under British employment. Besides having their own grievances the Sepoys and Sowars (Cavalry) shared the general discontentment of the people. Soldiers, irrespective of their caste, creed and religion — without exception — rose in revolt. Trouble started first in Barrackpore, Bengal and Mangal Pande, the first hero to defy the British Rule was executed. Meerut rose next, the Sepoys were court-martialled and jailed. They were set free by their comrades who raised the slogan — 'Delhi Chalo'. The Sepoys reached Bahadurshah — secured his support. Gradually the soldiers of Mathura, Kanpur and Allahabad and Western Bihar joined the fray. The Revolt brought out new leaders — Nana Sahib, Tatya Tope, Rani of Jhansi. Short-lived free governments were set up. But after initial successes, when the British fought with their back to the wall, the revolutionaries lost their strength — and the tide slowly turned against them. Bahadur Shah surrendered. Kanpur, Lucknow, Jhansi and Gwalior fell. The Great Revolt was crushed; but revolution triumphed. A new spirit of patriotism lurked in every human breast.

Here, in passing, we must mention some other heroic movements of the masses. The most militant of these came from the tribals. The tribals are very much a part of Indian society. They belong to the lowest stratum of the peasantry. They are mostly engaged in cultivation – of course landless; some of them are recruited as coolies to work in mines, factories and distant plantations. They are mostly found in Chota Nagpur in Bihar, in Assam hills, in Gujarat, in Visakhapattanam, in Andhra and the Madhya Pradesh. Of the many tribal revolts, the most outstanding and inspiring is of Birsa Munda of Ranchi. The Mundas were mercilessly exploited by *jagirdars* and *thikadars* — aided by the corrupt British administration. When all their appeals and prayers were turned down by the benevolent British Sarkar, they organised themselves under the inspiring leadership of Birsa Munda. Birsa asked his men always to be prepared with their bows and arrows. Mundas were all prepared for the final assault. They burnt the effigies of the British Raj and sang:

" 'O father, kill the Europeans, kill the other castes — Kill, Kill...."

The Mundas started fighting on Christmas Eve, 1899 — and tried to burn down Churches in Ranchi and Singhbhum. The Police stormed Ranchi and the adjoining forests. The armed and violent struggle — on one side arrows and bows, and on the other the latest sophisticated weapons — went on till January 9, 1900 and Birsa was captured. Birsa died in jail — some of his comrades were hanged and many others sent to the Andaman.

In Maharashtra, Vasudeo Balwant Phadke collected some peasants and raised armed protests against forcible taxation. His followers included Brahmins, Ramoshis and Dhangars. After his capture and life sentence, his followers found another leader named

Danlata Ramoshi. Bengal and Bihar got the severe taste of Indigo Rebellion. Here we find a brilliant unity of Hindus and Muslims. European planters of Indigo engaged Indians on a slight pittance and used them as slaves. Ultimately, when the torture and exploitation became unbearable, the people refused to submit to forced cultivation. The planters were attacked; their bungalows burnt and some of them were manhandled and killed. The Calcutta Vernacular Press publicised the struggle; Dinabandhu Mitra wrote a drama — Neel Darpan – which was staged widely. It was translated by Father Long into English. The British government ultimately set up an Indigo Commission. The Commission spoke against the English Planters.

Another rebellion of merit was of Moplahs. The Moplahs, are the Muslims of Malabar; they revolted against their landlords. These landlords were mostly Hindus and they were regularly aided by the British Raj. The British Raj tried to transform the rebellion into a communal issue. But the Moplah rebellion was essentially agrarian in nature as were the Deccan Riots towards the end of the last century. The Pabna League in Bengal was another such movement. These were no-revenue movements. In many of these movements — there was a high degree of harmony and unanimity between the two communities — Hindus and Muslims. Both communal and caste consciousness was there, but a proper study of facts reveal that in moments of distress and revolt — all differences were forgotten.

There was large scale discontentment everywhere. The discontentment gave rise to social reforms. In Bengal there was the Brahmo Samaj, and later on the Ramakrishna Mission — with its Visionary Sanyasi Swami Vivekananda. In Punjab there was the Arya Samaj — the founder being Swami Dayanand Saraswati. In Bombay and Poona there were Ranade and K.T., Telang. In Madras there was the young Madras Party. These organisations helped in the spread of education and collective consciousness in the middle-class. Many of these movements were fundamentalist and revivalist in character — which often contributed to the assertion of an aggressive Hindu identity. At the same time fundamentalist trends in Islam were also visible. The U.P. Muslim landlords were scared of the rising Hindu *mahajan* and trading community and organised themselves under the leadership of Sir Sayyid Ahmed who had started the Anglo-Mohammadan Oriental College in Aligarh. Two heroes of the 1857 Revolt Md. Qasim Nanawtawi and Rashid Ahmed Gangohi founded the Deoband Darul Ulam. Thus education was spread among the upper and middle classes of the two communities. However Deoband attracted ordinary muslims and became a seat of anti-British temper—but Aligarh was pro-British and largely anti-Hindu. The British Raj took advantage of the Muslim animosity to Hindu and carried on successfully its Divide and Rule Policy.

The English-educated elite of India — mostly located in Bombay and Calcutta formed the nucleus of the Congress leadership. It came into existence at Bombay in December 1885 with some moderate demands and without any pretension to be anti-British. For three days each year, the Congress met — in a way it was an exhilarating social gathering — ridiculed by the revolutionaries as a *'tamasha'*. High caste Hindus, big zamindars and industrialists flocked at Congress sessions and passed certain pious resolutions without causing any embarrassment to the British Raj. However, this could not last for long. Young enthusiasts in Bombay, Calcutta, Punjab and Madras — men like Tilak, Surendra Nath Banerjee, Motilal Ghosh, Lajpat Rai, T. Prakasam, Krishna Rao and others tried to bring in new blood and new consciousness to the already sterile Congress. In Bengal, disillusionment with Congress was complete. Aurobindo Ghosh, Ashwini Kumar Dutta and Bipin Chandra Pal started the Swadeshi Movement in 1905. Rabindranath enthused and inspired the people of Bengal through his poems and songs. Tilak in Bombay and Poona launched the Boycott Movement, with memorable words : 'We will not achieve any success if we croak once a year like a frog' and further addressed the working class — "Though down-trodden and neglected, you must be conscious of your power of making the administration impossible if you but choose to make it so. It is you who manage the railroad and the telegraph, it is you who make settlements and collect revenues...'. Thus the Congress was coming out of its shell — new voices were heard with new possibilities.

The partition of Bengal brought the *Swadeshi* and the Boycott movements at their highest peak. Lord Curzon brought in the partition with the imperialist motive to perpetuate the colonial system by alienating Muslims from the main anti-British current. He assured the Bengali Muslims — 'the prospect of unity which they have not enjoyed since the days of the old Mussalman Viceroys and Kings'. On the day of partition, i.e. October 16, 1905, Rabindranath moved out of his house with *Rakhis* and tied them in the hands of every Muslim that he met. Thus *Raksha-Bandhan* symbolised the unity of Hindus and Muslims. In an unprecedented move for unity, the whole of Bengal observed *'Arandhan'* on that day. The hearth of every house in Bengal was kept unlit — another symbolic protest against partition. People moved through the streets of Bengal chanting 'Vande-Mataram' and the patriotic songs of Rabindranath. People arranged bonfires of British cloth; small-scale indigenous industries were set up. The labour was also not sitting idle. A series of strikes in Calcutta and other places marked the active participation of the working class in the National Movement. The first real Labour Union – the Printers Union was set up on October 21, 1905 and a strike followed in government presses. Railwaymen's Union was formed in July 1906 and the Jamalpur workers, on strike, were fired upon. A leader exclaimed 'The workers of Russia are to-day teaching the world the methods of effective protest in times of repression — will not the Indian Workers learn from them?'

The efforts of British Raj to break the united *Swadeshi* and Boycott movement did not succeed. Muslim associates and leaders like Liakat Hussain, Abul Hussain, Deedar Bux, Abdul Gafur fought against the Raj unitedly with their Hindu brethren. Of course, the big landlords and the budding capitalists of both the communities remained cautiously aloof from the movement. Rabindranath, once again, warned the Congress against the elitist-intellectual-middle-class approach. He called upon the leaders to bridge the gulf that separated them from the masses — "a great ocean separates us educated few from millions of our country".

Meanwhile, revolutionaries were grouping themselves in different provinces. In Bengal, the leading groups were *Anushilan* and *Yugantar*. A group of firebrands comprising of Barin Ghosh (Aurobindo's brother), Bhupendranath Dutta (Swami Vivekananda's brother) and Hemchandra Kanungo made secret plans to remove the British Raj. Hemchandra went abroad and took training in arms and bombs from a Russian emigre in Paris. Kshudiram Basu and Prafulla Chaki murdered Kennedy — while trying to remove Kingsford. The whole group, including Aurobindo, was arrested. The great sacrifice of Kshudiram and Prafulla enthused and inspired the common people of Bengal. In U.P. only in Banaras, the revolutionaries could organise themselves under the leaderships of Sachindranath Sanyal — who very successfully recruited a brilliant revolutionary — Sunder Lal. In Punjab, many youngmen protested against the prosecution of the Punjabee; there were mass protests, demonstrations and attacks on Englishmen in Lahore. Several strikes were organised — the strike of the Revenue Clerks and then the North-Western State Railway strike. In Maharashtra — mass picketing of liquor shops was organised; the working-class was contacted and it was brought to the arena of struggle. The Nasik-based Abhinava Bharat group got pistols from V.D. Savarkar who sent them from London. The Nasik District Magistrate was killed in 1909.

The partition of Bengal was abrogated in 1911, but revolutionary activities were on onward march. Rash Behari Bose and Sachindranath Sanyal successfully spread out their anti-British organisation from Bengal to U.P., Delhi and Punjab. A bomb-attack was attempted on Hardinge when he was making his official entry into Delhi on December 23, 1912. Indian revolutionaries organised themselves in London — Shyamji Krishan Verma, V.D. Savarkar and Madan Lal Dhingra being the prominent personalities. In Paris, Geneva and Berlin also groups were formed — Madam Cama and Virendranath Chattopadhyaya were the leaders of these centres.

A special mention must be made of the Ghadr Party. The Ghadr movement was started in San Francisco in 1913. A weekly *'Ghadr'* was brought out. The top leadership included Sohan Singh Bhakna and Har Dayal. The first issue stated : 'What is our name? The Ghadr (Revolution). In what does our work consist ? in bringing about a rising. Where this rising will break out? In India. When will it break out — in a few years'. There was activity all around. Hyndman, the British Marxist addressed meetings at Indian House. Har Dayal wrote the earliest Indian article on Karl Marx — in the *Calcutta Modern Review* of March 1912. The Ghadr Party arranged to send arms to India. The arms were to be received by Rash Behari Bose, Sachindranath Sanyal and Jyotindranath Mukherjee. The Komagata Maru incident took place on September 29, 1914. At Budge-Budge in Calcutta, the Sikhs and Punjabi Muslims were killed. The plan fell through. Bose fled to Japan, Sachin Sanyal was transported for life, while Bagha Jatin — or Jyotindranath Mukherjee sacrificed himself after fighting a heroic battle with the British at Balasore in Orissa. Further efforts to send arms were made by Har Dayal, Mahendra Pratap, Obeidullah Sindhi and Bhupen Dutta. But the efforts proved abortive. In the Ghadr trials 46 revolutionaries were executed. Great were the last words of Kartar Singh Sarabha — a 19-year old lad — "If I had to live more lives than one — I would sacrifice each of them for my country's sake".

Mahatma Gandhi entered the Indian political arena during the war years. He came with his celebrated weapon of *Satyagraha* which he successfully practised in South Africa. He won the people of India by his sweet persuasiveness, by his invincible faith in Truth and *Ahimsa* and by his indomitable courage. Gandhi did not like the extremists like Tilak, Lajpat Rai and Bipin Chandra Pal. He first concentrated on specific grievances — campaigning against the 'indenture' system; fought for the Indigo cultivators of Champaran; led a successful *satyagraha* in the Kheda district in Gujarat. He wanted the capitalists and industrialists to work for the masses and succeeded in bringing a settlement between the mill-owners and the workers in Ahmedabad.

The first global war further impoverished the Indian economy. There was all round famine and hunger. Living standards of the common people fell sharply. But fabulous profits accumulated in the hands of the Business groups — the top of them being G.D. Birla, Swarupchand, Hukumchand, Goenka, Tata, Walchand, Hira Chand, Ambalal Sarabhai, Kasturbhai Lalbhai and others. The new strength of Indian capitalism wanted close involvement with nationalist politics for its survival against the possible labour unrest. G.D. Birla, Ambalal Sarabhai, Jamnalal Bajaj and several others became votaries of Gandhi and contributed liberally to Congress funds. The class character of the Congress was amply demonstrated. The post-war years saw the real start of the Trade Union movement. The October Revolution brought message, life and enthusiasm to the suffering humanity. Mahendra Pratap, M.N. Roy, Abani Mukherjee, Virendranath Chattopadhyaya and Bhupen Dutt went to Moscow. Some of them met Lenin and Trotsky and discussed with them the problems of India. The Soviet Union became a source of great inspiration to the toiling masses of India.

The British Raj introduced the Rowlatt Act on March 18, 1919. People were restive. They wanted to react violently against this pernicious act. Gandhiji wanted to organise a mass protest. Swami Shradhanand suggested for a no-revenue call. But the suggestion was turned down by Gandhiji. Dinshaw Wacha did not like the idea of mass-protest; he requested Gandhiji only to make a petition against the Act. Gandhiji told him — "the growing generation will not be satisfied with petitions, etc.... *Satyagraha* is the only way, it seems to me, to stop terrorism."

However, people resorted spontaneously to mass protests and hartals. Peace was disturbed in the Punjab, Ahmedabad, Delhi and

Calcutta. Punjab was the most affected province — where a tremendous unity of Hindu, Sikh and Muslim — frightened the British Raj, represented by General Dyer. Saifuddin Kitchlew and Satyapal were deported from Amritsar and Gandhiji was asked not to enter Delhi or Punjab. On April 13, 1919, an unarmed mass, ignorant of the proclaimed Martial Law, was suddenly attacked in Jallian Wallah Bagh — and butchered by the orders of General Dyer. Unofficial assessment stated some 2000 killed, while the official estimate spoke of 379 killed. The grim tragedy of Jalian Wallah Bagh silenced everybody. Rabindranath voiced the agony and anger of the Indian through his famous letter renouncing his knighthood. Gandhiji accepted the Satyagraha to be a 'Himalayan Blunder' and declared that 'Cooperation in any shape or form with this satanic government is sinful'.

In March 1920, Gandhiji gave a call for non-violent non-cooperation. Labour and peasant unrest surfaced themselves everywhere. The first session of the All India Trade Union Congress was held on October 31, 1920 — presided over by Lajpat Rai and attended by Motilal Nehru, Vithalbhai Patel, Annie Besant and M.A. Jinnah. Gandhiji did not attend, nor did he, send any message. In fact, he had entirely different notions about the working-class. He had established his Majdur Mahajan at Ahmedabad and he wanted the industrialists to be the trustees of the interests of the working-class. Kisan Movements started in Bihar, U.P., Bengal and in the South.

The non-violent, non-co-operation movement was, however, called off after the incidents of Chauri-Chaura. Gandhiji declared — "I would suffer every humiliation, every torture, absolute ostracism and death itself to prevent the movement becoming violent."

Here we must refer to the emergence of the Indian Communists, who played some very vital part in the freedom struggle. At first, most of the Communists came from the national struggle; there were some disillusioned extremists. The first name that comes to mind is that of M.N. Roy — previously known as Naren Bhattacharyya of the Yugantar group. Roy met Borodin — in Mexico in 1919; had a hand in the foundation of the Communist Party of Mexico. He went to Russia to attend the Second Commintern International; met Lenin and Trotsky and discussed with them the Indian problems. The main problem was that of the 'National Bougeoisie' of India; Lenin had differences with Roy regarding the Indian National Bourgeoisie.

Lenin felt that the Indian National Bourgeoisie had yet a vital role to play in the Indian emancipation movement. History proved that Lenin's approach was correct. In October 1920, M.N. Roy with Abani Mukherjee, Mohammad Ali and Mohammad Shafiq founded a Communist Party of India in Tashkent. Later he went to Berlin where he was joined by Bhupen Dutta, Virendranath Chattopadhyaya and Barkatullah. The same year three prominent Ghadr revolutionaries Rattan Singh, Santokh Singh and Teja Singh Swatantra joined the Communist Party.

M.N. Roy could establish secret links with the separate young Communist groups in India through Nalini Gupta and Shaukat Usmani. These groups operated in four big cities — Bombay-leader S.A. Dange; Calcutta leader Muzaffar Ahmed; Madras (Singaravelu) and Lahore (Ghulam Hussain). *Atmashakti* and *Dhumketu* (editor Nazrul Islam) came out in Calcutta and Guntur brought out *Nayayuga*. The Indian Communists were regular members of the National Congress. In the Gaya Congress in 1922, Singaravelu severely condemned the Bardoli retreat.

The British Raj was very much afraid of the Communists. It jailed S.A. Dange, Shaukat Usmani, Nalini Gupta and Muzaffar Ahmed in the Kanpur Bolshevik case. The first open Indian Communist conference was held in Kanpur in December 1925, and this, at present, is acknowledged as the formal foundation of the Indian Communist Party. The party began sincere work in the labour and Kisan fronts-though there was a paucity of party cadres. M.N. Roy very clearly laid down the party's priorities in 1924:

> "The immediate task of the communists in India is not to preach communism but to organise the national revolution; the role of the Communist Party of India is to be the heart and soul of the revolutionary nationalist party."

In the twenties, revolutionaries mustered their strength in Bengal, U.P. and Punjab. In Bengal, the killing of Englishmen was a daily occurrence. In U.P., Sachin Sanyal, Jogesh Chatterjee and Ram Prasad Bismil organised the Hindusthan Republican Association. The Kakori case took place in August 1925 and many of the HRA's important members were arrested. The new recruits were there; they moved under the leadership of Ajoy Ghosh — (General Secretary of the C.P.I. for some years after independence). Ajoy Ghosh established contacts with the brilliant young revolutionary, Bhagat Singh – the founder of the Hindusthan Socialist Republican Army in 1928. Other associates of Bhagat Singh were Chandra Sekhar Azad, Rajguru, Sukhdev and others. Bhagat Singh had a singularly Marxist commitment. In 1928 Bhagat Singh killed Saunders in Lahore — the British Police Officer responsible for the death of Lajpat Rai. He and Batukeshwar Dutta threw bombs into the Central Legislative Assembly. The H.S.R.A. organised the Nawjawan Bharat Sabha and through the Sabha tried to spread its message to the masses. Bhagat Singh made his approach clear in his trial. He said that he wanted to bring about a total change to the existing society culminating in the overthrow of the British Raj and the Indian Capitalism and securing the establishment of the Dictatorship of the Proletariat. His last brave words were — "Revolution is the inalienable right of mankind. Freedom is the imprescriptible birth right of all. The labourer is the real sustainer of society. To the altar of this revolution we have brought our youth as incense, for no sacrifice is too great for so magnificent a cause. We are content. We await the advent of revolution. *'Inquilab Zindabad'"*. Meanwhile Jatin Das who taught the soldiers of H.S.R.A. the technique of bomb-making, died in Lahore Jail on the 64th day of his hunger-strike. He had undertaken this hunger-strike as a protest against the maltreatment of prisoners in jails.

Another, unforgettable revolutionary upsurge was witnessed in Chittagong. The Chittagong group of revolutionaries, under the able leadership of Surya Sen — popularly known as Master-da, created a new history by capturing the Chittagong Armoury and proclaimed independence. For four days, the first free government on the Indian soil operated with a cry 'Gandhiji's Raj has come'. There was pitched battle on Jalalabad Hill on April 22, 1930. Twelve Revolutionaries were killed, Surya Sen escaped and continued guerrilla warfare for another three years. Finally he was arrested in 1933 and executed. Others like Ganesh Ghosh, Ambika Chakravarty and Kalpana Dutt were transported for life. After release they all joined the Communist Party of India.

Congress politics took a new turn in the thirties. It gradually moved towards the left. In the Lahore Congress of 1929, Jawaharlal Nehru declared the goal of Congress to be full independence. Meeting on January 2, 1930, the Congress Working Committee decided that January 26 should be observed as the day of Complete Independence. The Civil Disobedience Movement under the leadership of Gandhiji started on March 12, 1930. The movement continued for too long a period and it generally petered away when, in May 1933, Gandhiji suspended it. Nehru's comments are worth remembering.

> "The initial push of inspiration was far less than in 1930. It was as if we entered unwillingly into battle. There was a glory about it in 1930 which had faded a little two years later".

The growing economic depression led many Congressmen to lose faith in capitalism and they came to agree with Jawaharlal Nehru that socialism 'held the key to the solution of the world's problems'. Some young Congressmen embraced the ideals of socialism and formed the Congress Socialist Party. The prominent members of this group were Jayaprakash Narayan, Acharya Narendra Dev, Ram Manohar Lohia and Yusuf Meharally. They became active on the Kisan and Labour fronts. On both these fronts the official Congress leadership was playing a hide and seek game. The Leftists organised the U.P. and Bihar Kisans to fight against the atrocities of Zamindars, and asked them not to pay rent to the landlords. Gandhiji advised them — "let me warn you against listening to the advice if it has reached you that you have no need to pay the Zamindars or talukdars any rent at all". But the Kisans heeded him not. Hence in 1936, the U.P. leadership advocated the abolition of Zamindari — at least in theory. In the South also, Kisan Sabhas were being successfully organised by Prof. N.G. Ranga and Sri A.K. Gopalan.

Meanwhile, the Rightists were not sitting idle. They consolidated their position with their money-bag satraps at their back. Jawaharlal Nehru's Lucknow address, glorifying socialism and the Soviet Union was not liked by the Bombay Business group — H.P. Mody, Walchand Hirachand, Shroff and others. But G.D. Birla pacified them. He wrote to Purushottam Das Thakurdas — "Mahatmaji kept his promise . . . he saw that no new commitments were made. Jawaharlalji's speech in a way was thrown into the wastepaper basket . . . Jawaharlalji seems to be like a typical English Democrat . . . out for giving expression to his ideology, but he realises that action is impossible and so does not press for it. Things are moving in the right direction". During the next few years, Indian capitalists took more and more interest in the Congress. Rightists like Bhulabhai Desai, B.C. Roy, Vallabhbhai Patel and Rajendra Prasad openly helped G.D. Birla, Mody, Walchand Hirachand,

Purushottam Das Thakurdas, Jatia and Khemka to further their business interests. They were having lip sympathy with the working-class and the peasantry. The irony of the situation was that on foreign policy the Congress was left decrying the rise of fascism, but internally it was behaving somewhat otherwise. It was also involved into factional struggles. Subhas Bose won the Presidential election at Tripura by a vast majority, but with the defeat of Pattabhi Sitaramyya, Gandhiji declared 'Pattabhi's defeat is my defeat.' The old working Committee resigned; Nehru was indecisive as usual. Subhas failed to nominate a new Working Committee. Pant Resolution was passed in the steering Committee expressing confidence in the old Working Committee. Bose resigned and formed a separate party of no consequence. The Second World War was declared. Bose finally left India incognito, went to Germany and Japan and formed the Indian National Army which played such a vital role in achieving India's independence.

Gandhiji gave a clarion call to Indians to do or die. His words on passing the Quit India Resolution are memorable:

> "Every one of you should from this moment onwards consider yourself a free man or woman and act as if you are free. I am not going to be satisfied with anything short of complete freedom. We shall do or die. We shall either free India or die in the attempt."

The whole of India rose in revolt. There were hartals, strikes and clashes with the police, First the cities and urban areas were affected. But soon the fire spread to the countryside — U.P., Bihar and Midnapur in Bengal carried on the struggle relentlessly. Brutal oppression was unleashed. Secret parallel governments were established in Tamluk in Midnapore, Satara in Maharashtra and Talchar in Orissa. The Tamluk Jatiya Sarkar survived till September 1944. Lord Linlithgo had to order the use of machine-guns in and around Patna, and aeroplanes were used in Bhagalpur and Moongher in Bihar, Nadia and Tamluk in Bengal and Talchar in Orissa.

The war ended with the victory of the allies. The Indian National Army under the leadership of Netaji Bose reached the soil of India when the war came to an end. Bose disappeared, and it is believed that he died in a plane crash. The I.N.A. men were taken prisoners and they were put on trial.

But now, India was actually 'on the edge of a volcano'.

Everywhere there was united mass action — the I.N.A. Release Movement, the Rashid Ali Day in Calcutta, the R.I.N. Revolt, the Tebhagha andolon, the Telengana upsurge. The whole country was in a state of mass agony, turmoil; the whole country seeking a radical change. And the change came there in the shape of Partition of our body.

Yes, we have achieved freedom; we are proud of our country and our achievements. What we want is a proper appraisal of our freedom movement. We must recognise the fact that our freedom is the achievement of the various struggles in various parts of our vast land. Our history books should enumerate all the struggles launched to free the country. For example, the roles of the revolutionaries have seldom been properly appreciated. The R.I.N. Mutiny has been very scantily mentioned; perhaps if the R.I.N. Revolt could get the support of our national leaders, the country might have been saved from being partitioned. Seldom is the Hindu-Muslim unity so brilliantly displayed as in the I.N.A. release movements and in the R.I.N. upsurge. The R.I.N. Revolt had involved 78 ships, 20 shore establishments, more than 29000 ratings participated. The last message still rings in our ears, enthuses us and inspires us —

> "Our strike has been a historic event in the life of our Nation. For the first time the blood of men in the services and in the streets flowed together in a common cause. We in the services will never forget this. We know also that you, our brothers and sisters, will not forget. Long live our great people! Jai Hind."

We pay our deep homage to all the martyrs of our land, who have laid down their lives for the cause of our mother's freedom.

24

NEHRU ON EDUCATION

J.L. RAINA

One of the interesting aspects of Nehru's personality is that during the course of his eventful life he exercised his mind on virtually every vital issue concerning man's development and growth as a distinct social being. Soon after his return from England, he rejected to play the predetermined role of a lawyer that his father had planned for him, and for which he had been trained there, for he thought that he needed to apply his physical and mental energies to the realization of social and political ideals which he thought were the need of the hour. He jumped into the national struggle, became an ardent disciple of Gandhi, lived through difficult times, even denying himself the comforts of a settled family life. During the long years he spent in British prisons and the years after the Independence of our country as our first Prime Minister, Nehru wrote and talked a great deal about his experiences, about several aspects of our society and culture and of the world at large. As a man who was exposed to the best in the East and the West, Nehru also said several interesting and thought-provoking things on education. But it is important to keep in mind that he wrote on the basis of his perception and understanding and not because of his innate fancy for any theory or a dogmatically fixed ideological position. He was more of a pragmatic thinker than a systematic philosopher. What I attempt to present in this short piece are his views on education which can be gleaned from his occasional writings, addresses to various institutions and educational bodies, and his letters to his friends and acquaintances.

Nehru knew that in the India of his day the pattern of education had been devised by the Britishers as a part of their comprehensively thought-out colonial policy, in which they wanted the system to train Indians for administering their empire. This had made it very limited in its objectives and given it an unhealthy rigidity. Needless to emphasize, it was prejudicial to our national interests. It is true that this system produced many individuals who became distinguished beings very learned and knowledgeable, but Nehru did not give much importance to individual attainment as in his views the primary aim of education is to awaken in young men and women understanding of themselves and of their times. Nehru practically emphasised the social goals of education: "All education must have a definite social outlook and must train our youth for the kind of society we wish to have".[1] Education was thus looked upon by him as something much more than mastering this or that kind of knowledge or acquiring competence or proficiency in any particular field of education or research; it was conceived of as a process which trains people to understand their environment so as to establish a desired social order.

Nehru fully understood the unhealthy aspects of a highly competitive and acquisitive society in which individuals are toughtened to think only about themselves – their social and material advancement – to the exclusion of everything else. Keeping in view that many of us think in terms of individual attainment even now, as was and is evident by a pungent comment of E.M. Forster, a vociferous critic of the culture of "Public School Education" which produces 'a well developed body, fairly developed minds, but underdeveloped hearts',[2] it is a tribute to Nehru that in spite of the socially-advantageous position he had, he thought of the goals of education in very ideal terms: to create a cooperative order in which "we think not in terms of individual profit but of common good; where individuals cooperate with each other and nations and people work in cooperation for human advancement; where human values count far more and there is no exploitation of a class or group or nation by another".[3] For imparting education of this kind, Nehru thought of the teachers also in very ideal terms: a teacher would not be following a profession only to earn a livelihood but work "in the ardent spirit of a missionary in a sacred cause which fills his being".[4]

To mould young people to perform the task of shaping an environment which is in tune with the demands of their time, Nehru stressed two basic qualities which education should aim at: building "strength of character" and the "right out-look on life". The strength of character would imply the development of all those traits which make people into honest and courageous beings with a sense of integrity. And the right out-look would mean developing a mind which is receptive and tolerant and capable of grasping things in their entirety — that is, looking at things from different perspective. This Nehru thought, would lead to the growth of integrated human beings, and integration, in his words "means not only a process within themselves, which of course is highly important, but also a measure of integration with the environment".[5]

Nehru conceived of this goal-oriented educational system in various stages:

> The stage of pre-basic training which begins when a child is one or two year old. Obviously, in this stage, the child cannot be in a regular school. This is where the role of the family, especially of the mother, acquires significance in educational planning. Nehru regards this education of the highest importance, because it lays the foundation of a child's character which affects the course of his future education.
>
> The second stage he calls the stage of basic education. For every boy and girl in the age-group of 7 and 14, Nehru proposed a course of basic training which would aim at shaping their character. This would involve several things: building in them a fairly comprehensive awareness of their cultural past; inculcating in them the right attitudes to work; especially in their willingness to undertake manual work without any hang-ups; and providing them education which would enable them to acquire a reasonable intellectual ability.[6]

Two significant things which emerge are: (i) Nehru thought of education for everybody, for males as well as females, and for people of every class. In a country steeped in orthodoxy and groaning under the burdens of tyrannical past, Nehru was bold enough to declare unequivocally: "I have always been strongly of the opinion that while it may be possible to neglect man's education it is not possible or desirable to neglect women's education".[7] It is essential because mothers would contribute to the growth of better human beings, especially during the basic training period of a child. (ii) Nehru's plan of basic education lays stress on a person's willingness to do manual work. He had to emphasize it because one of the popular misconceptions about education which unfortunately persists even to this day is that of relating education with white-collar jobs. An educated man was good enough only to sit at a desk or to work in situations where he was not supposed to do any manual work. Nehru regarded it as baneful and clarified it repeatedly that true education produced "coordination of the mind with manual work". This alone he felt would make possible the speedy implementation of the developmental programmes of our country.

Nehru's plan of basic education was thus a very balanced programme to produce people who would have basic minimum training and adequate background to do something in life. But more importantly they would be responsible citizens of their country. Since Nehru regarded it to be essential for everybody, he advocated imparting such education free of cost.

In the final stage comes higher education and technical education. In this stage people would go in for attaining higher degrees in humanities or sciences or take to engineering or medicine. In this context, Nehru out-lined the role and functions of universities. These institutions had the primary function of shaping the intellectual atmosphere of a country. In carrying forward the work of teaching in the higher rungs of the educational system and for carrying out productive and fruitful research, Nehru pleaded that universities should not encourage only individual effort, but should create a climate of team work. This alone would help in lifting the falling standards of education in our country and brighten the future of higher education. He visualised a frequent interchange of the research teams between the various regions of our country. This, he thought, would provide another plank for the integration of our variegated people.

Nehru knew that the heads of our universities — the Vice-chancellors — have to be chosen carefully. They should not merely be good administrators, but men of learning and imagination who should be capable of providing academic leadership and earning the respect of students and teachers. In the present-day politicisation of the universities and the Vice-chancellors, it is important to remember that Nehru had to issue a special circular in 1961 to emphasize the high value he placed on the fact that "our Vice-chancellors should be men of learning and high academic standards".[8]

This brief exposition of some of the significant features of Nehru's thinking on education demonstrates that Nehru approached the problem of education from the standpoint of a man who was clear about the fact that it has to be thought of in relation to the times in which one is living. His enunciation of its aims and objectives and the various ways in which these could be realized amply prove that Nehru was no pedagogue, but a visionary who, like the Greeks, emphasized that education should contribute to the all round and integrated development of human beings. Since education has already degenerated in our country into a mechanical ritual, I hope that Nehru's views will be taken as a refreshing reminder to all of us that we ought to rethink on our educational system.

NOTES

1. From An Address at the All-India Educational Conference, Baradari, 27 December, 1939.
2. Passage to India.
3. From "An Address at the All-India Educational Conference, Baradari, 27 December, 1939".
4. Ibid.
5. From A message to the Hindustani Talimi Sangh, 28 November, 1957.
6. The discussion on Nehru's concept of basic education in his speech which he delivered at the AICC Session, Avadi, 23 January, 1955.
7. From a speech delivered in Madras on 22 January, 1955.
8. From a circular of 3 July, 1961.

25

NEHRU AND SCIENCE

A.K. KHARE

Nehru had a queer personality — an agglomeration of various qualities — sometimes conflicting and contradictory — a statesman — with all the mental windows wide open — a literary artist and a lover of poetry — who read and could quote freely Shakespeare and Tagore, Eliot and Frost; but at the bottom he had a scientific temper and he always nurtured a belief that only science could solve the mysteries of the Universe. In his self-introspection, which we find very fervently flashed in his inaugural speech of 1955 Science Congress in Baroda, he spoke of his inner contradictions and mental tensions in his search after reality and truth and he submitted that no truth was whole and final and that he was always ready to correct himself. This, he said, was the scientific temper – though he categorically stated that he was not a scientist.

This scientific temper was closely related to his humanism. He had a deep understanding of the undercurrent of India's cultural heritage. He had deep faith in science as the 'motive force' in the regeneration of India's social and economic life and situations. At the same time, he always kept his mental windows wide open to let the fresh air in. Nehru, we should remember, secured his tripos from Cambridge University — and his subjects, were Chemistry, Geology and Botany. No doubt, he studied law after that, but he soon got attracted to the studies of Scientific Socialism and set up his ideals for the achievement of freedom democracy and socialism. In the achievement of these ideals, he felt that 'it was science alone that could solve the problems of hunger and poverty, of insanitation and illiteracy, of superstition and deadening customs and traditions, of vast resources running to waste of a rich country inhabited by starving people *(The Discovery of India)*.

Nehru became the Prime Minister of India on August 15, 1947.

Immediately he started working out programmes and plans for the development of research in Science and Technology — 'The three fundamental requirements of India, if she is to develop industrially and otherwise, are a heavy engineering and machine-making industry, scientific research institutes, and electric power'. Therefore, he set up the National Physical Laboratories, the National Chemical Laboratories, Indian Institutes of Technology, because he earnestly felt that for the creation of a scientific temper and for the spread of science in our country, various research and study centres are to be immediately set-up. We still remember the great enthusiasm, that our people demonstrated and the welcome that they accorded to Prof. Joliot-Curie, Prof. Irene-Joliot Curie, Prof. Bernal and others when they came to inaugurate the N.P.L. The Nobel Laureates stressed the need for both fundamental and experimental research. In 1948, under Nehru's patronage the Atomic Energy Commission was set up. In 1950, he organised the Council of Scientific and Industrial Research (C.S.I.R.). In 1954, the Department of Atomic Energy started functioning. Various Research Institutes started functioning under the aegis of C.S.I.R. to meet the food problem. Nehru strongly felt the need of the use of the latest scientific methods in agriculture and he set up the Indian Council of Agricultural Research with the ultimate aim of having the green revolution.

But this scientific temper never allowed him to make compromises with basic human values. Says he — 'we should like to take all the latent scientific talent of the country and give it opportunities for growth and service to the community. Yet I know how difficult it is for a line to be drawn between scientific work for peace and for war'. Again, 'Science has its destructive side and constructive and creative side. Both have gone on side by side and both still go on. No one knows which will ultimately triumph. Hiroshima became a symbol of this conflict'. Nehru concludes — "I, myself, am convinced that there is going to be no very great progress either in science or in other ways unless certain fundamental changes take place in the social structure".

Subhas Chandra Bose could very well understand and appreciate this scientific temper of Nehru. Hence, he as President of the Indian National Congress in 1938 during the Haipura Session, set up the National Planning Committee under the Chairmanship of Nehru. Nehru, while working as the Chairman of the Council came in close contact with scientists of the calibre of Prof. M.N. Saha, Prof. P.C.

Mahalanobis, Prof. Bhaba and others. He could well realise the imperative requirement of the future Independent India — i.e. rapid industrialisation. He was not against Cottage Industries; but he felt the urgent necessity of having dams, steels and fertiliser plants and he strongly recommended the importation of technical know-how, and setting up of thermal projects to make Indian Scientists and Engineers to learn and adopt the best ways to put India on the road to real success. That's why he organised the Planning Commission and set up high ideals and targets.

Hence, Nehru always emphsises on the study of history. He feels that only the study of history can make us aware of the various phases of human development, of the basic causes of the two global wars, of the apprehension and hopes of the future. He is of firm conviction that one day science will equip man 'with weapons' with which he *'may be able to alter human nature'*. But for this attainment 'a scientist, like another person must develop some kind of organic knowledge of human history and human advance'.

26

NEHRU'S CONTRIBUTION HAD INDEED BEEN GREAT

JAGDISH KODESIA

November is indeed a month of inspiring memories. It reminds us all primarily of the first Prime Minister of the country, Pandit Jawaharlal Nehru, sincere champion of the downtrodden and a beloved leader of the masses. His birthday falls during this month. The memory of his deeds still look fresh.

In human history there have been very few individuals who lived a life of glory true to their name. Shri Jawaharlal Nehru was one such person. He was a real "Jawahar", a pure jewel. His name was true to his deeds.

His stepping into the turmoil of political arena leaving a life of luxury was regarded as a big surprise then. In a country where an average man is poor, his act of denying himself a life of affluence created a great impact amongst the farmers and the downtrodden.

Jawaharlal's entry into the world of politics and joining the Congress gave the freedom struggle a large army of fervent followers, who were ever ready to give their all for the leader. The leader in return steadfastly stood for their cause. The rapport he could establish with the people was simply great.

The popularity of Jawaharlal Nehru was greatly enhanced with the story prevalent in those days that his clothes, which he used for daily wear, were dry-cleaned in Paris and he wiped off the tears from the eyes of poor, men and women, using his kurta and sherwani. He was the leader of the people and countless legends of this type grew around him.

Though Panditji, as we all addressed him, denied the Paris story but the wide publicity these stories commanded and Panditji's quality of rare humanity and many other similar attributes made him the hero of the countless millions.

When India attained independence Nehru became the Prime Minister. There was all round relief at his elevation in spite of the numerous problems faced by the people primarily caused by the partition of the country. The comparative political stability and the great strides in industrialisation the nation enjoys today is without doubt a gift of Nehru to the nation. All this could not be achieved unless the people went all out behind the leader.

Panditji's concept of planning centred around improving the lot of the deprived millions. This could be achieved by improving nation's agriculture which in turn could better the living conditions of the common man. Under his inspiration the First Five Year Plan laid great stress on agriculture. It envisaged the fulfilment of nation's material goals through the traditional Indian way of shramdan. These ideas, however, proved short-lived. The farmers and agriculture were soon to occupy a backseat.

Have we progressed the way he planned? We did make progress. It has only been because of the foundations laid during the period that things are still moving forward and not coming to a standstill. The progress could have been more rapid if specific tasks and goals had been assigned. One hopes efforts to remedy the mistakes will be initiated even now.

Panditji was actually the inspiration behind the green revolution, a proud national achievement. Like many other spheres of national activity, agriculture too saw a sea-change under his inspiring leadership. He encouraged the import of high yielding seed varieties from abroad. This proved to be the key step towards multiplying nation's foodgrains productivity. Agriculture has been the greatest national achievement since independence.

Panditji's keen interest in the welfare of farmers was evident when he came forward to inaugurate the first national convention of Bharat Krishak Samaj in New Delhi in 1955. This was an organisation formed to look after the interests of the farming community. This brought together the farm leaders on one platform for the first time. The problems of the farming community for long neglected started coming into focus. The farmers were now in the news.

But Panditji did not stop here. He was a modern man. He could divine what lay ahead in future. He realised the importance of communication with the people. The idea of holding Agricultural Fairs to spread the message of new Agricultural technology owed much to the support extended by him. The World Agricultural Fair held in New Delhi in 1959 was inaugurated by the President of India and was graced by the President of the United States of America, General Eisenhower, Prime Minister of U.S.S.R. Mr. Kruschev and other world personalities. Panditji visited this Fair on eighteen occasions. Later on, a series of National Agricultural Fairs were also organised in different regions of the country. The Fairs helped in bringing the farmers from different parts of the world together. Panditji's presence on important occasions was a real source of inspiration for farm leaders.

Throughout his long political career, Pandit Nehru in spite of his elite up-bringing had tried to establish personal rapport with the farming community. He was well aware of the sacrifices the farmers had made in the struggle for independence. The real fight for nation's freedom had gathered momentum through the various isolated struggles launched by farmers in different parts of the country.

Panditji loved farmers in his lifetime but could not forget them even afterwards. He willed his ashes to be strewn all over the country in the farm fields to be of some use. This was an act of great import even though symbolic. It spoke of his love for his land and the people.

Nehruji's interest in agriculture was so deep that while inaugurating the Bhakra Dam, a water management venture, he hailed it as a 'temple of modern India'. The mighty dam has not been all beneficial. Perhaps, a different approach for solving national water management requirement was needed. But Panditji's picturesque description was indeed apt at the time this project of hope came up.

After the first plan, the objectives of the plan seemed to have undergone a metamorphosis. They became primarily urban-oriented. No wonder, the quality of life in rural regions started deteriorating. The situation has deteriorated to a degree that the farmers seem to be now in ferment. The recently organised farmers ' dharna in Delhi should be taken as a forerunner of the state of things to come. An agricultural nation like ours cannot do with a planning which ignores rural regions.

Yet another contribution of Panditji towards national resurgence was his message urging people to develop a scientific temper. There can be no two opinion on the efficacy of this idea. But in practical application the idea has turned sour. This has made people forget the time-tested ancient way of living without replacing it with anything worthwhile. The social upheaval currently witnessed may be symbolic of this development.

A true assessment of an individual's contribution to human progress can only be made after a long lapse of time. Panditji did great many things during his long illustrious career. The fruits of his actions are yet in the process of being reaped fully. He knew the people and the people loved him. He could get away with anything he did. This lack of check may not always be good in a democracy.

The conditions now are vastly different than what existed when Panditji led the country. He inherited all the ills left by a foreign ruler. He had to make good under adverse conditions. That he was able to channellise people's energy towards constructive goals in itself is a great tribute to his leadership. If he gave the same attention to agriculture as he did to industries, the health of the nation would have been much better.

During the long period of freedom struggle, he had come in direct contact with the farming community throughout the land. He had developed a deep insight in the problems of the agriculturists. Whenever he addressed big gatherings of farmers, over-whelmed by their enthusiasm, he used to leave the high dais to move into the general enclosure below to be with the people. Even when he assumed the office of nation's Prime Minister, this habit of his continued to rule his actions. His rapport with farmers was complete.

An event of great significance for our agriculture, the holding of the 17th general conference of International Federation of Agricultural Producers in 1959 came off because of Panditji's whole-hearted support. He not only agreed to address the delegates but agreed to become the patron of the international body.

The faith of Panditji in *shramdan* was pointedly demonstrated when he came to inaugurate the training camp of Congress workers in Alipur near Delhi. He refused to give a speech on the occasion but urged everybody present to come out of the meeting to do shramdan. He believed in doing what he preached.

The country is short of practical economists in the field of politics. Economies and politics are inseparable. The need of the hour is to plug wastages witnessed throughout the country. A frugal administration can do a lot to improve the quality of life of the people.

The farmers of the country are engaged in the dual role of defending the country on the borders and producing more and more for the hungry mouths of the millions. But no priority is given to the demands of farmers, nothing is being done for the fulfilment of assurances to the farmers and real help, which is required by them, is not reaching them.

May be this is happening because of the rampant corruption prevailing or due to the white-ants of administration or because of the shortsighted policies of self-centred politicians. Whatever be the reason, the interest of the farmers must receive priority if nation's peace, progress and the productivity are to be ensured.

For too long the interests of the farming community continued to remain unattended. No wonder, the farmers after decades of neglect, are now in ferment all over the country. The farming community, a traditionally peaceful lot, is resorting to agitational methods. Now the vast untapped energy of the farmers, unless channellised towards constructive activities, might create chaos in an otherwise peaceful countryside.

The healthy base Nehru gave to the nation was really strong. He gave the nation an enduring unit. On the foundation laid by him, a great nation can rise. Let us not lose a great opportunity. There is still time to act for achieving our nation's destiny.

We all admire Jawaharlal and Jawaharlal was an admirable man. But today in his centenary year his legacies are not only being ignored but the basic principles he stood for are not even cared for. When the country attained independence, the British played the same game of Divide and Rule as they played for practically 200 years of their misrule.

The real liberator of India, Netaji Subhas Chandra Bose, who had the courage and conviction had hoisted the flag of independent India at Kohima. In a big international conspiracy he was declared dead.

Nehru got the first position as Gandhi had declared him to be his successor. The democracy, which we have in our country, is his gift to the countrymen. He could have chosen to be a dictator but as he was close to the masses, he had faith in the destiny of the country to be developed through democracy, and that too by giving franchise to all men and women of the age of 21 without any consideration of caste, creed or sex.

Nehru had already discovered India but it so happened that in January 1962 at the All India Congress Committee session at Patna I discovered Nehru. It happened like this.

The A.I.C.C. session in January 1962 was arranged by one of our ablest administrators, Shri Jagjivan Ram who was Chairman of the Reception Committee of the A.I.C.C. A huge maidan was selected to accommodate 5 to 10 lakhs people expected to attend the open session.

This was an election year and the elections were to take place soon after. Thus elaborate arrangements were made not only to make the session successful but to send its message to voters.

Since there was a danger of a conflict with China, security arrangements were also very tight. There were only two gates, one for the common man and the other for the V.V.I.P. Though the gates were big enough and had two bags each for entrance and exit. The crowd was so big that it soon became difficult for the common man to move in and out.

The crowd at the open session was more than 5 lakhs. The proceedings were going on when all of a sudden the crowd started moving towards the dais just like a human wave. We, who were on the dais, felt that there could be a stampede. A large number in the audience, women and children, seated in front, felt the push from the back and to save themselves moved towards the dais.

This was a frightening situation. I took up the mike and asked the audience to sing Ram Dhun, which I myself started "*Raghupati Raghav Raja Ram........*"

Panditji, feeling greatly disturbed, about what might happen next moment, came up to me and asked what was to be done. I replied that the crowd was very eager to see him from near. He could kindly stand in a conspicuous portion so that people at the back may also have his *darshan*. "*Raghupati Raghav Raja Ram*" started in a big way but the movement forward continued.

I requested Shri Lal Bahadur Shastri to kindly order the removal of all tin sheets by the security staff from the sides of the dais so that people could move out and avoid a stampede.

I jumped into the crowd, which had now reached the dais and were crying for help. Though I got hurt in the process yet I started picking up small children, old men and women and putting them on the dais. The volunteers of the Seva Dal also came to help.

With the *Ram Dhun* in full swing and tin sheets removed, the stampede was avoided, and very few people were really hurt.

But I discovered Nehru when I picked up a very aged Harijan, who wanted to have a glimpse of Nehru from close quarter. He told me that the he should be given an opportunity to see Nehru. When I told him that he would be crushed in the crowd, he said "MARTE HAIN TO MARNE DIJIYE, NEHRU KO DIKHA DIJIYE". It was just like a lightening. I could see the picture of Nehru painted in the mind of the poor and downtrodden masses of Bihar.

I had read and had been told that during the earthquake in 1934 Panditji had gone to help the victims and had organised the Congressmen in Bihar and other provinces to come for rescue operations. The common man had not forgotten the angel in white.

27

PANDIT NEHRU AND INDIAN NATIONAL FEELING

L.B. RAM ANANT

Pt. Jawaharlal Nehru was born in 1889 when India was ruled by Britain. His father was Pt. Motilal Nehru, one of the leading and famous barristers of the day and his mother was Swarup Rani. Motilal Nehru was a law graduate from Kanpur with a good grounding in Persian, Arabic and Urdu. Walter Crocker has given a picturesque description of Nehru's family background which shaped his childhood. He says, 'Contrary to what is often said, Nehru's background was not aristocratic. He himself always spoke of it as middle class; in English terms of that day it would have been upper 'middle class'. His personal standards were aristocratic though he gave his life to destroying one set of conditions, and to creating another set, which could result only in the end of aristocracy. Anand Bhavan, abode of happiness, seems to have been not an incorrect name for the Nehru house'.

This type of family background was surely a very strong factor in shaping his body and mind, much different to those of average Indian children of that period. Motilal Nehru himself was enthusiastic westernizer so Nehru was living in Anand Bhavan in English style as regards food, speech and dress and he was educated by English tutors or governesses. Jawaharlal's tutor Brooks was able to influence him much by creating in him a taste for science, Theosophy and perhaps anti-imperialism. At the age of 13 he was initiated into Theosophical Society by Mrs. Annie Besant herself. 'Islamic Flavour' was an important element in his upbringing. He got this flavour living with Muslim members in Anand Bhavan. At the age of 15 in 1905 he was taken to England and put in Harrow School. For the first time in his life he felt that his social status was lower than those of Englishmen because he was an Indian. He was forced to think that an independent country was more honourable than a dependent country like India. He was not aware of this fact while living in Anand Bhavan. He was speaking English, Hindi and Urdu without knowing that even these languages might be made basis for the division of human society. In Anand Bhavan he loved and was loved by Hindu, Muslim and Christians without any distinction. At Harrow the idea of nation dawned on the horizon of his mind. There he was looked down upon only because he was an Indian; so the seeds of his nationalism were sown in Harrow.

At Harrow his vision of Indian nation must have been an image of English nation, a powerful and an honoured one. It may be guessed that the nation of his vision must have been whole of India including present Pakistan and Bangladesh. He came to know that India was a despised nation because it was not independent so he must have been restless in his heart to see India a free nation as early as possible.

In 1912 he returned to India and started working in his father's chambers at Allahabad. He was continuously thinking to do something to get India free and so to his father's disappointment his heart was never in law. But his legal background and his caste both were important. Because the good majority of the fomenters and leaders of anti-English nationalism were products of that new thing introduced by British-raj – the English Legal System, including the profitable and honourable profession of lawyers. These leaders showed a brilliant aptitude for using English law for their own cause against the British rulers. Pt. Jawaharlal Nehru was happy to join them and to find out a way leading to his cherished goal to get India free.

In 1918 when he was 29, he became the Secretary of Home Rule League in Allahabad. The aim of this League was not to his satisfaction because it was a moderate movement by Mrs. Annie Besant advocating India to remain a part of British Empire. In 1919 he got some money from his father and started a paper 'The Independent'. The very title of this paper showed his courage, revolutionary spirit and his noble ideals.

Though nationalism was growing more and more a strong driving force among leaders and even among common masses of cities and villages yet there was no clear concept of nation which might be defined in clear words and projected before the masses to attract them. In spite of this, the movement for independence was growing stronger with fast speed and was spreading like a wild fire throughout India including the present Pakistan. This movement was gradually brought at par with those national movements which were going on in other countries of the world. Those movements were based on principles which were developed by thinkers and fighters and were accepted by nations as acceptable ones. Indian National Movement also inspired intellectuals to think over national problems and to define nation in clear words. In 1920 Pt. Nehru attended the special session of Congress at Calcutta which was held in a hurry after the Jallianwala Bagh massacre. Here he became a follower of Gandhi and left Annie Besant. From this period up to 1946 when he became the Prime Minister of India, he was in the forefront of the Independence Movement. He held high office in the Congress during most of this period. He was the President of Congress in 1929, 1936 in 1937 and in 1946. After Independence also he held that office in 1951-54. During this period he thought deeply about the framework of Indian nation, problems regarding making her strong and united and defining her future shape. Walter Crocker has rightly said about Nehru's conception of Indian nation: 'Nehru had a vision of India in which getting the British out of it was merely the preliminary stage. What he was concerned with was a modernized India, with an industrialized economy and an egalitarian society. Nationalist leader though he was he hated many of the things which most Hindus hold dear-cow worship, subordination of women, temple, *Sadhus*, astrology and caste. He remained remarkably consistent in these aims, as his Bunch of Old Letters shows'.

It was quite new and revolutionary thinking in status oriented Indian Society where egalitarian relation of society was never even dreamt of. All Hindu religious books and other literature too were against this type of concept. Even Islamic thought was not in favour of egalitarian relations. It was Dr. B.R. Ambedkar who was thinking seriously like Nehru about the future shape of Indian nation and establishing a society which might develop itself economically, socially and politically on the basis of egalitarian relations. Keeping this vision alive Dr. Ambedkar defined nationality as follows:

> "Nationality is a social feeling. It is a feeling of a corporate sentiment of oneness which makes those who are charged with it feel that they are kith and kin. This national feeling is a double edged feeling. It is at once a feeling of fellowship for one's own kith and

kin and anti-fellowship feeling for those who are not one's own kith and kin. It is a feeling of consciousness of kind which on the one hand binds together those who have it, so strongly that it over-rides all differences arising out of economic conflicts or social gradation and, on the other, severs them from those who are not their kind. It is longing not to belong to any other group. This is the essence of what is called a nationality and national feeling."

No doubt, this type of national feeling was strong in castes and religious groups in India. But this feeling was never named 'national feeling'. Hindu castes numbering thousands have above type of feeling of kith and kin. But is it all right so say that if castes might be proved nation according to above definition, they may be conceded the right of self rule or right to have their own homeland? If the answer is in affirmative, then we should be ready to accept that in nation's interest India should be divided in thousands of caste states. It is clear that this type of thinking is quite against the true Indian national feeling. It is quite obvious that caste feeling cannot be named a national feeling. Similarly religious feeling too should not be confused with national feeling. But Muslim League and Mr. Jinnah were successful in getting accepted that Indian Muslims were a nation. No influential Muslim or Hindu leader opposed this wrong national concept of Muslim League and Jinnah. Both became stronger and stronger. Hindus instead of opposing the formation of Muslim League framed a 'Hindu Mahasabha' which was in a position to prove that if there was a Muslim nation, there was a stronger Hindu nation too.

Keeping in view his own definition of nation which was acceptable to European thinkers also, Dr. Ambedkar put the Muslim case as follows:

"Now apply this taste (national feeling) to the Muslim claim. Is it or is it not a fact that Muslims of India are an exclusive group? Is it or is it not a fact that they have a consciousness of kind? Is it or is it not a fact that every Muslim is possessed by a longing to belong to his own group and not to any non-Muslim group?"

If the answer to these questions is in affirmative, then the controversy must end and Muslim claim that they are a nation must be accepted without cavil.

Needless to say that the above questions may be asked regarding any Hindu caste or Hindu religious sects including *Buddha*, Jain, Parsee, Sikh, Christian and so many others. If Muslims are nation, then these too are nations. Dr. Ambedkar's definition does not clearly differentiate between caste, sect and religious social relations and national relations. Caste and social relations are developed by economic, social and political relations. Sects and religions also are economic, social and political relations developed by classes of men in their own interest using traditional beliefs, faith, gods and rituals etc. National feeling is comparatively a modern feeling, a product of capitalist system. Its etymological meaning indicates that nation was consisting of those men who were bound by a strong feeling that their ancestor was one. This type of concept also was the product of tribal life. Their caste, sect and religious relations are not opposed to national relations when we accept the definition given by Dr. Ambedkar. But this definition of nation is not acceptable to those Indians who do not wish to see India being divided and being made weak enough to be the prey of strong nations. Because they have seen how Mr. Jinnah proving Indian Muslims a nation divided India into three parts with the legal plea that every nation had its birth right to get a homeland for its inhabitants.

Pt. Nehru could not accept this type of definition of nation. We may look at his definition of nation in words of Mr. Walter Crocker:

> "His first concern was to see that India did not fall apart. To this end he encouraged a nationalism which would make Indians feel that they were Indians instead of feeling that they were Tamils or Punjabis or Dogras or Assamese or Brahmans or Kshatriyas or this or that caste, as they opt. He gave special consideration to Muslims so as to induce them to feel Indian. For the same reason Christians and other minorities could always be sure of Nehru's unflinching protection. The 'Secular State' that is to say non-Hindu and All Indian State, was fundamental to his concern."

All unbiased readers will feel that Nehru's concept of Indian National feeling was quite correct and acceptable to all. His concept of nation was like this because he was not only a politician to be guided by certain interests but was a literary genius also who had deep and wide knowledge of both Indian life and history. He always tried to peep into the darkest corners of Indian history. He was rightly convinced of that fact that the European type of national feeling could not be aroused in India because history had shaped her society in such cultural groups that it was a very difficult task to weaken their caste and other traditional relations and in place of those generate a national feeling dominating them. This was why he chose a new way to teach the Indian his own nationalism which was to make him feel that in spite of traditional and regional relations he should develop a new relation also which would be named 'India relation'. This would be able to create the true citizens of India, a secular democratic state. No one can say that Nehru's thinking was wrong or misleading.

Mr. Walter Crocker has defined Nehru's nationalism thus:

> "For Nehru nationalism as has been seen, was largely a preliminary step to the major step, which was to modernize India, and, especially, to bring in socialism. Nehru's socialism has been held with such conviction that he would have been a communist were it not for the rigid dogmatism on the one part – his favourite taunt to the communists was that they were a old-fashioned and out of date – and the mixture of coercion and violence on the other which go, or which have gone, with the communist's sort of socialism. For Nehru the end rarely justified the means."

It is true that to arouse national feeling for feeling's sake is fruitless. This cannot be the aim of any nation. In Nehru's time Indian national feeling many times rose to its high pitch. During national movement for independence this feeling was marred by Hindu-Muslim conflicts which was aroused by their leaders and masses in the name of Hindu and Muslim national interests. This conflict led to the formation of Pakistan, which created so many problems for both Hindus and Muslims that the pace of development of both the countries has been arrested so badly that poverty of these countries is no where seen in the world. Owing to this Hindu and Muslim anti-national feeling till now thousands of Hindu, Muslims and Sikhs have been killed and properties of unestimated value destoryed.

In Nehru's time true national feeling arose when the smaller state of Rajas and Nawabs were included in the Indian national state; when Hyderabad, Goa, Daman and Diu became integral parts of India, making it an undivided strong nation. Kashmir issue was not tackled so wisely. Though Muslim leaders and some foreign nations too, blamed Nehru for arresting and imprisonning Sheikh Abdullah and not allowing plebiscite there. In this respect too he was not on wrong side. Because Pakistan was not created on the basis of religious feeling. If this feeling would have been accepted Hindus of Pakistan would have been transferred to India and Indian Muslims to Pakistan. In the world Muslim population is divided into different nations so Muslims of Kashmir may live happily with their Muslim brothers in India. Attack of China was another occasion when true national feeling was aroused. This time Nehru was blamed for not helping Dalai Lama and keeping Tibet a buffer state but situation was really not favourable for this type of action; so it is not right to think that Nehru was quite wrong then.

We may say that true national feeling is a force which is quite essential for the development and protection of any country but in the name of national cause to arouse caste, sect and religious feeling for economic and political ends is quite wrong and anti-national. Pt. Nehru was always enough powerful to suppress this wrong tendency. After Nehru this tendency was encouraged and no ruler or no party leader was able to suppress it. It has been so because Nehru's path has been abandoned. Nehru was able to get done what he thought was in national interest. Walter Crocker has observed, 'Nationalism for instance; he gave the biggest part of his life to fomenting it, yet the great causes he stood for when he was Prime Minister, such as world government, or the control of the thermo-nuclear arms race, coexistence both inside and outside India, were damaged or frustrated by nationalism. Nehru however, would almost certainly have had no power except his nationalism or again, industrialization'.

We cannot agree with Walter Crocker that Nehru's nationalism was damaging or frustrating to his great causes. Reality is this that Pt. Nehru always kept himself burdened with heavy workload, perhaps, because he was not able to trust any man who might work with integrity to his own satisfaction. No doubt he put faith in Krishna Menon but we cannot say that this faith paid him in good coins. Owing to over-work he was not able to give enough time to great causes for which he was fighting throughout his life. In reality his nationalism was the only nationalism which could make India great, strong and honoured. In respect of India his nationalism cannot be replaced by any other kind of nationalism or national feeling. Because Nehru's national feeling and industrial development is quite essential for the proper development of this most poor, divided and backward country. In this respect Pt. Nehru is the only true guide. He should not be ignored by any one who wishes to work in India's interest. In this context Mr. Walter Crockers forecast should always be kept in mind:

> "It is unlikely that there will be a place in India again for ruler like Nehru – the aristocratic liberal humanist. If India is not run by Dictators, Rightist or Leftist or Militarist, she will be run by politicians, more and more drawn from, or conditioned by the outcast and the low castes. For this is the majority which will set up and pull down governments; votes won through promising more and more to the needy and the many. Some saviour of the people, an individual or groups, could conceivably carry, in due legal form, a plebiscitary election to abolish elections altogether. The convergence of unemployed or discontented, neo-literates with industrialization is a favourable condition for a mass revolution. Food shortages could precipitate it. In abolishing British-Raj and in propagating ideas of equality, so hastily and in way they did, Nehru and the upper class Indian nationalists of English education abolished themselves. Nehru destroyed the Nehrus!"

This prophecy of Walter Crocker may or may not come true but we should be careful to fulfil the task Nehru has left for us. Pt. Nehru and nationalists of English education were great because they destroyed Nehrus and themselves and in their place created a vast army of true nationalists in whose hands future of India is safe. It is also true that new type of Nehrus have come into prominence who are not working for construction but destruction of poor people and nation itself. We should be aware of them and follow the path which Nehru created sacrificing himself and his class too. If the out-caste and low-caste people are going to be rulers then we must be ready to be one of them because it is their natural right and Indian national democratic state demands it for her own existence. We are to fight for an Indian egalitarian Socialist Society which was the cherished dream of great Nehru. It will only be the appropriate contribution to the memory of Pt. Nehru, the first great nation builder.

28

NEHRU : A Literary Genius

HARISH SHARMA

There are two dimensional approaches to assess a Literary Artist. On the one hand, it is expected of him that he has got an aptitude to read and digest the expressiveness of the creative artists and thinkers in the field of creations with aesthetic appeal, and on the other hand he is supposed to have an urge from inside to express himself in a lucid manner. From these two angles, we are obliged to say that over and above being a political thinker-philosopher, Nehru was a literary giant, because he had a vision, which had imbibed the very spirit of humanism, enriched by his fascination for beauty. His works are the real testimonies of what we have said of him.

First of all, we would like to mention that he was a voracious reader. During his periods of imprisonments, he read several thousand books on all kinds of subjects ranging from Astronomy to Marxism. Wherever he went, he was always in search of books of his taste and those worth reading. How strange it is that he had read Gerard Manley Hopkins and T.S. Eliot, at a time when quite a few teachers of English in Indian Universities had hardly heard of them, whereas he had quoted from Hopkin's Sonnets and Eliot's 'Hollow Men'. Here we quote from his Autobiography —

> "Thou art indeed just, Lord, if I contend
> With thee; but, sir, so what I plead is just
> Why do sinners' ways prosper? and why must
> Disappointment all I endeavour end?
> Wert thou my enemy, O thou my friend,
> How wouldst thou worse, I wonder, than thou dost
> Defeat, thwart me? Oh, the sots and thralls of lust
> Do in spare hours more thrive than I that spend,
> Sir, life upon thy cause. . ."
>
> –Gerard Manley Hopkins

Failures, generally, break down a man, but Faith comes to his rescue. This is what Nehru wants to uphold by quoting Hopkins. He is of the opinion that without faith, the life of man may become like a desert where there might not be even a drop of water. For him Faith had been a deterrent to all kinds of obstacles.

If we go through his autobiography we find that he has quoted from Walter de la Mare, Richard Garnett, Swinburne, Thomas Moore, Le Ta Poe, La Fontaine, E. Markhem, Robert Browning, Byron and many more. It shows how wide the span of his reading was. He was well conversant with the vital traditions of India, because he had studied upnishadas along with the modern Indian Rishi-Philosophers like Aurobindo. Sarvapalli Radhakrishnan and Coomarswamy were his other favourites. If we go through his *'The Discovery of India'*, we come across many descriptions in a very lucid style, which speak of his keen observations. The descriptions of Lord Buddha and his teachings are so picturesque that one is amazed when he says that loving hands have portrayed the Buddha in paint and carved in stone as 'seated on the Lotus Flower, Calm and impassive above passion and desire, beyond the storm and strife of this world, so far away he seems out of reach unattainable. His eyes are closed, but some power of the spirit looks out of them and a vital energy fills the frame' — It is an example of the superb verbal equivalent of the painting as well as of carving. This sort of writings, at length, exhibit the impact of the *upnishadas*, wherein God Himself has been described as *rasovaisaha.* Further more, when we deliberate upon his views about the teachings of *Geeta*, we reach the conclusion that Nehru was a unique combination of Thought and Action. The quote from *'The Discovery of India'* is self-explanatory – "I cannot write about the present so long as I am not free to experience it through action. It is the need for action in the present that brings it vividly to me and then I can write about it with care and a certain facility". If we deliberate upon the echo of these lines, we are proudly convinced that he, unflinchingly, adhered to the unbreakable matrimony between Thought and Action.

These cursory references are enough, for the time-being, to prove the veracity and vividness of his reading-compass along with his digestive capability. Most of his readings and writings were in jail. What jail-life proved to Nehru is clear from the letter written to his daughter Indira on 9th August, 1933, wherein he quoted Benjamin Disraeli — the great English statesman of 19th Century — "Other men condemned to exile and captivity, if they survive, despair, the man of letters may reckon those days as the sweetest of his life". And, in fact, those days were the sweetest of his life. Nehru utilized 'his time in prison by keeping himself intellectually informed and mentally active'. He proved that his brain was an apt and exquisite instrument for receiving, absorbing and generating new ideas.

In this context the remarkable aspect is that he was very modest and humble because he further wrote — 'I am not a man of letters, and I am not prepared to say that the many years I have spent in gaol have been the sweetest in my life, but I must say that reading and writing have helped me wonderfully to get through them. I am not a literary man, and I am not a historian; what indeed am I ?' The fact, that he finished writing his *'The Discovery of India'* in five months when he was in Ahmednagar jail, proves that what indeed he was ! All his writings during prison-terms radiate vitalizing freshness.

To sum up this dimension of Nehru's personality, we conclude that Nehru's knowledge of English literature, Greek drama and poetry and world-history was very deep and extensive.

Before we deal with the other facts of Nehru's personality, we would like to quote him from his brilliantly drafted statement at his Gorakhpur trial in 1940. 'I am a lover of words and phrases and try to use them appropriately. Whatever my opinions might be, the words I use are meant to express them intelligently and in ordered sequence.' These words remind us of Matthew Arnold who defined the efficacy of style — 'Best words in Best order'. In our opinion the greatness of a literary figure depends upon his unison with the language he uses, and we are proud to avouch that Nehru was superb that way.

If we look at the basic themes of his writings and speeches, which are also rich with highest quality of literary flavour, we can safely say that Beauty in all its forms and Humanism have been the themes of his writings — be they political, historical, scientific or philosophic or otherwise.

He craves for the day when he would go across the Himalayas to look at Mansarovar and have *darshan* of Kailash, but feels gloomy to find the sand of life slipping away under the feet of time, there he quotes — Water de la Mare.

"Yea, in my mind these mountains risé,
Their perils dyed with evenings' rose;
And still my ghost sets on my eyes
And thirsts for their untroubled snows".

What an emotional touch!

While in Lucknow jail, he wrote in his autobiography that stretching himself in the open during rainy season he looked at the floating clouds in the sky. He felt thrilled to find the clouds changing their colours every moment. The following lines slipped out of his pen —

'To watch the changing clouds, like clime in clime;
Oh! sweet to lie and bless the luxury of time.'

Throughout his writings, we find that he had an everlasting love for nature and it remained a constant pre-occupation of his that the modern man had lost contact with nature. He always sensed the 'mysterious life of Nature, to hear her whisper, close to the ears, thrill and quiver at her touch?' He had an emotional affinity with nature and it would not be out of place to mention that he seemed to have the burden throughout, 'Human destiny appeared to become a part of Nature's rhythmic energy'. For him Nature had always been like a living entity. In the 'Unity of India', the description about the loveliness of Kashmir is like a lyric in prose:

"Kashmir is like some supremely beautiful woman, whose beauty is almost impersonal and above human desires, such is Kashmir in all its feminine beauty of river and valley and lake and graceful trees. And then another aspect of this magic beauty would come to view, a masculine one, of hard mountains and precipices and snowcapped peaks and glaciers and crude and fierce torrents rushing down to the valley below. It had a hundred faces and innumerable aspects, ever changing, sometimes smiling, sometimes sad and full of sorrow. The clouds would throw out their arms to embrace a mountain top, or creep down stealthily like children at play.... It was like the face of the beloved that one sees in a dream and that fades away on awakening".

He has personified nature with such an exquisiteness that one feels mesmerized. Although, he seems hilarious at the beauty of Kashmir, yet we find that . . . 'in the very temple of delight veil'd Melaneholy hath her sovran shrine', because he cannot fail to see 'the appalling poverty and misery and the man made ugliness of the politics in Kashmir. Here his humanism over-powers his lust for beauty. If we look at the man, in whose life thought and action had become so unified that no line of separation could be drawn within. He was an embodiment of struggle within and struggle without. The lines from Matthew Arnold quoted by him depict the real Nehru –

'Men will renew the battle in the plain
Tomorrow; red with blood with Xanthus be;
Hector and Ajax will be there again;
Helen will come upon the wall to see'.
Then we shall rust in shade, or shine in strife,
And fluctuate 'tween blind hopes and blind despairs,
And fancy that we put forth all our life,
And never know how with the soul it fares'.

His attitude towards nature-at-large and human nature in particular made him entirely philosophic, due to which he could not be what practical politics expected of him. We can have the glimpse of Hamletonic Character from the following lines —

'When the stars threw down their spears
And water'd heaven with their tears,
Dare he laugh his works to see?
Dare he who made the lamb make thee?

Sometimes his melancholious mood makes us quiver, but it is all due to his humanistic characteristic. The following lines are replete with the same burden. Quoting Robert Browning, he speaks out his feeling which persisted through out.

'Already how am I so for
Out of that minute? Must I go
Still like the thistle-ball, no bar,
Onward wherever light winds blow,
Fixed by no friendly star?'.

From all his writings, we can unhesitatingly say that literature, in the real sense, flowed out of his tongue and pen spontaneously. Here we are reminded of what Sheikh Mohammed Abdullah said about him: ". . . he is the Shelley of our times, with the added capacity of being able to translate his ideals into action. . . . Panditji is a poet at heart possessed of a refined sensibility and a Catholic intellect, he has all the ingredients in his personality which constitute a poet. . . . Whenever he could get opportunities to recollect emotions in tranquillity, i.e. in the Cloistered Solitude of a prison-cell, he poured forth lyrics in prose, which his writings are".

To prove the authenticity of this gesture, we quote from his speech at the time of death of the father of the Nation — Mahatma Gandhi.

> "Friends and Comrades! the light has gone out of our lives and there is darkness everywhere.
>
> A glory has departed and the sun that *warmed* and brightened our lives has *set* and we shiver in the *cold* and dark. Yet, he would not have us feel this way. After all that glory we saw for all these years, that man with the divine fire, changed us also — and such as we are, we have been moulded by him during these years; and out of this divine *fire*, many of us took a small spark which strengthened and made us work to some extent on the lines he fashioned.
>
> All we know is that there was a glory and that it is no more, all we know is that for the moment there is darkness, not so dark certainly because when we look into our hearts, we still find the same *flame* which is lighted there. And if those *living* flames exist, there will not *be darkness* in this land and we shall be able, with our effort, remembering him and following his path, to illumine this land again, small as we are, but still with the *fire* that he *instilled* within."

If we look at this homage, we are amazed that at the moment of national disaster, he, on the spur of the moment, could constantly hold up the images of glory, light and darkness, warmth and shivering, as does a poet, in blank verse. Only he could write 'when we look into our hearts we still find the living flame, which he lighted'. 'And if those living flames exist, there will not be darkness in this land'. How astounding and profound awareness regarding his immediate task as the leader of such a vast nation, who has got the responsibility to wipe the tears of the nation and steel the heart thereof!

On flashing back, we find that Nehru was very much concerned with the sad and miserable plight of the middle class people of India and particularly the labour class and the peasantry, who were fated to pass their miserable lives, enshrouded by the unfathomable span of darkness, with no hope of ever getting the chance to see the dawn signalling the advent of happiness. This moved him to the core of his heart and he quoted the lines from the poem "The man with the Hoe" of an American poet E. Markhem:

"Bowed by weight of centuries he leans
Upon his hoe and gazes on the ground,
The emptiness of ages on his face,
And on his back the burden of the world.

* * * * *

"Through this dread shape the suffering ages look
Times' tragedy is in that aching stoop,
Through this dread shape humanity betrayed
Plundered, profaned and disinherited,
Cries protest to the powers that made the world,
A protest that is also prophecy."

His humanism did not rest only to the extent of sympathizing with the ill-fated countrymen, moreover, he wished to raise up their stature and status to the height of those who were considered to be the honourable section of the society. He is emotionally moved and as a protest, questions the validity of keeping the deprived ones in the pitiable condition by administering the dose of 'simple living and high thinking'. In the mental state of sacred annoyance he quotes –

'Who made him dead to rapture and despair,
A thing that grieves not and that never hopes,
Stolid and stunned, a brother to the ox?"

Thus we see that his humanism is multi-faced. Sometimes it is mingled with his attitude towards nature and sometimes with his clear-cut sympathy with those who are down-trodden and are always in want of the bare necessities of life.

Finally, we look at his 'Will and Testament', which is one of its own kind in the world of literature. It is a unique combination of poetry and prose replete with refinement of feeling:

"My desire to have a handful of my ashes thrown into the Ganga at Allahabad has no religious significance, so far as I am concerned. I have no religious sentiment in the matter. I have been attached to the Ganga and Jamuna rivers in Allahabad ever since my childhood, and as I have grown older this attachment has also grown. I have watched their varying moods as the seasons changed, and have often thought of the history and myth and tradition and song and story that have become attached to them through the long ages and became part of their flowing waters. The Ganga, especially, is the river of India, beloved of her people, round which are intertwined her racial memories, her hopes and fears, her songs of triumph, her victories and her defeats. She has been a symbol of India's age-long culture and civilization, ever-shining, ever-flowing, and yet ever the same Ganga . . . as my last homage to India's cultural inheritance, I am making a request that a handful of my ashes be thrown into the Ganga at Allahabad to be carried to the great ocean that washes India's shore."

Lastly, we humbly submit that Nehru was a great man who knew no fatigue and who was an unparalleled man of Action dedicated to the Good of entire mankind. He always kept the final lines from Robert Frost's poem 'Stopping by Woods on a Snowy Evening':

'The woods are lovely, dark and deep,
But I have promises to keep,
And miles to go before I sleep,
And miles to go before I sleep.'

This short introduction about Nehru's literary genius, is potent enough to motivate the conscious mind to unveil his mastermind which had the potentiality of creating the best of literature. His prose is very rich in content and form. One feels that Beauty, Love and Humanism are like musical whispers, which touch both mind and heart and fill the vacuum with ever-resounding echoes.

29

THE MAN ALIVE — THE MAN IMMORTAL

N.B. DAS GUPTA

Pandit Nehru — our first Prime Minister and the chief architect of the Planning Commission — was a multi-coloured personality — an astute statesman, a man intensely devoted and deeply committed to Indian freedom movement and her development, an internationalist with socialist ideals, rather impulsive, at times a prisoner of indecision — the Prince Hamlet of our age, but a poet, a romantic revolutionary — with a lyrical aroma about him — at times a lonely crusader for the great ideals of liberty, justice, equality and secularism, — sometimes in the chasm of despair — but again having the shining faith that 'To-morrow is ours'. He is physically dead — but he is still with us with his ideals — he is the Man Alive, he is the Man Immortal.

The best tribute to him in this Centenary year is our self-introspection, is our self-criticism. We have achieved something, nay, we have achieved much — but we have also lost much — and much has yet to be done to reach the ideals set up by our three great men — Tagore, Gandhi and Nehru.

Nehru is highly self-introspective, he very honestly and masterly draws his self-portrait. He writes an article on himself — as far back as in 1938 under a pen name. This throws a light on the Man — the enigma of our century:

"Jawaharlal has learnt well to act without the paint and powder of the actor. With his seeming carelessness and insouciance, he performs on the public stage with consummate artistry. What is this going to lead him and his country to? What is he aiming at with all his apparent want of aim? What lies behind this mask of his, what desires, what will to power, what insatiate longings? Is it his will to power that is driving him from crowd to crowd and makes him whisper to himself: I drew these tides of men into my hands and wrote my will across the stars? Men like Jawaharlal with all their capacity for great and good work, are unsafe in democracy. He calls himself a Democrat and a Socialist, and no doubt he does so in all earnestness; but every psychologist knows the mind is ultimately a slave to the heart and that logic can always be made to fit in with the desires and irrepressible urges of men. A little twist and Jawaharlal might turn a dictator. He may still use the language and slogans of Democracy and Socialism, but we all know how Fascism has fattened on this language. Jawaharlal cannot become a fascist. Yet, he has all the Makings of a dictator in him — vast popularity, a strong will, energy, pride, organisational capacity, ability, hardness and, with all his love for the crowd, an intolerance for others and a certain contempt for the weak. His overmastering desires to get things done will hardly brook for long the slow processes of democracy. He may keep the husk, but he will see to it that it bends to his will. In his revolutionary epoch, caesanism is always at the door and is it not possible that Jawaharlal might fancy himself as a Caesar? Let us not spoil him by too much adulation and praise. His conceit, if any, is already formidable. It must be checked."

(Quoted in *Men I Met* — M.N. Roy, pp 6-7)

Hence self-introspection is the need of the moment to-day.

Nehru on Planned Economy and Socialism

It was in 1938 that Subhas Chandra Bose first formed a National Planning Committee with Nehru as Chairman. Nehru got himself committed to socialism years back. In fact, his mental make-up was born out of three forces: Fabianism; Gandhism and Marxism (Soviet Planning). He attended the International Congress against colonial oppression and Imperialism in Brussels in 1927. He was deeply influenced by the Bolshevik Revolution and quoted Wordsworth:

"Bliss was it in that dawn to be alive
But to be young was very heaven"

He formed the Independence for Indian League and wrote:

"The League aims at the socialist democratic state in which every person has the fullest opportunities of development and the state control of the means of production and distribution."

(*Selected Works*, 3rd Vol. pp. 287)

After the achievement of independence, Nehru wanted to usher in for India the era of planned economy. The basic contents are the ideals of Socialism. He said, "Our economy and social structure have outlived their day and it has become a matter of urgent necessity for us to refashion them so that they may promote the happiness of all our people in things material and spiritual. We have to aim deliberately at a social philosophy which seeks a fundamental transformation of this structure, at a society which is not dominated by the urge for private profit and by individual greed and in which there is fair distribution of political and economic power. We must aim at a classless society based on co-operative effort and opportunities for all".

Again: — "The picture I have in mind is definitely and absolutely of a socialistic picture of society. I may not be using the word in a dogmatic sense at all, but in the sense of meaning largely that the means of production should be socially owned and controlled for the benefit of society as a whole."

Again: "When we talk of Socialism or a socialist pattern of society — we mean social justice which is so lacking to-day, in spite of our efforts and declarations".

(Letter to CMS, 1961)

Nehru on Secularism

The danger is not of communism, but of communalism. The need is to secularize the intelligentsia at least and proceed on secular lines in politics. 'How long that will take I cannot say, but religion in India will kill the country and its people if it is not subdued' (*Nehru* Vol. I – Biography, S. Gopal, pp. 99).

About Urdu: "For some mysterious reasons, Urdu is supposed to be the hall-mark of the Muslims. With all due deference, I am not prepared to admit this. I consider Urdu as my language which I have spoken from childhood. Why is that whenever such so-called cultural and similar questions are pushed to the front, political reactionaries take a lead in them?"

(Qouted in Nehru – M. Brecher — p. 235)

Nehru has a deep humane sense and he puts humanity above everything — 'Humanity is the object of worship. Man is raised above the animal because he shares in humanity and finds by growing knowledge that he must live for humanity.'

Again: 'We have to think outside our narrow grooves of thought and action and face the situation squarely. History has cast a role upon us and we cannot escape from it'. (S. Gopal Vol. 2, pp-150-151).

Again: 'If any person raises his hand to strike down another on ground of religion, I shall fight him till the last breath of my life, both as the head of the government and outside.' (Ibid p.155)

He writes to P.D. Tandon on August 8, 1959 : "I think the major issue in this country to-day, if it is to progress and to remain united, is to solve satisfactorily our minority problems; unfortunately you are to a large number of people in India, some kind of a symbol of this communal and revivalist outlook."

The passing of the Hindu Code Bill, Nehru regarded — to be his supreme achievement. 'But I have miserably failed to do anything for Indian Muslims'.

Let us first mention the achievements of Nehru in the growth of our planned economy. We feel proud of Nagarjun Sagar, Hirakud, Damodar Valley Corporation, Bhakra Nangal, Bhilai, Rourkella, — these are our new temples. We must also mention the establishment of the Industrial Finance Corporation, 1948; the Reserve Bank of India under the State control, the nationalisation of the L.I.C., the Bank Nationalisation, the establishment of the Unit Trust of India, etc.

To-day, in our self-criticism, we find ourselves drifting away and away from the great ideals of Nehru. Nehru could well realise his failures on two counts before his death — his inability to remove the disparity between the high ups and the common people, and his inability to curb 'Black Money'. Perhaps his failures are due to the fact that he was a lone fighter — being surrounded by men with myopic vision and self-interest. Even after 25 years of the death of Nehru, we find ourselves in a worse situation than we were in 1964. We are fastened in the den of corruption, blackmoney, disintegration and communalism. The fundamentalists are raising their heads every where. The huge allocation of money for any welfare — measure becomes a misnomer, because the money hardly reaches them for whom it is meant. 'We fall upon the thorns of life, we bleed'.

Nehru's poetic bent of mind would express his loneliness in quotations from poets of eminence. Long back, the withdrawal of the non-cooperation movement made him utter the lines of Eliot:

> This is the way the world ends,
> Not with a bang but, a whimper.

Frustrated towards the end of his life — he uttered:

> There is nothing at all to
> be done about it
> There is nothing to do
> about anything.

And the four lines scribled on his pad before his death:

> 'The woods are lovely, dark and deep,
> But I have promises to keep,
> And miles to go before I sleep,
> And miles to go before I sleep'.

This same feeling of loneliness would perhaps take him again and again to Rabindranath, from whom he would gather comfort, inspiration, strength and vigour. Rabindranath could well understand the impulsive, the impetuous, but sometimes indecisive Nehru. He called Nehru — *Ritu raj*. Nehru called Shanti Niketan — 'an oasis in the midst of much barrenness'. Rabindranath wrote to Nehru after going through his autobiography:

Shanti Niketan
May 31, 1936

Dear Jawaharlal,

I have just finished reading your great book and I feel intensely impressed and proud of your achievement. Through all its details there runs a deep current of humanity which overpasses the tangles of facts and leads us to the person who is greater than his deeds and truer than his surroundings.

Yours very sincerely,
Rabindranath Tagore

Jawaharlal's admirable reply:

Anand Bhavan
Allahabad
June 10, 1936

Dear Gurudev,

My sister has sent me your letter. Need I say how proud and grateful I feel to have your commendation in such generous language? Many friends have used words of praise for my book, some have criticised it. But what you have written goes to my heart and cheers and strengthens me. With your blessings and good will I feel I can face a world of opposition. The burden becomes lighter and the road straighten.

I go tonight to my sister at Mussoorie for a few days.
With homage and affection.

Yours
Jawaharlal

Here is the Man Alive, the Man Immortal.

(Summary of the speech delivered at the Seminar)

INDEX